MW01008134

What Readers Are Saying About *Gen Y Now*

"Great leadership is the one sure thing that separates truly exceptional organizations from the rest. Hobart and Sendek have nailed it with this book. We are in a new century and leaders need new skills and capabilities to lead their current—and future—workforce. This book shows you how to be a 21st century leader."

—Stephen J. Kontra, vice president,
Global Learning & Development, Pfizer Inc.

"Insightful and well-conceived, Hobart and Sendek blend unique perspectives about the often misunderstood, yet talented crop of Gen Y workers. A must read for educators, employers, administrators, and leaders who seek guidance on effectively blending old-school concepts, work ethics, and technology with today's vibrant and creative next generation. The book is positive, upbeat, and optimistic about where this generation can take us if we effectively partner with them."

—Dr. Rick Brandenburg, Wm. Neal Reynolds Distinguished
Professor, North Carolina State University

"As I read *Gen Y Now,* I kept thinking, 'Exactly! I wish my boss knew this.' The book shows leaders exactly what they need to do to attract and retain Gen Y workers, and any organization that has seen an exodus of Millennials should read *Gen Y Now* to figure out what they're doing wrong and how to make it right."

—Annie Siebert, former newspaper reporter, freelance writer, and editor

"Hobart and Sendek provide a great resource for leaders and consultants navigating the ever-changing landscape of generational challenges in the workplace."

—Nicole Lipkin, Psy.D., author, *What Keeps Leadership Up at Night* and *Y in the Workplace*

"Gen Y is firmly in the workforce and leaders better understand them to be successful. Hobart and Sendek show leaders how to respond to Gen Y's need for learning, recognition, fairness, and flexibility and take advantage of their willingness to collaborate and innovate. The book is must reading for managers in all types of organizations."

—Manuel London, Ph.D., dean, College of Business, State
University of New York at Stony Brook

"It's not that corporate America can't afford to ignore generational differences anymore; it's that corporate America can't afford *not* to harness them. If youth are our future, that future belongs to organizations that know how to manage, motivate, and mentor Millennials into leaders. Hobart and Sendek are here to show you how it's done."

—J. M. Henderson, author and contributor, *Generation Meh, Forbes*

"Hobart and Sendek absolutely nailed the challenges and joys of working with Gen Y. It is a must read book for any business leader."

—Dave Kinnear, CCE-Board Certified coach and Vistage chair

"Hobart and Sendek have teamed up to author a remarkable book on an 'evergreen' topic. It promises to put you on the path to managing Generation Y employees and their impact on the future of your success as a leader!"

—Carol Hacker, author of fourteen books, including the best-selling, *Hiring Top Performers*

"*Gen Y Now* reframes the workplace canvas by painting generational differences as diversity, not adversity."

—Melissa Hider O'Brien, learning specialist, Black & Veatch

"I've hired and managed a lot of Millennials and this new edition is invaluable and insightful. Read it and profit!"

—Andrew Wood, LegendaryMarketing.com, author, *Traits of Champions*

"The case studies and practical research alone make this new edition a winner. As a bonus it's a fun read as well."

—Rick Crandall, editor, *Thriving on Change in Organizations*

Praise for the First Edition of *Gen Y Now*

"I have long appreciated Herb Sendek's ability to unite and inspire his players to perform at a higher level. That degree of selflessness is only possible when true leadership is present. Herb and Buddy have taken these concepts and applied them to business strategy. *Gen Y Now* provides leaders with real-world tools to build a winning plan."

—Jeff Van Gundy, NBA analyst for ESPN and former NBA head basketball coach

"Buddy Hobart and Coach Sendek have delivered a slam dunk. By providing such keen insights into this all-important generation, they have developed a leadership guide for everyone looking to build a team in the new economy."

—Tom Booth, Schering-Plough Consumer HealthCare, VP of International Marketing

"If we look back across the generations that came before us, we recognize that each confronted unique challenges and, for better or worse, shaped the world. As a university president now welcoming freshman classes that have never known a time when the Internet was not ubiquitous or when an unlimited scope of information was not at their fingertips, I can attest to the fact that Generation Y operates in a different modality. Buddy Hobart and Herb Sendek offer astute commentary on the implications and potential of this generational sea change for those who seek to operationalize leadership."

—Dr. Michael M. Crow, president, Arizona State University

"Gen Y is who will replace our leadership in the coming years. This book should be on every leader's list."

—Bradley D. Penrod, AAE, executive director, CEO, Pittsburgh International Airport

"Competitive companies and lean nonprofit organizations need to attract and retain the best talent, especially in tough economic times. Hobart and Sendek provide a clear message: don't confuse Generation Y employees' desire for progress, need for feedback, and insistence on meaningful work and work/life balance for self-centeredness, slacking, or disloyalty. Read this book and you will recognize the value Generation Y brings to the workplace. Learn how to engage Generation Y. Their talent will bring you technological expertise and continuous innovation."

—Manuel London, College of Business, State University of New York at Stony Brook, author, *Job Feedback*

"*Gen Y Now* is a compelling account of the demographic trends facing the organizations of tomorrow, coupled with strategies for the managers and leaders of today."

—Michael McQueen, author, *The New Rules of Engagement*

"*Gen Y Now* provides important insights into the realities of tomorrow's workforce, realities that dispel some of the common myths about this generation and guide you to understand their real value and importance."

—Bette Price, CMC, coauthor, *GenBlending: Ten Surprising Trends About Generation Y That Will Make or Break Your Business*

"Gen Yers are potential champions for any business. I've had great success with giving people goals and letting them go at them. With this book, you can, too."

—Andrew Wood, author, *Traits of Champions*

"It is natural to push back against the habits of Gen Y, but *Gen Y Now* presents a compelling motive to do just the opposite. Read this book to tap into the advantages of Gen Y—ahead of your competition."

—Jeff Taylor, MillennialMarketer.com

"*Gen Y Now* is like a great mentor in a business culture that requires every manager to step up to the plate and oversee Generation Y employees. Those who succeed will earn the strategic, competitive advantage. Hobart and Sendek offer practical insight and dozens of ideas for turning Gen Y employees into world-class performers!"

—Carol A. Hacker, author, *Hiring Top Performers—350 Great Interview Questions for People Who Need People*

"This book is right on target. It not only helps leaders gain an awareness of the challenges, it also provides real-world strategies for success."

—Doug Collins, four-time NBA all-star, head basketball coach, and sports analyst

Gen Y Now

MILLENNIALS AND THE EVOLUTION OF LEADERSHIP

SECOND EDITION

John W. "Buddy" Hobart
and Herb Sendek

WILEY

Published by Wiley

One Montgomery Street, Suite 1200, San Francisco, CA 94104-4594

www.wiley.com

Cover image: Wiley
Cover design: Wiley

For additional copies or bulk purchases of this book or to learn more about Wiley's Workplace Learning offerings, please contact us toll free at 1-866-888-5159 or by email at workplacelearning@wiley.com.

Wiley also publishes its books in a variety of electronic formats and by print-on-demand. Some material included with standard print versions of this book may not be included in e-books or in print-on-demand. If the version of this book that you purchased references media such as a CD or DVD that was not included in your purchase, you may download this material at http://booksupport.wiley.com. For more information about Wiley products, visit www.wiley.com.

Library of Congress Cataloging-in-Publication Data

Hobart, John W.
Gen Y now : millennials and the evolution of leadership/John W. "Buddy" Hobart and Herb Sendek. — Second edition.
pages cm
Includes bibliographical references and index.
ISBN 978-1-118-89946-5 (hardback); ISBN 978-1-118-89983-0 (pdf);
ISBN 978-1-118-89982-3 (epub)
1. Personnel management. 2. Generation Y—Employment. 3. Young adults—Employment—United States. 4. Intergenerational relations. 5. Supervision of employees. 6. Employee motivation. 7. Diversity in the workplace—Management. I. Sendek, Herb. II. Title.
HF5549.H5175 2014
658.4'092—dc23

2014007578

Printed in the United States of America
HB Printing 10 9 8 7 6 5 4 3 2 1

This book is dedicated to our Coach, Dave Maloney. He was our coach, mentor, and, most importantly, our dear friend. We miss him every day. We hope we made you proud.

CONTENTS

INTRODUCTION

A few years ago, Herb Sendek and I were talking about leadership when the subject of Gen Y came up. Herb had asked me about our consulting practice and whether we were seeing anything in the marketplace that was universal across industries and geographies. Solutions 21 has partnered with firms around the world, ranging from start-up to Fortune 500. We have worked in manufacturing plants, law firms, executive boardrooms, and nearly everything in between. While there are similar issues in every industry, seldom are the challenges identical across industries, and even less often across the globe. Until Gen Y.

I answered Herb by telling him that we are seeing businesses having a hard time attracting and retaining young talent. When he asked me why I thought that was, I must admit I allowed my Baby Boomer prejudice to show through and said things like, "These kids are different. They are not loyal, will quit in a minute, and expect things they have not earned. They think they are special, are entitled, and do not have an 'old fashioned' work ethic."

Herb then challenged me to think differently. He challenged me, as a leader, the same way we will challenge you in this book. The challenge of attracting and retaining Gen Y talent is not about Gen Y. It is about *leadership*. Gen Y is attracted to strong leaders and want to associate themselves with folks who display timeless leadership. This book is about timeless leadership every bit as much as it is about Gen Y.

We wrote the first edition of this book in 2009, and much has changed since then. Generation Y is fully in the workforce, the Great Recession has had a huge impact on business, and Baby Boomers are quickly retiring. Technology has grown exponentially and has impacted the work world in many exciting and unforeseen ways. This book reflects our many years of research in addition to the experience we have gained talking about leadership and Gen Y around the world. By 2025 nearly 75 percent of the global workforce will be Gen Y. Gen Y is the future of work.

Since 2009 we have been able to strike a very unique balance as it relates to Gen Y. We are Boomers who advocate for this cohort. You will see they have much to offer. They will challenge leaders to continually improve their leadership skills and they will find new, innovative, and productive solutions to business challenges. They will work hard, be extremely loyal, and be some of the best team players you have ever worked with . . . when led correctly.

Gen Y also brings some unique challenges. We have not shied away from addressing these leadership challenges. Gen Y needs to be led, coached, and mentored. When we have worked with Gen Y around the globe, they have told us we "get it" as it relates to attracting and retaining their generation. We "get" what they are looking for in a job, company, and leader. We have not shied away from challenging Gen Y on their developmental issues, and they have appreciated that input.

Gen Y *is not* afraid of challenges, input, feedback, and strong leadership. Just the opposite. They are looking for it.

This book is a leadership book. It will help leaders understand Gen Y, create a plan to attract and retain the best talent, align the culture to support *all* employees (not just Gen Y), and show you how to execute on the plan. This book is about the future of work.

Buddy Hobart

March 2014

CHAPTER ONE

THE PLATFORM IS BURNING

Sam started with Walter Manufacturing right out of high school. He wanted to attend college, but he didn't have enough for tuition and he needed to earn money to support his future family. Shortly after joining the company, he married his high school sweetheart.

As with all new hires, Sam was on the maintenance crew and was assigned some of the most difficult and dirty jobs in the plant. The plant worked three shifts, and all new maintenance employees were required to work rotating shifts for at least three years.

While the work was hard, Sam was eager to learn and take on more and more responsibility. He was always asking, "What's next?" and was never afraid to take on a new challenge or assignment. In fact, Sam often stayed late to make sure his work was properly transitioned to the next shift.

After "putting in his time" on the maintenance crew, Sam's hard work and dedication were rewarded and he received his first promotion. Fast forward many years and Sam is still at Walter Manufacturing. He's progressed steadily, taken on many roles and is currently a general foreman. In addition to his steady rise in the company, Sam found time to go back to school and earn a bachelor's degree.

Back to the Future

If we were to tell you Sam's story was from 1975 you would easily believe it. There were a lot of Sams in 1975. Maybe you have not seen many lately. Well, Sam is thirty-five and has worked at the same place his entire life. He is a real person, and we simply changed his name and company.

Sam's generation, Gen Y, is the future of work. When we asked Sam why he stayed at the same job, put up with shift work, took on the dirty tasks, and worked unpaid overtime, his answer was simple. He wanted to. He wanted to because his managers and the business owners were true leaders and he simply wanted to work for them. They earned his loyalty.

When we probed further he told us his leaders pushed, challenged, corrected, coached, and, maybe most importantly, trusted him. They gave him several jobs to tackle and recognized his good work. He was encouraged to go back to school, even though a degree might have him looking for other opportunities outside the company. They also "called him on the carpet" when his work was sub-standard. In short, his leaders were true leaders.

This book, when all is said and done, is a leadership book for a new generation of employees and a new generation of leaders. Gen Y (also referred to as Millennials), all eighty million, demand a new leadership style. What worked in the past and passed for leadership will no longer work. Gen Y does not accept sub-standard leadership and will "vote with their feet." They will leave your company rather than work for someone who is not a good leader.

The Time Is Now

When we wrote the first edition of this book in 2009, businesses still had time to put their plans and strategies in place to attract and retain the next generation of talent. That window has closed. The time is now. Gen Y (born between 1977 and 1995) is fully in the workforce. In 2013 the youngest turned eighteen. In 2009 the youngest was only fourteen, so the full impact of this generation was still in the future. Not now. Every Gen Yer is working, looking for work, or earning an advanced degree to enter the workforce. To paraphrase John Kotter, the inventor of Change Management, "The platform is burning."

Since our first edition, much has changed and we will address it in this edition. The Great Recession* has had a major impact on Gen Y and how they view the world. Much like the Great Depression impacted the "Greatest Generation" for their entire lives, the Great Recession will impact all of Gen Y's decisions, careers, and spending choices.

Not only has all of Gen Y entered (or are prepared to enter) the workforce since 2009, but the oldest of this cohort has gained many years of experience and vast amounts of education. In addition to being the most well-educated generation of all time, starting in 2013 every eight seconds *for the next eighteen years*, a Gen Yer will turn thirty-six. We certainly are not talking about "these kids" anymore.

As Gen Y matures and gains experience, Baby Boomers and Gen X are marching toward retirement. Gen Y will be replacing this lost knowledge capital. Boomers began to turn sixty-five in 2010 and a Boomer will turn sixty-five every 8.5 seconds until 2029.

Leadership for a New Generation

In many ways leadership is timeless. Many of the things we will discuss in this book are not new. However, many leadership tenants have evolved over time and no longer resemble the original intent.

*According to Wikipedia—The Great Recession is an ongoing marked global economic decline that began in December 2007 and took a particularly sharp downward turn in September 2008. The recession affected the entire world economy, with greater detriment to some countries than others, but overall to a degree that made it the worst global recession since World War II. It was a major global recession characterized by various systemic imbalances, and was sparked by the outbreak of the U.S. subprime mortgage crisis and financial crisis of 2007–2008. The economic side-effects of the European sovereign debt crisis, austerity, high levels of household debt, trade imbalances, high unemployment, and limited prospects for global growth in 2013 and 2014, continued to provide obstacles for many countries to achieve a full recovery from the recession.

This evolution** has left us with some things that, at times, are not even recognizable as leadership. In fact, many of the leadership practices organizations *say* they do (and may even do as a part of their culture) end up having a very negative impact on Gen Y.

Over the past fifty years many organizations have said things like, "People are our greatest asset" or "We have an open door policy" or "There is no such thing as a stupid question" to motivate and communicate with their employees. In practice, people never hear feedback, are made to feel stupid when seeking input, and the boss's door, while physically open, might as well be nailed closed.

First and foremost, this book is about leadership and aligning your words with your actions. We will challenge you to evaluate your leadership, get your peer leaders on board and, finally, to develop the next generation of leaders. All of this can be built into your culture. It's the next step in the evolution of corporate leadership (see Figure 1.1). The opposite of evolution is extinction.

As a consultant and a coach, we have the opportunity to interact with many different people from all walks of life. We have also had the good fortune of working with some of the best leaders in the sports and corporate worlds. They have one thing in common. When it is time to change something in their organizations or on their teams, they first look in the mirror. Bear

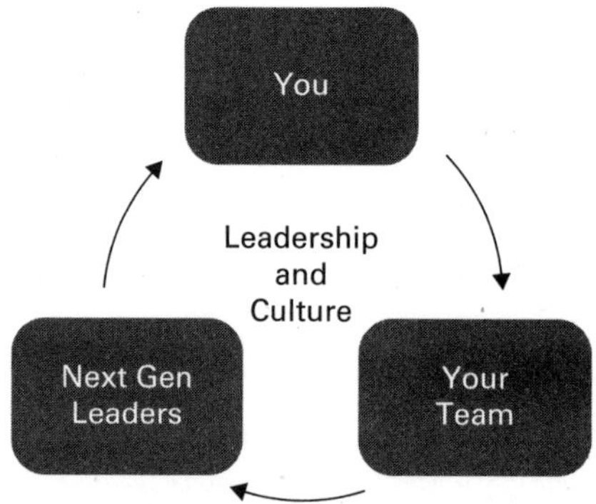

FIGURE 1.1. 21st Century Leadership: An Ongoing Process

**http://i.word.com/idictionary/Evolution

Bryant, the legendary football coach, used to say, "When we win the team played great. When we lose I coached a bad game." And he meant it. Change and leadership start in the mirror.

> "Management is about coping with complexity. Leadership is about coping with change."
>
> John Kotter, Harvard University,
> Author, *Leading Change*

Consultant's Corner

Since the publication of the first edition of this book in 2009, I've had the good fortune of speaking to groups around the world on the topics of leadership and Gen Y. One of the things I do is ask the audience to write down the adjectives they think of when they think of Gen Y in the workplace. They are instructed to throw political correctness to the wind.

Without fail, the results are always the same. Folks start off with one or two nice things about Gen Y, like "tech-savvy" or "well-educated." From there it is usually an out-of-control train wreck. The audience says things like "spoiled, lazy, entitled, soft," and some things not fit to print.

I then relay my "road to Damascus conversion" regarding Gen Y. Coach Sendek had me open my mind and look in the mirror.

When we first started to discuss writing a book, I had very similar prejudices toward Gen Y. As the youngest of six children, born to Greatest Generation parents in a working class neighborhood, I did not think highly of Gen Y. In fact, the book was intended to be a "point/counter-point" book, with Herb giving the virtues of Gen Y and me challenging him every step of the way.

(*continued*)

Herb forced me to look in the mirror. As a lifelong student of leadership who makes his living working with Gen Y every day, Herb posed a simple point for my consideration. He said, "By definition, leaders have followers." Then he asked me, "If one cannot adapt his leadership to the new followers, guess what that means?"

It was time for me to look in the mirror. You may well have some of the same feelings I had about "these kids" and "Why can't they be more like us?" I pose the same question to you, "If you can't adapt your leadership to new followers, what does that mean?" The answer is obvious: you won't have followers for long, which means you will no longer be a leader.

The Right Kind of Change

Key Point

Gen Y will force businesses to align words and actions.

Let's, right up front, tell you what this book is NOT about. This book is NOT about coddling a new group of employees. It is NOT about compromising your values. It is NOT about giving in or acquiescing to a new generation. It is about leadership and leading the right kind of change.

"When we are no longer able to change a situation, we are challenged to change ourselves."

Victor Frankl, Author,
Man's Search for Meaning

Leading this change will have several very important benefits. An important thing to know is that any changes you put in place that motivate Gen Y will also be well received by *all* of your employees. Gen Y has been more vocal and demanding than previous generations. Previous generations would "put up with" poor leadership and simply disengage. We call this "retiring on the job." They may well stay and not quit, but they are not engaged and they are certainly not as productive as possible. Leading your organization in ways that will attract Gen Y will also increase your overall productivity from *every* generation.

This book will help you align your organization in ways that attract Gen Y, increase all employee productivity, and create a more engaged and motivated workforce. You will see that hiring and retaining folks like Sam is possible. Sam may eventually leave his current employer, and you will also lose quality employees who move on to other challenges, but you will have maximized your investment along the way and will be known as an employer (and leader) of choice. This is not something "warm and fuzzy" and "nice to do." This may be the single most important thing a business can do to positively impact its bottom line.

Key Point
Every generation wants what Gen Y demands.

Exhibit 1.1. Families Want to Understand Gen Y, Too

As we worked with leaders throughout the country and around the world lecturing on how to better understand Gen Y, both of us have been amazed at the unexpected benefits our work has produced. While we set out to help business leaders create better recruiting and retention strategies, we found we were accomplishing much more: we were also helping Baby Boomer parents better understand their children.

Senior executives have approached us after our talks to thank us for the insights—not as business leaders, but as parents! While this book isn't aimed at parents, we would feel deeply honored if even one person improved his or her relationship with Gen Y children as a result of the contents of this book.

Conclusion

Beginning in 2013 the last of Gen Y turned eighteen and is either in the workforce or preparing to join the workforce. They are the future of work and at eighty million strong will define talent acquisition and retention practices for decades. Business leaders in the 21st century will be challenged to adapt to several new realities and to discard 20th century management practices that no longer work. Business leaders must learn how to integrate four generations of "breadwinners" into their workforce and adapt their leadership in order to attract and retain the best talent available. Talent retention is critical for many reasons, including financial/bottom line profits. Turnover is costly and has a direct impact on the financial performance of any company.

At the end of the chapters, following the traditional conclusion, we include a brief biography of a real Gen Y individual that describes his or her work situation. These bios are designed to provide you with an additional perspective on the points brought out in this book.

Ann's Gen Y Profile

Name: Ann

Location: Northeast

Age: 27

Background:

- Graduated with a bachelor's degree in English from a large state university
- Served as editor-in-chief of the university's daily student newspaper during her senior year of college
- Worked for nearly six years at a major metropolitan daily newspaper as a reporter and editor
- Currently working as a copy editor at a worldwide business publication owned by a large corporation

After graduating from college in 2008, Ann was thrilled to land a job as a copy editor at a major newspaper near her hometown, calling it her "dream job." After just a few years, though, Ann was seeking work at a new organization.

While she enjoyed reporting and editing, Ann was frustrated with the newspaper's operations. There was no formal mentoring program or focus on professional development, so Ann felt like there was little room for improvement and even fewer opportunities to move up.

The paper's newsroom was unionized, meaning Ann brought home a higher salary than a lot of her peers, but it also fostered a sense of complacency among her colleagues. Her editor, for example, arrived later and left earlier than Ann nearly every single day, leading Ann to feel resentful and disillusioned.

Additionally, the union focused on protecting older workers, which meant that Ann wasn't enjoying some of the benefits of her peers working in other industries. A percentage of her pay went toward a pension fund she was not a part of, and the fund will likely never be solvent enough for Ann to count on it as a retirement plan. Because Ann is planning to start a family at some point, the newspaper's less-than-stellar maternity leave policy also left her wanting to find an organization with more progressive benefits.

Ann sought new work for more than two years before deciding to leave the paper to work as a copy editor for a larger publication owned by a major corporation. This job comes with a higher salary and better benefits, including a 401(k). Ann's bosses at her new job have also told her there will be opportunities for professional development, as well as chances to move into new roles with the company.

For Ann, the characteristics of a good job are

- Opportunity to learn and grow professionally
- Recognition that her development is good for the organization's success
- A fair salary and progressive benefits, including flexible work schedules, paid time off, retirement plans, and maternity and paternity benefits
- Flexible work arrangements, including the ability to work from home

(*continued*)

Ann is motivated by:

- Feedback and constructive criticism
- The ability to affect long-term change
- Collaboration at work

CHAPTER TWO

FOR THE FIRST TIME IN HISTORY

Leaders throughout history have always had to face and overcome challenges. This is the nature of leadership. When faced with an obstacle, leaders call on their teams, advisors, instinct, and past precedent to determine the best course of action. Rarely do leaders face a challenge that has never, in some form or another, been addressed by someone else. Usually, there is some sort of past experience to draw upon. Until now.

As a leader you are faced with a very unique challenge. One that has NEVER before in history been faced by business leaders. For the first time in history, there are four generations of workers in the workforce. Four distinct generations of people who bring their own personal and generational challenges to the work world.

You may or may not be leading all four generations at the moment, but it is a near certainty that someone you interact with employs all four. As we have worked with organizations around the world, especially when we are speaking to groups, it is very rare if all four generations are not represented in the room.

As a leader, you know how much of your time and energy are spent on directing your people and dealing with the interpersonal issues that arise. You now must not only lead through the traditional "people issues," but you must also be aware of the generational issues that exist.

Having four generations in the workplace will not go away soon. In fact, there will soon be five generations as the generation after Gen Y comes of age. Even when the Traditionalists retire in total, there will still be four generations for you to lead.

The Generations

There are many ways to slice the generations, and several publications may have different years here and there. Our research, and what we find to be the most widely accepted years, shows Gen Y to make up over 25 percent of the population in the United States. This group was born between 1977 and 1995, representing eighty million people. They are the largest generation, surpassing the Baby Boomers (born between 1945 and 1964) at seventy-eight million.

The other two generations in the workplace are Traditionalists (born between 1922 and 1944) at forty-four million and Gen X (born between 1965 and 1976) with forty-eight million. Our research shows that of the Traditionalists born during these years, nearly twelve million are still working or could/would work. Table 2.1 gives an overview of the numbers.

TABLE 2.1. Table of Generations—United States

Generation	Dates of Birth	Number
Traditionalists	1922—1944	44 million
Baby Boomers	1945—1964	78 million
Generation X	1965—1976	48 million
Generation Y	1977—1995	80 million

Global Phenomenon

While much of this book has been researched using population data from the United States, the impact of Gen Y is a global phenomenon. We have worked with clients from all over the globe, and much of what we discuss in this book is applicable to leaders from around the world. In fact, we have presented to global forums that represented more than twenty-five countries and many of the conversations were the same. Whether someone was from Seattle or Slovenia, as business leaders they shared the same challenges.

By 2025, 75 percent of the global workforce will be Gen Y and a significant part of the remaining 25 percent will be the generation following Gen Y. It is important to note that the issues and leadership challenges will be the same for most organizations around the world, not just in the United States. We wanted this to be a leadership book, and not a demographic/data book. We chose to focus mostly on the population data from the United States in order to make certain points. We did not want to overdo the data at the expense of timeless leadership skills.

Why the Emphasis on Gen Y

While all four generations are represented in the workplace, Gen Y is the future of work. This generation brings new and different ideas to the workplace, and many of these ideas are not understood by the other generations. Many of the processes, procedures, and leadership practices were designed for the other three generations. The other three generations have accepted these practices, even if they have evolved beyond the original intent. Traditionalists, Boomers, and Xers, for the most part, accepted things as standard practice. Gen Y will not accept things the same way other generations have in the past. They WILL move on to find an employer who "gets it."

For organizations to attract and retain the best, it will be critical for leaders to "get it" and drive the necessary change. The future labor pool will be made up of Gen Y. By pure demographic numbers, there will be a high demand for this cohort. There simply are not enough Gen X workers to replace the retiring Baby Boomers and Traditionalists.

Donna Korenich, human resource/career management consultant, has already seen the shift for talent. According to Korenich, "Back in the 1980s and 1990s, we were still able to find several qualified Boomer candidates for every retiree. Replacing experience with experience was not that difficult. Now, the number of people who are retiring or just 'slowing down' cannot be replaced that easily. As Boomers retire, there will not be enough qualified candidates to replace them." Korenich continues, "It is critical for business leaders to understand this very real demographic shift if they are to sustain their organizations and their talent."

The High Cost of Turnover

Turnover of employees has always been expensive. Most business leaders have understood this fact for years. We see many leaders who do not factor in the hidden cost of turnover:

- Calculating benchmark employee cost
- Departing employee annual base salary
- Calculated annual benefits cost—estimated at 20 percent of base salary
- Calculated monthly salary + benefits
- Calculated daily salary + benefits—based on 230 (8 hr.) working days
- Cost of "covering" a vacant position (calculated costs of other employees "filling in" while the position is vacant)
- Number of days until the vacant position is filled—number of working days

- Calculated daily cost of "covering" a vacant position—33 percent of departing employee's daily salary + benefits
- Cost to fill a vacant position
- HR/hiring manager's annual salary—salary
- Calculated HR/hiring manager's hourly rate—based on 230 (8 hr.) working days and 20 percent fringe rate
- Cost of advertising (online and/or print)—cost
- Cost of résumé screening—number of hours
- Cost of interviews (telephone screening, first and second)—number of hours
- Cost of behavioral and skills assessments—cost
- Cost of background checks (criminal, credit, reference, education)—cost
- Cost of travel/moving expenses (if applicable)—cost
- On-boarding and orientation cost
- Trainer/manager annual salary—salary
- Calculated trainer/manager daily rate—based on 230 (8 hr.) working days and 20 percent fringe rate
- Total training days—days
- Cost of productivity ramp-up (During the first three months, an average new employee performs at 50 percent productivity of a tenured top performing employee)
- Daily employee cost (salary + benefits)
- Number of working days during first three months—number of days (avg. fifty-eight days)
- Cost of productivity ramp-up
- Total cost of turnover (per employee)
- Number of employees lost (in the last twelve months)—number of employees

Cost of Turnover Calculator—http://us.drakeintl.com/hr-tools/cost-of-turnover-calculator.aspx

Managing your talent and retaining your "best and brightest" is now much more difficult than in the past. In previous times, predicting who was retiring and who you wanted to exit the business were the primary concerns. Little thought was given to understanding who might just up and quit with little warning. Leaders were much more aware of why folks were leaving and much more in control of retention. Today, Gen Y is changing this equation, and it will be expensive for businesses.

Key Point

Turnover is expensive and is controllable.

You must have a strategy to retain your current Gen Y employees because it is extremely expensive to replace an employee. Estimates vary widely and depend on your industry, but employee turnover costs a lot of money. Whether turnover is due to retirement, resignation, or terminations, it is expensive. For example, according to the U.S. Department of Labor Statistics, the cost to replace an employee, at a minimum, is 25 percent of an employee's annual fully loaded compensation (salary, benefits, and taxes). It can cost thousands to hire and train a new hourly employee. It can cost much more to replace a manager. At the high end, some companies estimate the cost of replacing an employee is over $200,000.

The vast majority of the sixty or so employees of Weston Premium Woods of Ontario, Canada, are Generation X or older, making incorporating new Gen Y workers into the culture of the business a unique challenge, according to Michael Shapiro, vice president of purchasing and logistics. Shapiro said the wants and needs of the different generations vary to a certain degree, and the lack of understanding has lead to poor retention of Gen Y workers in the past.

Gen Y asks questions "not to challenge authority but to understand what they have to do . . . and perhaps do it better or more efficiently," Shapiro said. He said some Gen Y workers have left the company because of frustrations over management style, while older managers complained the company is failing to recruit employees who understand the work ethic required to succeed in today's ultra competitive business of buying and distributing wood products.

Shapiro said he worked to explain to the older leaders in the company how to manage Gen Y workers, noting, "You can't give a younger worker a job description and say, 'Go do your job.' They require an understanding of the why in their jobs, and the answer can't be 'because I said so.'"

Shapiro, who was born in 1980, said he tries to help the different generations understand one another. Although he considers himself to have the characteristics of Gen X, he understands Gen Y workers and helps to "bridge the gap" between younger workers and the older management team. "I don't have all the answers," he said. "What we realize is that the way we trained and managed employees from other generations will not work with Gen Y, but that should not be perceived as negative. This creates a new opportunity for us to get ahead of our competition in cultivating the next generation workforce."

Note: Canadian demographics are defined a bit differently from those in the United States. Gen Y is calculated as beginning in 1980 in Canada (vs. 1977 in the United States). Because of that, the Gen Y population is actually slightly less than the Baby Boomers. If the births in 1977, 1978, and 1979 were counted toward Gen Y, then Gen Y would slightly exceed the Baby Boomers. See Table 2.2.

TABLE 2.2. Table of Generations—Canada

Generation	Dates of Birth	Number
Traditionalists	1922—1944	4.9 million
Baby Boomers	1945—1964	9.8 million
Gen X	1965—1979	7.0 million
Gen Y	1980—1995	8.9 million

The Need to Retain Knowledge Capital

In addition to the high cost of replacing a worker, there is the problem of losing the experience and information uniquely possessed by that person. When you are replacing retiring, experienced workers with younger, inexperienced ones, you are losing an incredible amount of knowledge and experience, known as "knowledge capital." Experienced employees have inside knowledge of how your organization works, including how to deal with the internal, institutional bureaucracy. They have leadership skills. They have detailed knowledge of customers and prospects. Experienced employees have contacts and relationships they have developed and built over the course of their careers. They have product familiarity and knowledge. To some degree, Gen X employees will bridge the gap to Gen Y, but there aren't enough of them to do it fully.

Voices of Experience: Stephen D'Angelo

Stephen D'Angelo was in the "turnaround business" in the early 2000s when he was called in to get an international construction company back on track. The company found itself in some financial trouble after building power plants for companies like Enron, but instead of fixing the business and moving on, D'Angelo bought the company, now called dck worldwide.

The former company had been in business for nearly ninety years when D'Angelo, now president and CEO of dck worldwide, took over in 2008. After going through a name change, a rebranding, and an adjustment in the business model, dck worldwide looked a lot different by 2013.

D'Angelo said some employees of the former company didn't make it through the restructuring, but many did. He brought in a group of senior and mid-level managers, and he branded another group of people who were fairly new to the company as "to-be managers."

By 2013, some of the senior managers at dck worldwide were people who had worked for the former company for thirty years, and some of them had only worked for the rebranded company for about three years.

He said the management group that emerged after the restructuring consisted of members of all four generations, and they work together well, with the older managers mentoring and teaching the younger managers. In 2009, D'Angelo launched the Leadership Development Institute to take people who know a lot about the worldwide construction business and teach them about how business operates. He encouraged employees to nominate each other for "the LDI," to overwhelming success—there were thirty-five nominees, and he chose seven. "The fact that we got thirty-five nominees was a message that people are starting to understand what we're trying to accomplish," he said. He said the mix of younger and older managers made for a more efficient leadership team, noting that, while the younger managers might work better collaboratively, the older managers were essential because they transferred their knowledge to the Gen Y workers.

D'Angelo said the LDI allowed older workers to mentor younger managers in a "non-threatening" environment, because it was "outside the lines of authority," allowing managers to meet with each other on an individual basis to ensure everyone grows as employees.

One of the biggest things D'Angelo has tried to instill in his leadership team is the desire to achieve higher profit margins while keeping employees safe. In the construction business, the goal is often to be the cheapest while maintaining low profit margins, D'Angelo said. But if a project manager only thinks about profit margin, he likely won't treat the client in a way that will allow for repeat work.

But it doesn't have to be one or the other. "He can make a profit," he said. "He can be direct, *and* he can maintain a relationship, *and* he can satisfy the client, *and* he can get new work for that company." D'Angelo said a big part of his business is "keeping control of the outcome." "What is the outcome? People sometimes think too low," he said. D'Angelo said the outcome is not, ultimately, to make a profit, but to have a satisfied client, meet financial goals, and develop a repeat customer, which allows dck worldwide to have control over quality while achieving 100 percent safety and keeping customers coming back.

This is another reason you need to have a strategy to recruit and hire Gen Yers as well as a strategy to successfully integrate them into your organization. The new Gen Y employees you hire must be capable of accepting the transfer of knowledge capital from the workers they will eventually replace. You must create an environment in which this cooperative sharing can exist. This means making sure your current workers are comfortable with Gen Yers and vice versa.

Estimates of turnover costs per employee based upon our client's expenses:

- Construction $20,000
- Manufacturing $20,000
- Trade and transportation $15,000
- Information $24,000
- Financial activities $19,500
- Professional and business $25,000

Conclusion

Leaders are facing a new challenge; one that has never been seen before. Four generations of breadwinners are in the workplace. Leading such a diverse group is unprecedented, and leaders need to understand the demographic realities as well as the generational needs of each cohort. Failure to adapt will cause unnecessary turnover in the organization. Turnover is extremely costly to any business in terms of pure dollars and cents. In terms of lost knowledge capital, competitive advantage, and workforce engagement, the loss is nearly incalculable.

Bryan's Gen Y Profile

Name: Bryan

Location: Northeast

Age: 30

Background:

- Graduated with a bachelor's degree in English and history

- Works as a long-term substitute teacher, currently teaching English and Latin

One of Bryan's main concerns with his current position is that it is not permanent. His goal is to find a permanent teaching position where he can spend the rest of his career. Ideally, that would be a position that fits his "financial and mental needs" and offers room for growth.

Bryan said the culture at his current workplace isn't ideal. "The culture of schools typically is that, once you are in, you do not have to work too hard to keep your job," he said, adding that he's frustrated by older teachers who refuse to embrace technology. "Older teachers do not use a lot of technology and feel that it should be squashed," he said. "Teachers are unwilling to change what they have done for years, despite evidence that it is hurtful to the educational process of children."

He said that some of his colleagues "have no knowledge of how the outside world operates, despite attempting to prepare students for the workforce." Bryan would prefer to work with people who are motivating, willing to work with him to help him achieve his professional goals, and comfortable communicating by email, phone, and in person.

Bryan said his work and personal lives are equally important, and he shifts his schedule to accommodate both. "I spend time every day at home working on my career, either by taking work home or honing other skills," he said. "Whenever I have something coming up in my personal life, I organize my work so I have time to pursue activities I enjoy."

For Bryan, the characteristics of a good job are

- A long-term position, potentially one where he could spend the rest of his career
- Opportunities for advancement
- Focus on work/life balance

Bryan is motivated by:

- Working independently
- Constructive criticism and supervisors who motivate him to work harder

CHAPTER THREE

WHY THE NEGATIVE FEELINGS TOWARD GEN Y
The Science

prejudice (n., pre•ju•dice) An adverse judgment or opinion formed beforehand or without knowledge or examination of the facts.

Prejudices

There are a lot of negative attitudes about Gen Y. Most people know someone from Gen Y and have some sort of opinion about that generation. Some people are uncomfortable with Gen Yers because they seem so "different." Some just have a gut feeling that Gen Y is "trouble." In the business world, many employers honestly consider that hiring and working with Gen Yers is a problem.

It is human nature to fear or feel uncomfortable about something we don't really understand, and our research and experience show that Gen Y is, indeed, something people "don't really understand."

In speaking before business groups, and even in casual conversations, we have found that most Traditionalists, Baby Boomers, and Gen Xers not only do not understand Gen Y, but they have a very poor opinion of that group. It seems that most of us are, in the true sense, prejudiced against Gen Yers. That is, we are prejudging them and attributing overwhelmingly negative characteristics to them without knowing all the facts.

Believe it or not, this is not at all unusual. It happens all of the time. When you meet someone new, you make instant judgments based on subconscious triggers. In any merger and acquisition we have ever worked on, "the other" is usually the challenge/problem. Most people, without even knowing it, attribute negative characteristics to "the other" and positive ones to themselves. Think about rival schools, neighborhoods, teams, competitors, and just about everything else.

In social psychology this is known as "attribution."* Attribution is the process of inferring causes of events or behaviors without all of the facts, having just our immediate and observable inputs. This leads to what is known as the Fundamental Attribution Error (FAE).

Humans *fundamentally* attribute what is good to themselves and what is negative to "the other." If my team wins it's because we worked hard and played fair. If my rival wins, they got lucky or even cheated. If I receive the promotion it's because I worked hard and deserved it. If my rival receives the promotion, he or she "pulled strings" or "played the game." You get the idea. It's quite normal and natural to fall victim to the FAE.

There are many "attributions," but for our purposes we only want to discuss two—interpersonal and predictive attribution. *Interpersonal attribution* means we normally assign what is best and right and most attractive to ourselves (or our team, work group, company, and *generation*). Listen to someone tell a story about himself or herself. Often the story will be positioned so the teller is placing himself or herself in the most favorable light possible.

Next is *predictive attribution*. When an event happens, we tend to look at all of the variables and try not to repeat them. For example, a sales person is trying to break into a new market and her first

*In social psychology, the fundamental attribution error is the tendency to overestimate the effect of disposition or personality and underestimate the effect of the situation in explaining social behavior. http://en.wikipedia.org/wiki/Fundamental_Attribution_Error

few proposals are rejected. There is a tendency to conclude that this particular market is not viable. Or, on a more personal level, your coat is stolen from the coat rack at a particular restaurant. Your tendency will be to attribute the theft with the restaurant or neighborhood and you may unknowingly avoid both in the future.

You are trying to predict future outcomes based on your experience (or even what you have heard or read). You are looking at one variable, the restaurant, and attributing your lost coat to the establishment. You are simply not aware of the many other events that may have led to the theft. In fact, your lost coat may have had *nothing* to do with either the restaurant or the neighborhood. It may well have been other contributing factors, and you are simply unaware. Someone may have made a mistake and taken your coat, returned it later, and the restaurant has no way of contacting you.

There is another important psychological phenomenon at work as you look to align your culture to attract and retain Gen Y. It is called the "Actor Observer Bias."[**] Simply put, if something happens to us there is a natural tendency to blame outside forces and not our own actions/decisions. Even if we do not "blame" outside forces, we will often allow ourselves to think through the many uncontrollable factors that went into the final outcome. This helps us to psychologically accept the negative outcome and move on.

Conversely, we do not have this same depth of knowledge when we are simply observing "the other." When explaining the outcomes of others' actions/decisions, you have only your observations and attributions. Many times we draw a negative conclusion based on our lack of other key information.

Why is any of this important? Because each generation attributes what is right and good and correct to their own cohort. What "the other" is doing and feeling, since it is not like my generation, must be wrong. Different too often equals wrong. As a leader, your job is to recognize that different equals different . . . and then lead your troops to that same understanding.

[**] Actor–observer asymmetry explains the errors that one makes when forming attributions about the behavior of others. http://en.wikipedia.org/wiki/Actor-observer_bias

Here is one interesting fact about the Fundamental Attribution Error and the Actor Observer Bias theories. The more you know about "the other," the *less likely* you are to attribute negatives to their actions, decisions, methods, way of life, and so on. The more you know about someone, the better able you are to see his or her point of view and the better able to understand situations and outside influences affecting the situation.

Consultant's Corner: Mergers and Acquisitions

In our consulting practice we have worked with many firms in various stages of a merger or acquisition. We have worked on transactions ranging from one of our clients buying a small firm and rolling it up into their core business to one of the largest corporate mergers of all time. What we have learned is that, regardless of transaction size, there is one constant. People.

In large transactions there is a host of complexities to deal with that smaller transactions may not have. However, from large to small, there are always people to deal with. One mistake we find happens all of the time is ignoring this fact. If the human element is not taken into consideration quickly, then there is a near certainty that there will be an "us versus them" mentality.

Our advice to our clients is to humanize the process as quickly and as thoroughly as possible. Get everyone in a room. Make sure people get to know each other. Put names to faces. Start using inclusive pronouns (we and us) instead of "the other" (they and them). It is quite natural for people to judge "the other" as wrong or bad. Get that out of the equation as quickly as possible.

The Four Generations

Each generation tends to attribute what its cohort does, how they feel, how they view work and life as the "right" way. This is almost always subconscious. It's how the brain is wired.

In order for you to lead yourself, and then others, to a more engaged and collaborative workforce, it is important to know how all of the generations view certain areas of their lives. Knowledge is power and, in this case, knowledge is understanding. The more we know about "the other," the more we will see their viewpoints.

While the focus of this book is on Gen Y, this information works for all generations (see Table 3.1). Leading yourself and others to a greater understanding of Gen Y is only part of it. We can lead Gen Y to a greater understanding of Boomers, Xers to a greater understanding of Traditionalists, and so forth and so on.

For the Traditionalist, work was viewed as a sacrifice one needs to make for the family. It was an obligation and not an option. This generation says things like, "That's why it's called work. It's supposed to be hard." Fun at work was a foreign concept. Fun is for other times. Work is work.

While the Boomers were rebellious, they did look at work as an adventure. Something to be cherished. One's career mattered. It defined them. Climbing the corporate ladder was to be admired. Often Boomers described others by the company they worked for or the position they held.

Looking at the outcomes of the previous generation's "company loyalty" and seeing folks laid off and the loyalty not necessarily rewarded, Gen X took a radically different approach. This was the first generation to fully question the "one job/one company" social contract. They had witnessed how the "company" did not always reward, which Gen X deemed to be misplaced loyalty. Gen X looked at work as a contract and mutual agreement. I work for you. I give you my time, energy, and efforts. You give me a wage. After that, we are even. I owe you nothing else.

TABLE 3.1. Generations' Views of Work

Views of Work	Traditionalist	An obligation
	Baby Boomer	A lifelong quest
	Gen X	An employment contract
	Gen Y	A place to make a difference

Gen Y has taken what Gen X did (having multiple jobs as a career by choice) completely to the next level. Work is a place to make a difference, not just earn a paycheck. To work is to contribute. Not just to my employer but also to my co-workers, the local community, and the world. Gen Y works to live and not lives to work. The work ethics of the generations are outlined in Table 3.2.

Not only did Traditionalists look at work as an obligation, but they also looked at it as a place to put in maximum effort. They valued hard work. Hard work was defined as putting in both time and physical/mental effort. These folks respected authority and deferred to the boss or the "title." Traditionalists are the sons and daughters of parents who worked for the great industrialists. The boss was to be revered, even if he was not a kind or good person—or even a good boss.

The term "work-a-holic" was coined to describe the Baby Boomers. This generation went from protesting war to sex, drugs, and rock-n-roll to work-a-holics. Putting in time was important. This generation would say "in early and out late" is important and those who do that are hard workers. Time equaled effort. Being seen in the office meant you were committed and working hard.

Gen X saw things a bit differently than the Boomers did. This cohort did not want to give up control of their careers to the company. Xers were the first generation to want to take charge of their own careers. Things like "professional development" and "career planning" were invented by Gen X. Gen X was self-reliant and the first generation to fully question "the company man."

TABLE 3.2. Work Ethics of the Generations

Work Ethic	Traditionalist	Work hard
	Baby Boomer	Time equals commitment
	Gen X	Self-reliance
	Gen Y	What's next?

For Gen Y the evolution has continued. Gen Y is very goal-oriented and is always asking, "What's next?" This generation is very comfortable multi-tasking and, in fact, prefers to multi-task. Speed of accomplishment is important. Putting in hours is not seen as important. But doing your share, producing results, and pulling your weight are admired. This cohort wants to learn new things and take on new challenges—quickly.

In a word, Traditionalists who might be asked about "work/life balance" would respond "What!?" They looked at life and work as two separate things. There was work and there was family. Never the two shall meet. These folks prided themselves on leaving work at the office (or factory). Work was hard, and family provided a respite. "A man's home is his castle" and no one could tell you what to do in your own castle . . . not even a bad boss!

"Work/life balance" (see Table 3.3) became a popular term as Boomers matured in their careers. Boomers lived to work, and their profession/job/career was very important to who they were. There was no such thing as balance. At a certain point this cohort realized they might be missing out on other parts of their lives.

Gen X took the concept of "work/life balance" and made it a mantra. Previous generations had counted on relaxing once they retired. At that point they could travel, fish, paint, garden, or do whatever they wanted. Gen X said, "NO WAY! I want balance *now*, not when I am sixty-five. Travel will be more fun when I am thirty rather than forty, and forty rather than fifty, and fifty rather than sixty!"

Gen Y looks at work as a *part* of life. Work is not distinct and separate from other areas of their lives. Life is life. This cohort wants to make everything fit. They realize there are not two of

TABLE 3.3. Views of Work/Life Balance

Work and Family Life Balance	Traditionalist	What is that?!
	Baby Boomer	Live to work; balance when I retire
	Gen X	Balance now; not at retirement
	Gen Y	Everything should fit

them, just one and only one life to live. This cohort has coined a term "work/life blur," as in everything is connected and there is no separation. If they have to leave work with an unfinished project, they are quite comfortable opening the laptop and working past midnight.

"No news is good news" could be the unofficial slogan for Traditionalists as it relates to rewards and recognition (Table 3.4). As long as the boss is *not* talking to me, I must be doing OK. To go to the principal's, coach's, or boss's office was not a good thing. That only meant trouble.

Boomers did not have much of a different view about feedback. They also felt "nothing good came from a trip to the boss's office." However, in lieu of recognition, Boomers would simply say, "Pay me." Boomers liked titles and felt a promotion, with a higher title, was a form of recognition. This generation admired time spent at work and rewarded time. Often promotions happened simply because it was someone's turn. Tenure and years of experience were admired. Many annual meetings spent the majority of the recognition time on anniversary recognition, who has been here the longest, not who has produced the best result.

Gen X was the first generation to look at rewards and recognition and align these with their views on work/life balance. Early in their careers, technology began to make it possible to work remotely and the two-income family became commonplace. Time was precious. With both parents working, there just never seemed to be enough time.

A time crunch at home, coupled with technological advances, led Gen X to begin seeking professional opportunities that allowed

TABLE 3.4. Views of Rewards and Recognition

Rewards and Recognition	Traditionalist	No news is good news
	Baby Boomer	Don't tell me—pay me
	Gen X	Freedom is the best reward
	Gen Y	Real-time feedback

for more flexible schedules and awarded more vacation time. Being able to better control one's time was important for Gen X. The best reward they could receive was to have the freedom to control their work schedules. Gen X viewed "freedom" as true recognition and a reward for their accomplishments.

Gen Y looks at rewards and recognition much differently. Gen Y appreciates liberal vacation policies and time off for good work. However, Gen X made these kinds of policies standard and often commonplace. Gen Y has really never known a work situation that did not have the kinds of programs Gen X built.

Gen Y does not look at time *away* from work as recognition for doing good work. Gen Y looks at flex-time and vacation time as commonplace. What motivates Gen Y is receiving feedback, both positive and developmental, in real time. Organizations that provide input to their employees on a regular basis are attractive employers for Gen Y.

A "no news is good news" culture will not attract and retain Gen Y. They believe, if there is good news to discuss, discuss it. If there is something to be improved, tell them and they will work on it. Either way, just provide input. Real-time feedback is the best reward.

Overcoming Stereotypes

We realize our points are generalizations for each of the four generations. It is impossible to place millions of people into small descriptors. However, we have tested these descriptors with hundreds of audiences and thousand of participants for each of these generations. While not everyone from each of these cohorts fits *exactly* into our categories, the overwhelming majority do. We sincerely hope we are not stereotyping.

Gen Y has really been a victim, in our opinion, of stereotyping and negative publicity. We believe in many ways this is how the other three generations have assigned Gen Y attributes and have often judged them unfairly. We also believe that many negative feelings that have developed about Gen Y are driven by "urban legends" and by the media.

> **urban legend** (n., ur•ban le•gend) an often lurid story or anecdote that is based on hearsay and widely circulated as true. For instance, the urban legend of alligators living in the sewers.—also called, *urban myth*

First, let's address "urban legends." Sure, you may know of a thirty-year-old who quit his $100K job to tour Europe. Or maybe you had an employee who demanded the president's parking space. Or, better yet, who wanted to be president after a year with the company. If you did have this employee working for you, we have one small piece of advice: you should not have hired that person in the first place.

Just as with other urban legends (think kidney removal emails!), many of the stories you have heard are either exaggerated, out and out false, or repeated through someone's "attribution filter." Are there some crazy stories that are true? Absolutely! Again, our advice is, do not hire folks like that. Were there some crazy stories about Traditionalists, Boomers, and Gen X . . . *absolutely*! You should not have hired them either.

Next, let's address the media. As we researched Gen Y, we became acutely aware of the stories published about Gen Y. Many of these stories are intended to play into the other three generations' stereotypes about Gen Y. We have begun to collect some of these stories for our files.

The first thing to realize is that headline writers and reporters are not the same people. Reporters write the story and the headline writers make up what they think will attract readers. Often the headline and the story are not even in sync. For example, we recently came across a headline, "Gen Y Whoa Fully Ill-Prepared for Retirement." If that's all you read, and you already had a negative opinion about Gen Y, the headline would confirm your beliefs.

However, once you read the article, you would find out the author is referring to "eighteen-to-twenty-five-year-olds." While certainly a part of Gen Y, they are not the entirety of Gen Y (which by and large are great savers, see Chapter 5) Plus, we can't speak for others, but we both were "woefully ill-prepared for retirement" at eighteen!

As these anecdotes are repeated, Gen Xers and Boomers start to believe that all prospective Gen Y employees are the same. Examples like these are exaggerated in the retelling and become the image of Gen Y.

Are there Gen Yers who are spoiled, lazy, disloyal, and pampered? Absolutely—and you do not want them as employees. But we cannot paint the entire generation with so broad a brush. In fact, if we examine these negative traits closely, we will find one of two things. Either they are misconceptions and exaggerations or they are traits that can actually lead to positive and productive Gen Y performance in the workplace. In any case, Gen Y does not deserve the bad rap it gets.

We have conducted leadership seminars around the world, done word searches on Gen Y articles, surveyed managers and supervisors across the globe, and have found seven consistent stereotypes. In the next chapter we call them "myths" (because they are myths). The top seven stereotypes we uncovered are:

- Lazy/slacker
- Want a trophy for showing up
- Self-centered/narcissistic
- Disloyal
- Pampered/spoiled
- Lack respect
- Entitled

Conclusion

It is quite normal for any group to think the way they approach most everything is the "right way." The challenge for leaders is that there is an equal tendency for groups to think those who do anything differently than they would do it are doing things "the wrong way." Each generational cohort has certain attributes associated with their generation, and the tendency is to judge the other generations as being "wrong" when in fact they may just be "different." A leader's challenge is to make sure that "different" is judged as "different" and not "wrong."

Dan's Gen Y Profile

Name: Dan

Location: Northeast

Age: 31

Background:

- Earned a bachelor's degree, a J.D., and an MBA from a large state university
- After working at a small community newspaper after obtaining his bachelor's degree, Dan opted to return to school to earn a J.D./MBA to increase his earning potential
- Now works as a junior associate for one of the biggest law firms in the world

Dan has a history of "major, pervasive, and unending health problems," and a job that provides good health insurance was a top priority for him. "This is relevant to you and everyone else because, even though you don't realize it, you are one phone call away from being like me," he said. "And if you don't have real-deal health insurance when you get that phone call, your whole life will change for the worse."

Dan said he is fortunate to be in a position that not only adequately compensates him in salary and benefits but also provides him with "almost limitless opportunities to learn new and valuable skills."

Dan recognizes that, in his role as a corporate attorney, a healthy work/life balance is not something that is easy for him to attain, but he said his compensation makes up for his lack of free time and his "incredible wife does a disproportionate share of the heavy lifting at home."

When working with older generations, Dan said one of his biggest frustrations is that they struggle with technology. He said this is particularly challenging in the law firm setting, where it makes more sense to have a digital record of changes to documents, as opposed to passing edited print copies among different lawyers. He added that his older colleagues don't understand how different the job market is now. "They have no real internalization of the fact that some of us are hundreds of thousands of dollars in debt and that every one of us has a couple dozen equally credentialed and totally unemployed peers," he said.

For Dan, the characteristics of a good job are

- Compensation commensurate with his capacity
- Company benefits, including health insurance
- Room to learn and grow into a more competent professional
- Working with people who can help him become better at what he does and develop his professional network with an eye toward advancing his career

Dan is motivated by:

- Detailed feedback on his work performance
- Making enough money to adequately support himself and his family
- Working with people who are good at their jobs

CHAPTER FOUR

MYTHS

"Seek first to understand, then to be understood."

Habit 5 from *The Seven Habits of Highly Effective People* by Stephen R. Covey

There is a logical reason why Gen Y is the way it is and it is helpful to understand it. More important, whatever Gen Y's characteristics may be, if we are good leaders, we will be able to work with them and bring out the best in them. *There are no attributes possessed by Gen Y that cannot be successfully managed, nurtured, and channeled in a beneficial way by a good leader.*

We believe urban legends and misplaced media headlines drive much of the negative image of Gen Y. We also believe one or two "real life" examples that support these "urban legends" can quickly be seen as validation of one's prejudice and become viewed as the norm and not the exception. There may be a tendency to look at one or two exceptions

Key Point

A leader's job is to bring out the best in his or her people.

and ignore the tens of thousands of stories that are not in the media and do not "go viral" on the Internet. Only the unusual and extreme tends to "go viral."

Our research into the common myths has been supported over and over by our audiences when we discuss Gen Y. Around the county and around the world we hear very similar things. Let's look more closely at the seven major myths about Gen Y that have developed over time.

Myth 1: Gen Yers Are Slackers or Lazy

This is one of the most repeated prejudices we hear about Gen Y. In 2008 we conducted a national survey and asked Baby Boomers, Gen X, and Gen Y to rank what qualities make someone successful. (In 2008 we did not include the Traditionalists.)

We redid the survey, including Traditionalists, and asked folks to rank virtues like leadership, communication skills, efficiency, time management, and so on. The top virtue chosen by Traditionalists, Baby Boomers, and Gen X was "hard-working" (in 2008 we had nearly identical results).

It was not surprising that these generations, given their outstanding work ethic, chose hard work as the number one choice. What might surprise people is that Gen Y, just as in 2008, also chose "hard-working" as the number one virtue. They clearly understand the connection between hard work and success.

If this is the case, why do so many business leaders still believe Gen Y is lazy? Let's examine a few things we believe are attribution errors. In other words, leaders are *attributing* laziness to Gen Y without all of the facts. Also, leaders may be running the behaviors through their own generation's filter and drawing erroneous conclusions (FAE).

Two Common Attribution Errors and the Rest of the Story

First FAE. One thing we have heard over and over is that Gen Y will "run you over to get out at 5 p.m. Don't stand in the doorway at quitting time." This desire to leave at 5 p.m. is often interpreted as being a "clock watcher." If there was one thing other generations despised, it was a clock watcher!

Being a clock watcher meant your only concern was to get out of work as quickly as possible. If this meant something was left undone, or even worse, was done poorly, then so be it. As long as one got out of the door exactly at quitting time, who cared about quality.

Previous generations valued *time*. To be seen in the office meant you were working. In early and out late was admired. The 20th century probably did require presence in order to be productive.

The Rest of the Story. That is not so in the 21st century. Time does not equal productivity or hard work. Tasks can be completed from anywhere, at any time. Gen Y was born into this reality. It is the only thing they know. Equating presence with productivity is simply a foreign concept. Gen Y has been able to make significant purchases, communicate with people face-to-face, and earn a degree, all without being "present."

So why does Gen Y "run out the door at 5 p.m."? The short answer is because they can. The longer answer is because they have many other interests and obligations to attend to after 5 p.m.

Let's look at the short answer. Gen Y has always lived in a world where quality work can be produced from anywhere, at any time. Just because Gen Y leaves work at 5 p.m. does not mean they are done working for the day. Our research shows that engaged Gen Y workers put in an *average* of 1.6 additional hours per day either on weekends or after 5 p.m. This work just happens to be done out of the sight of bosses and co-workers.

Consultant's Corner: Words Matter

Twenty-first century leaders will have a challenge getting themselves and others from previous generations to see that time does not equal productivity. I do think this will be one of the bigger challenges leaders will face, convincing co-workers that their Gen Y peers are not slackers because they put in less time onsite. After all, "seeing is believing."

There is a very fun (and simple) test leaders can do to open the minds of the previous generations. Simply ask them, when they are working after regular work hours, how they would describe what they are doing. It might take some prompting from the leader, but what one will hear are things like, "putting in some OT (overtime)" or "burning the midnight oil." Previous generations have developed sayings to describe this extra time and in most cases the wording was meant to show how hard they were working and the extra effort they were putting in.

If one were to ask a Gen Y employee this same question, the answer would simply be "working" or "finishing a project." There are no sayings to describe the extra time because Gen Y does not see this as anything special. They are simply finishing a project and do not need any special recognition for doing the job after hours.

This test may be seen as a little too elementary, but it drives home the point. Putting in extra hours, after regular business hours, is seen from two completely different viewpoints. One is a sign of hard work and commitment; the other is just doing what is needed. It is nothing special.

Many studies, including our own, have concluded that Gen Y is the most family-centric of the four generations. Time must be made to share with family and friends. Work is not an excuse to miss Grandma's birthday.

It is not hard to understand this family-centric attitude. Many Gen Yers have maintained very close relationships with their parents. In fact, Gen Y *enjoys* interacting and spending time with their parents. When you add to this the extended family (grandparents, aunts, uncles, as well as possibly great-grandparents, and other relatives), Gen Y feels a need to make the time while the opportunity is available. They know their elderly relatives will not be here in twenty years, so the time is now. No regrets.

The longer answer is that Gen Y has a life outside work. Their careers/jobs are only one part of who they are. Projects, physical health, community projects, friends, and family are just a few of the things Gen Y attends to after 5 p.m. One of the biggest priorities for Gen Y is family.

Gen Y clearly knows the correlation between hard work and success. What they don't get, and we contend *won't* get, is the need to "be present" in a defined location in order to be a productive contributor. Gen Y will work just as hard, if not harder, than every other generation . . . just not on a traditional time schedule.

Second FAE. The second thing we often hear to "prove" Gen Y is lazy is, "They never want to dig out an answer. They are always looking to someone else to give them the answer." This is often followed by, "How will they learn anything if we are always giving them the answers? That's how I learned when I was getting started."

Gen Y is often viewed as lazy because they tend to ask questions and seek input from their superiors. This may be interpreted as trying to cut corners or not wanting to work at digging out the answer.

Gen Y simply views asking questions as being productive. In their minds, why should time, energy, productivity, and money be wasted to find an answer that already exists? If someone else knows the answer, then it is as simple as just asking him or her. They truly believe it is no more complicated than that.

Why might they believe that? First, because it is true. It is a waste of resources to reinvent solutions that already exist. Second, Gen Y has always been exposed to collaboration tools on the web. If there is a problem to be solved, go out to your network and find an answer. At work their manager and co-workers are simply a part of their network.

According to Wikipedia, the transitive verb to google (also spelled Google) means using the Google search engine to obtain information on something or somebody on the World Wide Web. However, in many dictionaries the verb refers to using any web search engine, such as Yahoo! or Bing. A neologism arising from the popularity and dominance of the eponymous search engine, the American Dialect Society chose it as the "most useful word of 2002." It was added to the *Oxford English Dictionary* on June 15, 2006, and to the eleventh edition of the *Merriam-Webster Collegiate Dictionary* in July 2006.

Finally, Gen Y would believe it is OK to ask because *we told them they could.* Things like, "My door is always open" or "There is no such thing as a stupid question" or even "If you need something, just ask." Often these things are said because we have always said them, knowing we were not going to be taken up on it.

Previous generations were told the same things. They just knew it wasn't true. They believed it was a sign of weakness to ask for help, or even worse, an answer to a problem. For years it has been an unwritten rule at many businesses: "We say you can ask questions, but we don't really mean it."

Gen Y takes leaders at their word. If you say I can ask questions, then I will ask questions. If you say you are available, then I will assume you are available. Gen Y believes what we say. Until we prove otherwise.

Myth 2: Gen Y Needs Instant Gratification and Wants a Trophy for Just Showing Up

The second myth is that all new Gen Y employees want everything now and do not want to pay their dues. We have heard literally hundreds of times from executives and managers, "They want it all without working for it. They want to be the president after six months."

Do not fall for this myth. Certainly, Gen Y has grown up in a world where "fast" is not only a virtue but a way of life. This generation has always known the technology to have instant access to nearly anything. These devices have allowed Gen Y to multi-task and find quicker ways to achieve a result.

They text, often finding email to be too slow. "Snail mail" to them is a 20th century relic. They do not drive to the mall and visit multiple stores in order to comparison shop. They go online, visit multiple websites, and often make their purchases in the time it takes to back the car out of the garage. They have information instantly at their fingertips via the Internet. Cable and satellite TV have made hundreds of television stations available. There is no longer a need to "go to the video store." That, too, is a 20th century relic. Smart phones have connected them instantly to an array of friends globally. The large number of shopping centers available, combined with online shopping, has shown Gen Y that if they can't get what they want from one source, they can immediately go to another. Technology has made Generation Y accustomed to getting what they need easily and quickly.

Consultant's Corner: Who Bought the Trophies?

One thing I hear over and over again from folks once they know I wrote a book about Gen Y goes something like, "Oh, you mean the kids who got trophies for just showing up?" I can hear

(*continued*)

the disgust in their voices. It is obvious to me they have little respect for someone who "always got a trophy" for just being on the team. No real need to accomplish anything, just be on the team and receive a reward.

Well, I usually have one question for these folks. Who bought the trophies? Did the eleven-year-olds pool their money together and buy their own awards? I don't think so. The parents bought the trophies (and these parents were most likely Gen Xers or Baby Boomers). If the parents did not buy the trophies directly, it is a near certainty that the awards were purchased with their knowledge and maybe even financial support.

My point is, Gen Y *did not* buy trophies for themselves. The adults did, and now these same adults are mad at Gen Y! Does that make sense?! Plus, over and over, we hear from Gen Y that they were not really proud of the trophies, but their parents were. I had one Gen Yer tell me "I knew I was in ninth place, I did not want a trophy for that. It bothered me when my mom put it on the mantel at home."

Gen Y can, and does, separate real results from meaningless accolades. For real results, Gen Y wants, and I would argue deserves, real praise. For meaningless accomplishments, like showing up, Gen Y no more wants a trophy than any previous generation.

Does Gen Y really need things to be instant or immediate on the job? Does Gen Y really expect to become a senior manager in the first year? The quick answer to both of these questions is a resounding NO.

The full answer is twofold. First, you may be able to use Gen Y's propensity for speed to your advantage. Second, some things like performance feedback do need to happen more quickly than you or your culture might be used to. For years most organizations have used a performance management system that has a thirty-day, ninety-day, and one-year review point for new employees. After that, a one-year review is the norm. The fact of the matter is, these review timelines do not work for Gen Y. And even if the timelines did work, rare is the organization that provides timely annual appraisals.

To go even further, annual appraisals do not work for the other generations either. This is a 20th century tool in a 21st century world. The evolution of annual appraisals has gotten so far off track that books and computer programs are now used to find the correct "phraseology" to fill in an appraisal.

Managers the world over are referring to programs/books to give them the wording to say, "Sally did a great job." This may be the most unauthentic management tool that exists. Gen Y is nothing if not authentic. According to sustainablebusiness.com, feedback is not just for Gen Y. Their survey indicated that "15 percent of Gen Yers would prefer three to four performance reviews per year in contrast with 5 percent of Boomers wanting the same." Sustainablebusiness.com goes on to say, "Now if we're talking genuine feedback on performance versus 'performance reviews,' I don't think the desire for more feedback is an exclusive right of Generation Y. They have just challenged the status quo more often and stood up and demanded their right to know how they are doing on the job."

Gen Y Loves More Feedback

You cannot wait for the one-year anniversary to evaluate Gen Y, give them a raise, or ask for their input. They want feedback sooner. Gen Y *does not* believe they must be president in six months. They *do believe* they should receive feedback regularly and be financially rewarded for their contributions.

To more fully understand this issue, let's look at a typical culture and performance management system:

- New-hire training
- Thirty-day evaluation
- Ninety-day evaluation
- One-year performance appraisal
- Annual raise
- Regularly scheduled annual reviews

Gen Y wants and needs feedback on a regular basis. They want to know how they are doing and whether they are progressing. Gen Y wants to progress as quickly as they deserve from their abilities to contribute and they want to see steady progress to the next level. The standard performance management system, in many ways, creates an artificial and arbitrary time constraint. To be successful, leaders must challenge the performance management status quo and make time for regular feedback.

"Apparently, Gen Yers differ from my cohort, as well as others, with a preference for more constant feedback—or that's the story being highlighted. However, the survey indicated only 15 percent of Gen Yers would prefer three to four performance reviews per year in contrast with 5 percent of Boomers wanting the same. Now, if we are talking genuine feedback on performance versus 'performance reviews' I don't think the desire for more feedback is an exclusive right of Generation Y. They have just challenged the status quo more often and stood up and demanded their right to know how they are doing on the job."

http://sustainablebusinessforum.com/tedcoine/186751/it-s-not-just-generation-y-experiencing-feedback-deprivation

---

Coach's Corner: Spend Time with Your Players

I think at early stages of my coaching career I would exhaustively pour through film. I would try to prepare for every possible contingency. Sometimes I would keep at it well beyond the point of diminishing returns. Almost to produce some type of security for myself should we not be successful I could at least say that I did everything I could. But there's only so much time. What I found in later stages of my career was that it's much more important to make sure that your own players are in the right place. As much as you can with the constraints of time, we try to stay connected with our players, talk with them. Really address their needs as much as the technical aspects of a game plan. Both are important; you have to have both. Early on I was more lopsided toward the Xs and Os. And as time has moved on I've tried to move more toward the middle. Spending time with my players is as important, if not more important, than spending time on the Xs and Os.

If you're not willing to give Gen Y timely feedback, they are willing to just put in their time until they jump to a situation that looks better. They are also willing to quit and go back to school, to train for a marathon, to travel, or to live at home for a while. They are not motivated to work just for the sake of working. They want to be in a "good" situation.

Leaders must also challenge the traditional idea that compensation is linked to tenure. Annual raises, based on simply surviving for another year

Key Point

How are you recognizing and rewarding your workers (not just Gen Yers)? Do you have a mechanism in place to provide timely feedback and recognition?

versus making significant contributions along the way, must be examined. Gen Y wants to be recognized for their contributions, not their tenure. We'll cover this point more in later chapters on issues like alignment. In order to recruit top talent, it is critical for your top candidates to know that you reward contribution, not just tenure.

Voices of Experience: Ret. General Dom Rocco

Retired Army General Dom Rocco was born in a coal-mining town in Western Pennsylvania, but he had no interest in working in a coal mine. At sixteen, Rocco said, he was "afraid they were going to throw my butt in the coal mine, so I ran away and joined the Army." He spent thirty-five years in the U.S. Army, commanding at every level from platoon to battalion brigade.

Rocco took the skills he learned in the military and applied them to business after his retirement, noting that his leadership style is different from that of most military and civilian leaders. He said he's tough—he specified a strict dress code for his workers—but also accessible—he commanded both soldiers and civilian employees by routinely walking among them.

Another thing he learned in the military is that respect and recognition can mean more than money, saying he could get more out of a soldier by bestowing him with an honor than he could by giving a civilian worker $30,000.

In the early 2000s, Rocco retired from the military and started a wealth management company, raising and managing $1.4 billion. He then retired again and started a small nonprofit company in Greensburg, Pennsylvania, that makes loans to people who'd struggle to get a bank loan. He also managed a ministry of churches, schools, and orphanages in India.

Despite all of his success as a military leader, business leader, and nonprofit leader, Rocco said most people aren't born with the ability to lead but it can be learned. As a businessman, he set rigorous standards for his staff—and enforced them. "If they didn't meet my standard, we would have a talk or I would put them on thirty or sixty days' notice," he said. Then, if they failed to produce, "I would terminate them."

Rocco taught weekly classes on economics during his time leading the wealth management company and said setting goals is key to productivity.

"You have to challenge the people," he said. "If the people are good, and of course that's what you wanted . . . you had to challenge them."

"You have to show this improvement, this betterment, that you can bring to the company," he added.

One frustration that Rocco, born in 1938, shares with many members of Gen Y is a focus on tenure over merit in the workforce, saying it's impossible to run a successful business with people who don't work hard. "The good guys always have to outnumber the bad," he said.

Rocco's advice for Gen Y? "Whatever you do, don't insult the boss by thinking you know more than he or she does," he said. "You may, but don't make it obvious in front of anybody."

In the meantime, Rocco said, Gen Y workers should try to work hard and learn from their elders.

Myth 3: Gen Yers Are Disloyal and Job-Jumpers

Gen Y has a reputation for leaving jobs after one or two years and moving around from job to job. As we will discuss shortly in Chapter 7, Gen Yers have the freedom to move from job to job because they are delaying the responsibilities of marriage and parenting and have a strong financial safety net in the form of parental support. They are also keenly aware of their other options.

Gen Y is constantly asking, "What's next?" It is true that they will jump from job to job more often than any previous generation. What is not true, and is an absolute myth, is that they will jump from company to company with reckless abandon.

The Great Recession has had a significant impact on Gen Y. Many business leaders thought the economic challenges would "break Gen Y" and they will conform to the previous generations' norms. This has proven *not* to be the case. However, the recession has had a major impact on Gen Y's desire for stability. (More on the recession's impact in Chapter 5.)

Gen Y does not *want* to jump from company to company, but they *do* want to have a varied work experience. While desiring stability, Gen Y will in fact leave an organization if their career development is blocked. There is a deep desire to continue to learn and grow at all times.

Leaders must be keenly aware of this fact. Boomers and Xers were born into a world that had "career ladders." The most ambitious of these cohorts "climbed the corporate ladder." If the next rung on the ladder was occupied, the standard order of the day was "be patient, work hard, and you will move up." Many Boomers' and Xers' careers stagnated as they "remained patient."

Leaders need to redefine the career tracks in their organizations. Gen Y will not allow their careers (or their talents) to stagnate waiting for an open rung on the ladder. Leaders must design "career lattices" that allow talent to move not only up, but sideways, and even down.

Key Point

Gen Y will make "lateral moves" and will be attracted to organizations with a "career lattice."

Previous generations were taught that a "lateral move" was a negative and maybe even career suicide. In a world that had ladders, a side step meant a fall. "If you were not moving up, you were going backward" was the standard belief. Gen Y is more than willing to make a lateral move if they will learn something new, be able to contribute, add new skills, and the work is meaningful.

What *is* different is Gen Y's requirement that their work be meaningful and interesting. Gen Y will not devote long hours to something they don't consider valuable or motivating. If you assign Gen Y a task that lacks substance, you will see a nonchalant, "slacker" approach to that task. If you give them boring, endless administrative work that is not linked to a more meaningful, important project, they are not going to work up to their potential. They will live down to your "lazy" expectations and then quit.

How to Inspire Gen Y

Many managers assume all new Gen Y employees only want easy, fun, and exciting work. The prejudices we discussed take over and there is a tendency to jump to unfair conclusions. Let us be clear: we are not saying Gen Y will only do easy and fun work. They want *meaningful* work. When needed, Gen Y will do mundane tasks. The key is linking these work assignments to a more important goal. Put another way, Gen Y wants to know why they are doing a task and *how* it contributes.

We understand two key realities. First, in any job there are tasks and assignments that are not exciting. Many times these tasks are downright difficult, boring, time-consuming, and mindless.

The second reality is that this work absolutely needs to be done. Any manager worth his paycheck will not assign work just to assign work. There is always a reason for the task.

There are two minor adjustments that all leaders must make if they are to successfully motivate Gen Y. The first adjustment is not new, but it is often overlooked or forgotten by leaders. Leaders must explain the *why* of these mundane assignments. Why is this task necessary, and how does it link to the bigger strategy?

This might be a good time to mention the important distinction between a manager and a leader made by Peter Drucker and others.

Managers get things done through other people. Their weakness tends to be trying to do the work themselves rather than training and supervising others. *Leaders* not only get things done through others, but they *inspire* others. Their weakness tends to be forgetting to inspire. They must set the vision for the task. Gen Y responds better to leaders than to managers. They want to be inspired.

Communicate the Big Picture

Traditional managers tend to overlook the important step of explaining the why. They think it's a waste of time to explain the bigger picture. They think the fact that they say something needs to be done is reason enough to cheerfully accept boring assignments. By taking just a few minutes to explain the bigger picture, managers will not only experience a more productive result, but they will exhibit more leadership traits and will keep their employees engaged and motivated.

Key Point

Leaders explain the why.

The second adjustment that needs to be made is to be open to suggestions about the task. As Gen Y employees tackle new tasks, they are continually thinking about how to do them better and faster. Gen Y is not at all locked into the mentality of "it has always been done this way." If there is a more productive solution, they will find it and they expect to both share their findings and help implement the improvement. Leaders take time and listen to these suggestions. If Gen Y reinvents the wheel with their suggestions, the leader explains why this is and encourages their initiative. If Gen Y invents a better way to accomplish something, the leader embraces the idea and celebrates the success.

If you assign Gen Yers jobs of substance and significance, you will see dedicated, hard-working performers. You just have to know what motivates them. They will put in long hours, but they have to care about what they're doing. They can be very productive if they are treated like independent contractors, given a clear goal that they buy into, and rewarded for great performance. As a leader, you need to enlist their interest and commitment. You have to learn about their values and personal goals, then incorporate these in some way into their assignments. Offer them challenges, teach them new skills, and enlist their fresh perspectives.

Gen Yers will not be disloyal or job jump if you give them the incentive to stay. If a job is relevant, they will stay. As discussed above, Gen Y employees also want to care about their work, have frequent communication, and experience career progression. When these requirements are met, Gen Yers can be loyal, stable, long-term employees.

Voices of Experience: Martin Zvirbulis

The 120 employees of the Cucamonga Valley Water District have some of the hardest, dirtiest jobs on the planet. CVWD is a public agency formed in 1955 for the sole purpose of providing potable water and wastewater collection services for 186,000 customers in an area of about forty-seven square miles in four Southern California cities.

Martin Zvirbulis, CVWD's general manager and CEO, said an oft-repeated maxim—Gen Y workers won't do "dirty jobs"—is completely false. "These are the guys who, on a day-to-day basis, clean sewer lines, make sure we don't have any blockages or overflows that would affect water quality," Zvirbulis said. "This isn't a glamorous job . . . but I've never met a prouder group of individuals." Zvirbulis said CVWD's board and management staff are dedicated to the organization's founding principles—people, service, water. Because the jobs at CVWD only get harder as you grow older, there are a lot of members of Gen X and Gen Y in leadership roles right now, and they're setting the bar and employing a new style of leadership that goes over well with the entire workforce, Zvirbulis said. The strong cultural fabric of the CVWD empowers leaders to adapt to get the best out of each worker.

(*continued*)

The Gen Y workers are "looking forward to a work environment that allows them to grow and develop their skills, take advantage of leadership opportunities, work in an environment where they feel empowered to do the work that needs to be done while not being micromanaged," Zvirbulis said.

For some of the CVWD's workers, they come in, learn how to do the job, and if advancement opportunities aren't there when the worker is ready, they go elsewhere.

With just 120 employees, there's not a lot of room to move up, so if an employee is ready to move on before the opportunity arises internally, they're encouraged to seek opportunities to meet their goals.

"I don't necessarily see that as a bad thing," Zvirbulis said. "Far be it from us as an organization to stifle the growth and development of an individual."

Myth 4: Gen Y Is Self-Centered and Narcissistic

Certainly some members of Gen Y have been convinced by their parents, schools, and friends that they are the center of the universe. However, the majority of Gen Y is not as selfish as we imagine. Most are not "all about themselves." They place a high priority on family and friends. Gen Y cares equally about career and family and less about "work only" like previous generations. They support and believe in social causes and want their employers to do so as well.

Gen Y is not simply looking for their companies to show they care. They are walking the talk and volunteering at record rates. The trends are overwhelming. Gen Y volunteers more than any previous generation.

Gen Y's goal is not simply to earn money. They want to contribute—at work, in the community, and in the world at large. If this generation were truly selfish, why would they give up their nights, weekends, and vacation time to volunteer?

As previously mentioned, many attributes are assigned to Gen Y based on urban legends and media positioning. We believe this misguided publicity is to blame for Gen Y's being labeled "narcissistic." In addition, many surveys are cited to confirm the "fact" that Gen Y is narcissistic. But if one reads the surveys carefully, most of them are surveying co-workers (Traditionalists, Boomers, and Xers). These surveys reveal what *others think* about Gen Y. The results are then posted as fact and not opinion.

We will not argue that many have a very strong opinion about Gen Y and find them to be narcissistic. We only take exception to opinion versus fact. We also take exception to the data which is used to "prove" Gen Y's narcissism.

For example, a major publication referenced that a majority of Gen Y, while in middle school, would rather be a celebrity's personal assistant than a U.S. senator. This was "proof" that Gen Y was self-absorbed. The point they were trying to make was that Gen Y (while in middle school) would rather have a "look at me" career, rather than a civic-minded career. The "research" concluded these middle school Gen Yers were self-absorbed. We are not sure about others, but when we were in middle school, we wanted to play in the NBA. The point is, how many folks in the previous generations would have responded any differently? Did Traditionalist, Boomers, and Gen Xers want to be Senators when they were in middle school? The "research" does not address that. If it did, we think the answers across all cohorts would have been similar.

We also believe there is a major difference between "individualism" and "narcissism." Gen Y is very individualistic and does not believe that "one size fits all." They more likely feel "my size fits me."

Another reason Gen Y is typed as self-centered and narcissistic is the tools they use. Things like Twitter, LinkedIn, and Facebook give the impression "it is all about me." Now, do some Gen Yers use these tools inappropriately and to show off (look at me)? Absolutely! Also, do many grandparents and great-grandparents out there use these tools inappropriately and to show off (look at my beautiful kids and grandkids)? Absolutely! Using social media tools to draw attention to oneself (or to one's grandchildren) is not reserved just for Gen Y.

As individualists, Gen Y finds it to be important to establish their own personal brand. Many people will view this as narcissistic. We would argue that branding has long been a part of our culture. Iconic brands, in and of themselves, have significant value. By establishing personal brands, Gen Y is looking to establish their value and individuality. More about branding in Chapter 8.

With all of that said, Gen Y also values collaboration and teamwork. Some of the same tools discussed previously also allow Gen Y to communicate and collaborate with others instantly.

Surveys we have conducted show an overwhelming majority (72 percent) of Gen Y wants to be on a productive team. Most responded that collaboration produces a better work product. Even when working alone on a project, many Gen Yers (62 percent) will reach out to their network for input when appropriate.

Working on teams creates an "even playing field." The traditional corporate hierarchy is broken down and team members can act as equals. Additionally, teams allow for social interaction and the opportunity to hear diverse opinions.

All of these traits do not add up to self-centered and selfish individuals, but to people who actually care about others and who have the capacity to care about you and your organization. Again, it is up to you to make them care, give them ownership of their jobs, communicate frequently with them, and help them buy into what your company is all about.

Key Point

Gen Y is individualistic, not narcissistic.

Myth 5: Gen Y Is Pampered and Spoiled

In some ways members of Gen Y really were pampered. They have Baby Boomer parents who indulged them and catered to their many wants and needs, from fixing traffic tickets to completing college applications for them. According to EmploymentReview.com, Gen Y's parents have spent more time with them, their fathers were more involved with rearing them, and their parents have been more hands-on with them than any prior generation. Naturally, some of them are spoiled. However, the majority of them are not. They simply have different priorities and see the world differently. They grew up knowing they were valued. They have high self-esteem and they have no need to do what you want just because you want it. They are used to being treated as if they mattered and being given reasons for taking a particular course of action.

All individuals want to be recognized for their accomplishments. Celebrating success by going out to lunch or dinner, and being recognized by key business leaders, goes a long way toward making young workers feel valued. Experienced employees may have grown used to not being acknowledged. Gen Y has not and won't!

According to the Families and Work Institute, Gen Y sometimes has a reputation for being pampered because they tend to put more emphasis on non-work areas of their lives like family and leisure. However, they work just as many hours—and in some cases more—than the Baby Boomers and Gen Xers did when they were a similar age. Gen Y is also perceived as spoiled because these individuals are not reluctant to live at home or take money from their parents. Gen Y simply views accepting help from their families as the logical use of available resources and a way to save money. To them it's not being pampered, but being prudent and practical.

Voices of Experience: Ron Lott of Lott Marketing

As a leader, I have thought a great deal about how we must adapt as we move forward. There is an analogy that works for me. A talented Gen Y candidate is like an untested, finely tuned motor in a sports car. This motor wasn't designed to perform at its peak in a school zone at 25 miles an hour. Nor was the engine designed

(*continued*)

to sit in a garage and have its performance measured by simply revving it up every once in a while.

Like a fine automobile, you must put it in gear . . . fully engage it in order to really understand its performance capability. With Gen Y, we, as leaders, must be prepared to engage our new, highly tuned talent. Only then can we truly judge their performance and contributions.

On a very personal note, my son, a Gen Yer, used a week's vacation to take a course to obtain certification to deal with children at risk. And one of our employees is taking all of his vacation and two weeks without pay to do missionary work in South America.

There are three other big things we hear that are meant to "prove" that Gen Y is spoiled. These three are what we call "the old school trio": timeliness, dress, and attention span. The truth is Gen Y will push timelines and dress codes and may well check their devices dozens of times during meetings while seemingly not paying attention (or even actually not paying attention!).

The issue here is not that Gen Y is spoiled and "wants their own way." It is something far more universal: time management skills, pushing limits, and distraction/boredom. These three elements have been around since the beginning of time. What is different now is how the behavior manifests itself and how it is judged.

There have always been people who are late for meetings. In fact, certain personality styles are prone to it. Folks have always fumbled the dress code, and people have always "doodled" during meetings. Many who exhibited these behaviors may even have been star performers (and maybe even you!).

If these behaviors were distracting and counterproductive to the group *and* the group had a strong leader, the behaviors were addressed. Nothing has changed. The "old school trio" still should be addressed through appropriate leadership.

As a leader, ask yourself about all employees: Do we tolerate tardiness? Do we put up with unprofessional attire? Do we tolerate distractions? If so, fix it. You may need to tighten up your dress code, have "no-device meetings" and stop tolerating meetings that constantly start fifteen minutes late (even if *you* are the one always late!). Gen Y feels that "if anyone can be late, including the boss, why not me?" Having been brought up in a "fair play" environment, what is good for one is good for all. This is only a natural conclusion.

Prepare yourself for push-back when you set the dress code and "device-less" meetings. Gen Y, just like every other generation, likes to push their boundaries. If your decision is sound, do not back down. Explain the "why" of your decision and make sure you do not allow exceptions. If you are the exception, either stop it or get used to seeing Gen Y model your poor behavior. If the leader acts "spoiled" and can make everyone wait, then this behavior must be acceptable.

Consultant's Corner: Explain the "Why of Devices"

One of my mentors, the late Ron Morris, taught me a valuable lesson about devices. Ron was a born entrepreneur who founded many successful businesses. He also founded *The American Entrepreneur* radio show. The first show I was on he invited me to talk about Gen Y. After that he called me "the Gen Y guy"!

Later on he invited me to host my own show, *The Consultant's Corner*, but no matter what topic I discussed, he still called me the Gen Y guy. Ron had a deep faith in this generation and even helped to found an entrepreneurial studies program at Duquesne University. One day he called me after a meeting he had with one of his new (Gen Y) sales folks. He was very frustrated because during the meeting/sales call, his new person was using her device the entire time. Ron felt this was rude and distracting. He also felt the prospect was put off, too.

(*continued*)

When Ron confronted the new sales person about "surfing the net" during the meeting, she explained she was *in no way* surfing the Internet and was, in fact, simply taking notes on the call. She opened her device and showed him the notes. He was floored, but also learned a valuable lesson.

After that, he learned to ask prospects whether they could take notes on the device and received their permission in advance. This also helped put the prospect's mind at ease and eliminated his or her frustration. Ron also learned that Gen Y is not always doing what he thought they were doing and were, in fact, leveraging technology in ways he had never considered.

He also learned to coach his Gen Y folks on how interfacing with a device at meetings might be perceived. While she knew what she was doing, Ron did not, and neither did the prospect. It is everyone's responsibility to make sure communications are clear and that no one is offended by the use of devices.

Ron learned to "explain the why" and also to have his new folks do the same thing!

Authority Figure vs. Authentic Figure

One very striking difference between Gen Y and every other generation is the way they view leadership and titles. To Gen Y, these are two *very* separate and distinct things. A title does not make a leader. Leadership makes a leader.

Gen Y makes managers face the fact that respect isn't given, it has to be earned. That's really true of all workers; however, past workers have given you the benefit of the doubt and been more willing to just put in time. Gen Y is willing to work hard and loyally, but these individuals expect to learn new skills, be part of something worthwhile, and be appreciated. While it takes a bit more of your attention, it can work out better for the organization, too. Leaders need to be authentic and wield "influence power" and not just position power. "Because I said so" is not an answer to a thoughtful question.

Gen Y is looking for authentic people to lead them. They have very little tolerance for doublespeak. "Talking the talk" is simply not enough. Gen Y will follow leaders who "walk the talk." Frankly, even if they disagree with some of your decisions, knowing you are authentic will be enough to gain their trust and loyalty.

In his bestselling book, *The Five Dysfunctions of a Team*, Patrick Lencioni lays out how to build great teams and uses his character, Kathryn, to illustrate strong leadership. One of the first things Kathryn does is get everyone together and have them complete some "game film." (More on that in Chapters 10 and 11.) The goal was to get everyone on the same page. Next she displayed her authority by allowing herself to be vulnerable. This part of her leadership, and the book, has always been most striking. Too many leaders are afraid to show vulnerability. As Lencioni notes, followers already know it and leaders just look silly ignoring it!

Coach's Corner: Allow Yourself to Be Vulnerable

When I went to college, we didn't tease with our coach, Dave Maloney. We may have teased behind his back—we may have laughed about some things—but not with him. As a grown man he became my dear friend. Why wait thirty years? Why not show a "humanness" with your players now? Have fun together.

(*continued*)

In other words, let's not let the disguise of respect impair us from being connected because every human connection is enhanced if both sides have an element of vulnerability. If there's an aspect of openness, Gen Y finds this really important. As a leader you could be much more effective if your team could see multiple sides of you—even sometimes your vulnerability—it makes you more human to them.

That doesn't mean that in the face of hardship you allow your fears to take over and fail to lead. You as a leader stay poised and positive. You can't allow your own fears to encroach on the people you're leading. What it does mean is that every interaction is not a crisis to be managed. When there is a challenge, step up as a leader and lead. However, during regular interactions it is OK to be human, even vulnerable.

People in authority sometimes, because of the need for respect, think it's important to keep those lines drawn. That could backfire and really create a distance between people.

Consultant's Corner: The Power of Laughter

As the Coach's Corner and Lencioni's book illustrate, there is nothing wrong with showing a little vulnerability. Having fun at work, no matter how you do it, engages the team. Allowing laughter and, if you so desire, creating laughter, brings energy to the workplace. It does not detract from one's "authority." In fact, just the opposite is true. It also makes the leader authentic.

Earlier in my career one of my mentors, Jack Bogut, a Hall of Fame radio personality, taught me about the power in laughter. I remember him saying "everyone knows laughter is the best medicine, but it is also a powerful leadership tool."

Jack explained to me that laughter relaxes people and allows them to become more at ease with any situation. In later years I learned that laughter may have evolved as a human response to the passing of danger. Following a "fight or flight" situation our earliest ancestors may have developed laughter in order to calm down. Whether this it true or not, the fact is that laughter does calm people down.

Laughter is also an important "team building tool." As a speaker I am often in front of rooms with hundreds of people. Jack taught me a long time ago that when an audience is laughing it is the only time all of their brains are "on the same page." Studies have revealed that when a group is laughing their brains are all lighting up in the same region. Laughter is the only thing that allows an audience to be mentally exactly in the same place at the same time.

As a consultant, I have observed another thing about laughter. Many of the leaders we deal with around the world, who have become quite successful, are humorous. This may seem coincidental, or maybe I just like working with funny folks (and that may be true!), but it is more than that. Humor is a display of power.

I have concluded, completely unscientifically, that if groups are all on the same page when they are laughing and if many of the best leaders I know are humorous, then making people laugh is a display of power. It allows the leader to have all of the team members "mentally together" at one time. This makes if far easier to lead the group, since it is starting from an aligned place.

Laughter helps create alignment, whether in teams, work groups, or large audiences.

Myth 6: Gen Y Lacks Respect for Authority

Gen Y is often viewed as disrespectful of authority and authority figures. The picture that is often painted of Gen Y is that they are always questioning authority, checking devices at meetings, tuning out the speakers/boss, dressing unprofessionally, and not deferring to titles. While much of this may be true, the conclusion that is drawn, one of disrespect, is not true.

Let's look at another point: Gen Y is always questioning authority. It is true that Gen Y is always asking "why" and wanting to know why a job needs to be done, how it fits, and so forth. The truth is, this question is often misinterpreted. English is a living language, and words take on different meanings and have different connotations. Take the question "why" for example.

Baby Boomers were a generation who rebelled. Protesting the Vietnam War and segregation were two of the many things Boomers protested. In the workplace, Boomers were also major change agents. When a Boomer asked "why" anything, it was to question authority and be defiant. A Boomer asking, "Why do I need to do this?" was not really asking a question. It was a rebellious statement that was delivered in a defiant tone of voice.

The Boomer generation, and by extension Xers, hear defiance when asked "why" questions (certain personality styles excluded, as you will see in Chapter 10). When an Yer asks, "Why do I need to do that?" what is often heard is, "I don't want to do that" or its close cousin, "Doing that is stupid." Defiance is heard where none is intended.

Key Point

Are you hearing defiance in questions where none exists?

Gen Y is asking the question "why" not to be disrespectful, but to actually gain understanding. They are asking for context. They want to know why a job needs to be done and why it has been done this way. This helps them understand where the task fits. It also helps them to think whether there might be a better way to accomplish it. "Why" is not push-back.

"Why" is curiosity. "Why" is context. The issue is *not* with the questioner, it is with the receiver. It is not necessarily the question that is off base, it is the interpretation.

Consultant's Corner: The Power of "Why": The Leadership Difference

A client of ours had a major sales opportunity that required them to act quickly. They developed a mail piece that needed to be sent, along with other details of the offer, to thousands of prospects. These pieces needed to be stuffed into a special envelope, sorted, and mailed. In order to maximize the financial opportunity, time was of the essence.

Two groups of college interns were assigned this task by two different supervisors. Each group had four participants who had been with the organization the same amount of time. On the surface, there were no variables that would have allowed one group to be more productive than the other.

The important variable turned out to be the up-front communication by the supervisor. One of the supervisors chose to be a leader. She took a few minutes and explained to her group (Group 1) the "why" of this task. She explained the opportunity, the strategic link, and the time-sensitive nature of the materials. She offered to stop back later in the day to help and wrote her cell phone number on the whiteboard, should there be any questions.

The other supervisor chose to be a manager in the worst of the "old-school" tradition. He assigned the task, explained what needed to be done, and left, leaving Group 2 to stuff envelopes. The supervisor who offered to join them in the afternoon was thanked for the offer, but told, "We have it handled." Group 1 worked until late in the evening and finished the task.

Group 2 went home at 5:00 p.m. on the dot with the task less than half finished. The next day they started on it again. Group 1 volunteered to join them and helped to complete the task.

(*continued*)

When senior management first described the above scenario, we were told how unmotivated Group 2 was and how the members of Group 1 were real winners. Words like "old fashioned" and "work ethic" were used to describe Group 1, and "lazy," "slacker," and "spoiled" for Group 2.

As we dug deeper with senior management, they began to realize the real issue—leadership. Group 1 was no more "old fashioned" than Group 2; they were just provided with a leader who displayed timeless leadership skills. She explained the why.

Myth 7: Gen Y Feels Entitled

In many ways we have saved the hardest and most often repeated myth for last. If we, as Gen Y advocates, were to be completely honest, this was the hardest myth for us to overcome. As we researched this book and discussed our own experiences, we struggled with Gen Y entitlement.

Based on our research, surveys, formal and informal discussions with both Gen Y and business leaders, we have concluded we are wrong to believe Gen Y has a sense of entitlement and is not willing to work for results. However, when we really looked into the meaning of the words, we were confused as to how to bust this myth. Gen Y *did* enter the work world as "entitled." There is a difference between "entitled" and entitlement.

Allow us to explain. Merriam-Webster's Dictionary defines "entitled" as

1: to give title to

2: to furnish with proper grounds for seeking or claiming something

Gen Y *was* given "title to." They were told by their parents, teachers, coaches, and even Mr. Rogers,* that they were special.

*Frederick "Fred" McFeely Rogers was an American educator, Presbyterian minister, songwriter, author, and television host. Wikipedia

Gen Y *did* have a title. They were special. Everyone said so. As young children, how were they to know any different? They had the title of "special." So the first definition is accurate.

The second definition is also accurate. Gen Y *was* furnished with what they believed to be "proper grounds for seeking or claiming something." They sought success and felt they could "make a claim" to their "rightful place" among the successful. The message Gen Y heard over and over was about how they could do anything, accomplish anything, be anything, if only they wanted to. This, in Gen Y's mind, was "grounds for claiming something." What was missing from this message was that "wanting to" is not enough. "Working for" was missing. Simply wanting something was not going to get anyone anywhere.

When we looked at the definition of "entitled," we have concluded that many Gen Y, especially the earliest part of this generation, may well have felt entitled. In the late 1990s and early 21st century, young college graduates may well have, at first, felt it was time to "claim" their rightful place among the successful. Looking at this situation through the eyes of twenty-two-year-olds in 1999 or 2000, it is not hard to understand how they might have felt entitled. If they were told since birth they were special and the message was supported by nearly every institution, it would *truly* be the special person who would question the message. Add to this equation Gen Y's education and life experiences at an early age, then it is easy to see how they might have wanted to "claim their rightful place." In fact, Merriam-Webster.com, when using "entitled" in a sentence chose, "This ticket *entitles* bearer to free admission." Early on, Gen Y may well have expected free admission. (Our apologies for mixing metaphors.)

The problem with calling Gen Y entitled is twofold. First, it assumes an entire generation has not learned from experience. The world is a much different place today than in 1999 when the first of Gen Y entered the work world. In 1999 they had to experience life and work the same as anyone else. Also, they had to learn just like everyone else. *Everyone* starts the learning process unconsciously incompetent (Figure 4.1). We "don't know what we don't know."

As Gen Y gained experience, they began to learn and move from unconsciously incompetent to consciously incompetent. As time progressed and their skills were refined, Gen Y moved to Stage 3 and possibly Stage 4. This knowledge, given the social media tools and natural collaborative nature of Gen Y, was shared with subsequent graduating classes. In our opinion, not only did individual Gen Y employees gain valuable knowledge and experience, but they passed it along to future employees. Employees who entered the workforce in 1999 are dramatically different from workers entering it in the 21st century.

The second issue we have with calling Gen Y "entitled" is it presumes they have a sense of "entitlement." Again using Merriam-Webster, we find the word "entitlement" defined as "the condition of having a right to have, do, or get something" and "the feeling or belief that you deserve to be given something (such as special privileges)."

Maybe, just maybe, early in the 21st century, Gen Y did feel entitled. However, in *no way* does this generation today have a sense of entitlement. Gen Y clearly understands the correlation between hard work and success. In fact, because of sheer demographic numbers, Gen Y has realized they need to work *harder* than previous generations to achieve the same results.

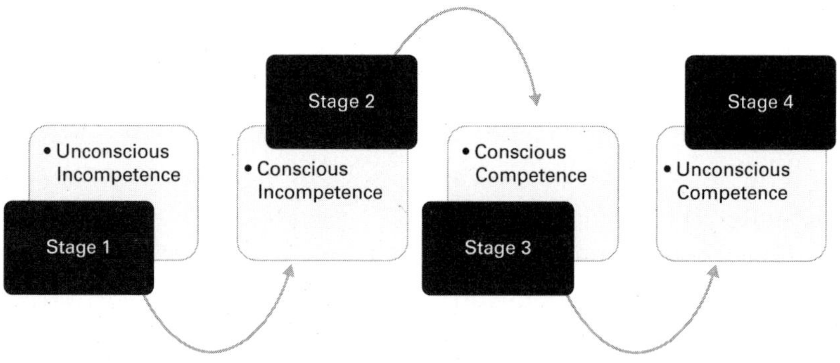

Figure 4.1. The Learning Process
Source: businessballs.com

The world Gen Y enters is truly global in nature. Gen Y must compete with not only their local peers, but with others from around the world. Pure numbers illustrate the challenges Gen Y faces in finding their place and achieving success. The world's population (7.2 billion) has grown by 2.8 billion since 1980. In the United States alone, the percentage of people twenty-five and older with bachelor's degrees has tripled in the last forty years, and this does not count international students in the United States or graduates from international universities.

Even if we ignore the global impact of demographics, there are simply more Gen Yers, with more education, competing for fewer opportunities. The supply and demand equation has made Gen Y acutely aware of the need to work hard and compete. This generation clearly knows it will not be "given something."

> "There are more people leisurely playing basketball in China than there are people in the United States. China has over three hundred million basketball players, playing at some level from recreational to professional. The competition is staggering."
>
> *Herb Sendek*

To further support our argument, not only does Gen Y realize they need to work hard to succeed, but they also realize they need to work hard on their developmental areas in order to succeed. Business.Time.com reported, "When asked whether they [Gen Y] need to build their strengths or fix their weaknesses in order to succeed professionally, 73 percent of Gen Y respondents chose to focus on their weaknesses—a much higher proportion than previous generations." It stands to reason that if Gen Y felt a sense of entitlement, then they should "have the right to" success just because of their natural gifts. This generation, however, to a much higher degree than previous generations, chooses to work on their weaknesses in order to earn professional success.

The Great Recession (see Chapter 5) has provided a huge learning experience for Gen Y. The realities of a worldwide recession have taught all of us, including Gen Y, some valuable lessons. While we will discuss some of the impact the recession has had in Chapter 5, we wanted to make sure to highlight that Gen Y does not have a sense of entitlement because of the Great Recession. The Great Recession has not "broken Gen Y." If anything, it has emboldened Gen Y. This generation, in spite of high unemployment, depressed wages, increased global competition, and a host of other challenges, *remains* optimistic, *retains* their belief in a bright future, and *continues* to give of their time and talent to others in need.

Key Point

Gen Y does have a sense of entitlement for the pursuit of happiness. It is spelled out in the Declaration of Independence.

If Gen Y feels entitled to anything, it is something spelled out in the Declaration of Independence. Something even Great Recessions can't shake. Gen Y, just like the founders of the United States, truly believe "We hold these truths to be self-evident, that all men are created equal, that they are endowed by their Creator with certain unalienable rights, that among these are life, liberty, and the pursuit of happiness."

How You Must Deal with These Myths

Gen Y has been unfairly stereotyped. It is crucial that these stereotypes do not exist in your organization or in the hearts and minds of your employees. All of us will live up—or down—to expectations about us. If we are treated as responsible people, we will act more responsibly. If we are treated as slackers, we will tend to act like slackers.

If your organization has a negative attitude about Gen Y, all the books, seminars, and guides in the world—including this one—will not help your staff accept and work with Gen Y.

Make no mistake about it, if anyone in your organization is prejudiced toward Gen Y, Gen Yers will pick up on it. You need to set a clear policy from the top or you can forget about attracting and keeping this new generation of employees.

Key Point
Leaders need to confront their own bias and then challenge others to confront theirs.

Coach's Corner: Don't Settle

When I was an assistant coach at the University of Kentucky, the recruiting coordinator for the football program was Coach Tommy Limbaugh, and he took a lot of time with Billy Donovan and me to share with us his philosophies on recruiting. He had spent a career studying recruiting and was a master at it. He told Billy and me that there were two kinds of mistakes that you can make in recruiting. One is OK; the other is not.

The first one is that you go after a talented person—someone who could really help your organization, your team, someone who could really help you win the championship—but in the end you don't get him. That's OK. On that same day, over 330 other basketball programs in the country didn't get him either. That mistake's fine. You're going after people who can help you win the championship.

If you make the second kind of mistake too often, you're going to be out of business. The second mistake is when you go after somebody and you get them and they're really not the answer. They're not good enough to help advance your organization, your team. They're not good enough to help you win the championship. If you make that mistake too often, you're in big trouble.

Conclusion

Whether you are a Traditionalist, a Boomer, or Gen Xer, it is incumbent upon you as a leader to check your pulse and your organization's pulse on this issue. How do your current employees feel about Gen Y? Have they bought into the stereotypes and misconceptions about Gen Y? What are their expectations for these future employees? Do they dread working with them or look forward to it? Do they understand why Gen Y is the way they are and what makes them tick? Do they understand the fresh skills Gen Y brings to the company? And, most important, can they accept Gen Y's differences and work with them?

You Have to Be a Role Model

You cannot eliminate prejudices and stereotypes about Gen Y that are latent in your organization until you confront them first in yourself. What do you honestly think about Gen Y? Do you consider this new generation of workers a problem to be solved, or a vital asset to be developed? Do you still believe the negative stereotypes? Are you resentful that you have to adapt to this new type of worker? Do you wish they would change instead of your having to?

Now is the time to shed those prejudices and negative feelings. These are the people you will be leading for the next few decades. They are the folks already working for you now. They are your future. Ultimately, you will need them more than they need you.

It is imperative that you set the tone unequivocally and welcome Gen Y with open arms. Your employees are watching and so are your current and future Gen Y workers.

Do Not Lower Your Standards

Putting aside unfounded prejudices with respect to Gen Y does not mean leaving behind your good judgment, common sense, or standards. It does not mean you will no longer recruit or retain qualified employees. Put another way, you do not recruit and retain unqualified employees simply because they are Gen Y.

Not every Gen Yer is a potentially great employee, and not every Gen Yer already on board should automatically be retained. Nor are we suggesting that you pamper or coddle Gen Y employees who lack the skills, the integrity, or the other intangibles that you require. Like any other generation, they have their weak links. The mark of excellent leadership is to be able to look beyond stereotypes to see the talent and potential within Gen Y, yet still hold them to the standards you have set for all employees.

There are Gen Yers who truly are self-absorbed, lazy, and spoiled and live down to the negative stereotypes. You do not want these people as employees. However, Gen Y as a whole has a good work ethic, wants to contribute and be productive, and can become an important asset to your company. It is important that you do not mistake Gen Y's legitimate desire to progress, their need for communication, or their insistence on meaningful work as self-centeredness, "slacking," or disloyalty. As a leader, it is your job to expose and eliminate any prejudice toward Gen Y that exists in yourself and your organization. You must be able to look beyond the superficial preconceptions you may have about Gen Y to harness and nurture the talent and potential that lies within. At the same time, you must still demand that Gen Y meet the standards you set for all employees.

Elizabeth's Gen Y Profile

Name: Elizabeth
Location: Midwest
Age: 36

(*continued*)

Background:

- Graduated with a bachelor's degree in family and community services and a master's degree in education
- Works in customer service for a large health insurance organization

Elizabeth faces a number of challenges in her job with a health insurance group that employs more than seven thousand people. While she said her immediate colleagues share her values, others within the customer service division do not, noting that she deals with a lot of unionized workers, meaning "seniority rules, and implementing change is extremely challenging."

Elizabeth said she carefully manages her expectations; otherwise, she'd feel "defeated and disappointed." "There is still a lot of dead weight, resistance to change, and far too many personal agendas," she said. "Our organization is the perfect example of a workplace with four generations under one roof."

She said older workers at her organization feel entitled and "demand respect, but they don't understand that respect is earned."

Elizabeth said that, while she communicates a lot by email and instant messenger, she feels "held hostage" by electronic communication and prefers to communicate face-to-face, noting that building relationships allows you to gauge people better. That said, a lot of her colleagues still believe that showing up to the office every day means they're producing, but that's sometimes not the case. "They believe that people should work a set schedule and they are definitely not open to working from home," she said, in contrast to Gen Y workers. However, she said, the current health care marketplace is forcing change within her organization.

For Elizabeth, the characteristics of a good job are

- Promoting and encouraging learning and development, new ideas, and new ways of doing things
- A team environment
- Recognition of skills, talents, and accomplishments
- Productivity and accomplishments counting more than seniority

Elizabeth is motivated by:

- Mentors who provide guidance and support
- The sense of accomplishment that comes from completing projects and tasks
- Setting goals and meeting them
- Feeling that her work makes a difference

CHAPTER FIVE

RECESSION GENERATION

It is not hard to imagine that the Great Recession has had a significant impact on Gen Y. It is safe to say the world has not seen an economic challenge of this magnitude since the Great Depression. It is also safe to say in both cases these financial markets had a profound effect on the young folks who began their lives in the midst of such challenges. The Depression molded the Greatest Generation and the Recession will mold Gen Y.

The full impact of the Great Recession will not be known for quite some time. Just like the Greatest Generation, it will take many years for us to understand all of the ramifications of the Recession on Gen Y. We will present this chapter in three different sections. First, we'll look at the statistics and try to make sense of the numbers. Next, we'll look at how Gen Y has responded. Finally, we'll offer our opinions and theories on how this will affect Gen Y and how you, as business leaders, can react.

There will be one over-riding theme in this chapter. Just like the Great Depression did not break the Greatest Generation, the Great Recession has not broken Gen Y. We are not suggesting that this puts both generations on par with one another (after all, there was this thing called World War II that was also a part of the

Greatest Generation). What we do hope to point out, though, is that these two situations in many ways brought about similar reactions and generational responses.

Some of the Numbers

The first Gen Y class to graduate from college was in 1999. By 2007 the United States, and most of the world, was starting into what we now know was a recession. This means that even the oldest Gen Yer (born in 1977) was thirty years old or younger when the recession began. At best, this cohort only had eight years (or twelve years, if no college) of work experience under its belt by 2007. As unemployment began to skyrocket around the world, Gen Y was particularly vulnerable and found themselves unemployed at a greater rate than the other generations.

Assuming 2007 as the start of the recession, nearly 25 percent of the entire population of Gen Y graduated into a recession. If we look at the slow recovery, then that number exceeds 40 percent who graduated into either a full-blown recession or a very slow recovery.

Even for the youngest of Gen Y (born in 1995), they were only twelve when the recession hit. While it may not have affected their careers, it did affect what they experienced. Family members laid off, long stretches of unemployment for mom or dad, and changes in family spending behavior, to name just a few. At the start of the recession some of Gen Y were early in their careers, some were just getting started, and some were growing up with the ramifications at home. The fact is, all were profoundly impacted.

Even the most jaded anti-Gen Y out there would not blame the Great Recession on this group. It is a situation they clearly had nothing to do with causing. However, what they inherited had to be overcome.

The unemployment numbers across all groups were very challenging during the recession and the slow recovery. Gen Y was particularly affected, with some publications publishing numbers as high as 50 percent. By 2013, according to American Student Assistance, a full 48 percent of those twenty-five to thirty-four were either unemployed or underemployed. Our research also revealed that college graduates are filling up to 50 percent of open jobs that do not require a college degree.

In addition to the high unemployment and underemployment that Gen Y experienced, this cohort was hit particularly hard by wage stagnation and depression. The average working adult has felt a 4.4 percent decline in real wages since the start of the recession. Gen Y has seen their incomes fall by over 8 percent since December 2007 or nearly double the total adult working population (Hawley, n.d.).

The final piece of this very discouraging puzzle is the rising cost of a college education and the soaring debt load that comes with it. Historically, in difficult economic times, more people delay entry into the workforce and seek a post-secondary education. Given that Gen Y was more inclined to earn a degree anyway *and* that a great many also went to school due to limited job opportunities, it's easy to see a crisis brewing.

Let's start with the rising cost of college. For Traditionalists, Baby Boomers, and Gen X, college was reasonably affordable. For many it was still a stretch, but affordable. Since 1985 the cost of a college education has soared by over 500 percent! This has outpaced every other purchase in price increases, including health care (Jamrisko & Kolet, 2013). Nothing has risen at the same rate.

The rise in tuition has also led the rise in student loan debt. In 2012 there were twenty million college students, with more than twelve million borrowing money to pay tuition. There are more than thirty-seven million outstanding student loans, 70 percent owed by Gen Y. The average debt for these loans, across all age groups is $24,301, according to American Student Assistance (asa.org.). We have seen several different estimates on the total student loan debt, ranging from $900 million to $1.2 trillion.

Many Gen Y college graduates have $250 to $500 monthly payments or more. One would think high unemployment, underemployment, and depressed wages for nearly the majority of Gen Y would cause this cohort to break. Except, that is not the case.

> "For our generation 'ball and chain' means something completely different. That is our school loans."
>
> Todd Barnett VP of Finance, Co-Founder of PortaBeer

Gen Y's Response

Gen Y has not in any way been broken by the Great Recession. Has it been a major challenge? Have they found themselves complaining at times? Have they blamed Baby Boomers and Gen X for these issues? Of course they have. And they probably have said and done things we can't print here. However, one thing we want to make perfectly clear is that they have not been broken, quit, rebelled, or given up. In fact, the Great Recession has, in many ways, emboldened them.

First, Gen Y has tried to cut corners and maximize resources. Now, some readers will point out that some of those resources are their parents and many Gen Y have moved back home. That is true. In fact, the standard for achieving financial independence in 1980 was always thought to be twenty-two. Now it is thought to be *at least* twenty-five.

However, as discussed, Gen Y looks at moving back home as a good use of resources. Also, in many cases (and we do not have anything but antidotal evidence for this next statement), the move home has been encouraged by parents. Finally, Gen Y is often encouraged to stay, even after achieving the ability to move out.

Gen Y has also responded eerily similar to the Greatest Generation when it comes to managing money, saving, and paying off debt.

"Those aged twenty-five to thirty-four showed the best improvements and cut their credit card debt in half. People in this age group had an average debt of less than $5,200 in 2012, compared with more than $10,400 four years earlier.

"The youngest surveyed, those aged eighteen to twenty-four, showed modest improvement but still had the lowest debt of any age group. Young Americans reduced their credit card debt by 15 percent, falling below $3,000 per person."

Debt Demographics–Statistical Breakdown of Consumer Debt in the U.S. www.debt.org/faqs/americans-in-debt/demographics/

Gen Y has managed their credit card debt better during the recession than any other generation. In fact, every other cohort's debt went up, and Gen Y's went down. In addition to credit card debt, Gen Y is aggressively paying off their school loans and forgoing other expenditures. This trend has been a boon to secondhand stores. Gen Y is shopping much more frugally than previous generations did. Very much like the Greatest Generation, if Gen Y does not have the cash to purchase something, they will wait and save.

Saving for Gen Y is not just for the short term in order to make delayed purchases. Gen Y has come to believe it will never retire. First, because they believe that to work is to contribute and, second, they have no faith that Social Security will be there when they are of retirement age. Gen Y realizes how important it is to save for their futures and the compounding nature of invested money. This generation is saving at a greater rate than any previous cohort, except for possibly the Greatest Generation.

SaveUp.com compares Gen Y to the Greatest Generation when it comes to savings. With their savings, Gen Y is taking a very balanced approach. One-third is going into retirement/long-term savings, one-third into taxable investments, and the final one-third into short-term instruments like CDs. Even with high college debt and depressed wages, Gen Y has the self-discipline to save what they can. These savings are not coming at the expense of racking up credit card debt or missing loan payments. It is being done the "old fashioned way" by forgoing spending.

Again someone might argue that it is easier to save when one is living for free or with a reduced rent payment in a parent's home. That is true. However, we would also argue that it is just as easy (in fact, perhaps easier!) to go on a spending spree instead of saving the money.

Gen Y's Post-Recession Attitude

The challenge of the recession and its aftermath has left Gen Y with a renewed belief in their futures. Having grown up being told, "You can be or do anything you choose," the recession provided a reality check. Gen Y clearly now know that just "choosing" is not good enough. One must put in the work and commitment to succeed. The recession provided Gen Y with a very real obstacle and some very real hurdles to success.

As problem solvers, Gen Y has used every available resource to not only survive tough economic times, but in many ways to thrive. Whether it was going back to school, taking part-time work, working two (even three or four) jobs, starting their own businesses, moving home, volunteering, or taking unpaid internships, Gen Y has found a way to ride out the storm. This has not beaten down this generation; it has given them confidence.

A Wells Fargo study (wellsfargo.com, 2013) mirrors many other post-recession studies we researched. A full 67 percent of Gen Y believes they will still achieve a greater standard of living than their parents have. This group looks at their careers as a marathon and not a sprint. Since they believe they will work their entire lives, they do believe they will make up the lost ground from the recession. Not only will their careers rebound, but as a new generation of savers, they understand the power of time and savings. By beginning to save early, they know their net worth will only increase as time goes on. A small amount invested now will be worth many times more in thirty or forty years (http://thefinancialbrand.com/30161/millennials-worry-about-financial-problems/).

The Great Recession was, for most of the world, the "Great Uncontrollable." If the recession affected someone because of lost employment, underemployment, compressed wages, and so on, it was most likely out of one's direct control. Outside forces were driving many situations.

One statistic from the Wells Fargo study surprised us. Given years of outside influences and situations out of Gen Y's control, it is a reasonable assumption that this generation would feel less, not more, in control of their futures. In fact, a full 75 percent of Gen Y surveyed feel in control of their futures. This cohort is *not* looking at outside forces and blaming their situation on something out of their control. Three-quarters of Gen Y feel accountable and in control of their ultimate fate.

The final statistic that has far-reaching ramifications for leaders is that, even with the difficult circumstances posed by the recession, Gen Y *still* feel their income can be replaced if they were to find themselves unemployed. An astounding 80 percent of this cohort believes they could find a job paying the same or more than their current income if they were to quit or be let go. Gen Y, even in the face of challenging employment opportunities, will not be led by leaders who act like "you should just be happy to have a job."

Don't get us wrong. Gen Y *is* happy to have jobs. Our research shows a great depth of appreciation for opportunities presented. The fact is, if a work situation is made toxic by managers believing the employee has nowhere else to go, that manager is sorely mistaken. Gen Y will leave. If it takes three or even four jobs to replace the income or shed a "toxic work environment," Gen Y will choose the multiple jobs.

Our Thoughts

We believe there will be many opportunities for leaders to attract and retain top talent post-recession. We also believe that the recession will prove, in the long run, to have been a turning point for Gen Y. We think in the years to come the recession and the slow recovery will be looked at as where and when Gen Y made their stand. They have not quit and have proven to be fairly resilient.

This resiliency will translate well to employers. We think Gen Y has developed a "thicker skin" in the past few years and will not be as "easily bruised" as they may have been early on. Given the sheer numbers of Gen Y in 1999, they were able to make changes to things like where they worked, who they worked for, where the jobs were located, and so on, quite easily. If they were unhappy, sometimes even for the smallest things, they could (and would) quit to find something better.

This "thick skin" means Gen Y has become more appreciative of having a job and will not allow meaningless things to drive them away. They have come to realize no situation is perfect and in any organization there will be challenges and temporary setbacks. Gen Y is far less likely to leave a good job because of a temporary setback today than in 2000.

We still believe Gen Y will leave bad situations or situations that just don't fit them. They will not be happy to just have a job. However, Gen Y has learned a few very valuable lessons. First is that sometimes there are situations, major situations, that are uncontrollable. The traditional support systems that may have helped in the past cannot help with everything. Parents, teachers, bosses, and peers who may have been able to offer support in the past are powerless against things like a recession. We have found that parents, in particular, are adjusting some of the advice and guidance they are offering. Our research showed a fairly dramatic shift in parental "hang in there" advice.

In 2008 we saw a much higher incidence of parental advice that approved of job jumping, even for little things like negative feedback or evaluations. Now we are seeing parents question the situation more and advising Gen Y to "work through it." We believe the recession has also had an impact on the parents of Gen Y and on the advice offered.

Secondly, Gen Y has been learning about the generations that proceeded them. Just as the previous generations have scratched their heads about Gen Y, the confusion has been mutual. Since we wrote the first edition of this book, we have seen a great many leaders working to understand, motivate, and lead Gen Y. The progress has been striking.

Additionally, we have seen a great deal of progress with Gen Y working to understand "their elders." This cohort has faith in their leaders and is working to understand "why" things are done the way they are done. Nearly 65 percent of Gen Y see their immediate supervisor as a great resource for mentoring and guidance. Gen Y, while not always agreeing with many things, has gained the wisdom to work for understanding. There is still much work to do, but we believe the situation has improved greatly since 2008.

When it comes to a job search, we think Gen Y will respond to the Great Recession much like the Greatest Generation did to the Great Depression. They will seek more security from their employers. We have uncovered several studies that show Gen Y is now ranking "job security" as one of the things they want from an employer. In 2008 this was not even on the radar. We do not have any hard numbers to support our theory, but we do strongly believe Gen Y will be looking for security much more moving forward. Our interviews of Gen Y have supported this theory.

This has several implications for business leaders. We believe that small- to medium-size firms will have a wonderful opportunity to recruit talent that in the past was "reserved" for larger, more prestigious companies. In smaller firms Gen Y can have more impact and more quickly. In larger firms Gen Y can feel like a cog in the wheel, but at small to medium-size firms they can be the wheel.

In addition, in smaller companies, Gen Y is more likely to directly interface with senior leadership more regularly. This will give them access to top management on a more consistent basis and allow them to "showcase" their progress and accomplishments. Leaders of these companies must understand the need to interact more regularly with Gen Y and communicate the big picture often. This includes business results and future opportunities. Knowing the results and future opportunities will give Gen Y a greater sense of security.

For larger firms it will be important to have a "small company feel," even if they have 200,000 employees. Managers must understand the need to communicate regularly with their teams and keep people informed. Lack of information leads to fear and insecurity.

All leaders will have to do some things to attract and retain top talent. The organizations that do it the quickest and the best will have a significant competitive advantage. Businesses must develop a career lattice. Job security is gained by knowing you have some place to go after the current role has been mastered. Dead-end opportunities, which is how Gen Y views the traditional "career ladder," do not provide a sense of security.

Next, business leaders must reward performance and not just tenure. Gen Y wants to know they are contributing to the bottom line and the greater good. Rewarding tenure only, whether with raises, promotions, or positions of influence, will turn off Gen Y. Gen Y will search out companies that provide security, not companies that reward "living long enough."

We also think the organizations that understand Gen Y's deep belief that they will be working their entire lives, and set up their systems accordingly, will have a head start in attracting talent. One key element is to have some sort of retirement/savings plan. Next is to recognize Gen Y's desire for "time." Vacations and flextime will be viewed very favorably. Company size is irrelevant. Those firms that are "secure" enough to allow someone to work from home (at least from time to time) will be displaying trust *and* security.

Voices of Experience: Jeff Wangler

In the days and weeks following the terrorist attacks of September 11, 2001, moving forward seemed unfathomable to the citizens—and businesses—of the United States. The leaders of AIReS, a company that relocates workers domestically and internationally, sat in a boardroom in the days after the attack. "What are we going to do here?" remembered Jeff Wangler, the company's president. When then-President George W. Bush encouraged Americans to move forward, that's what AIReS decided to do. The company recognized, however counterintuitive it might seem, that the years following 9/11 would be the best time to invest in the company's infrastructure and "make it better while everyone else is going the other way."

Additionally, Wangler said, they had to believe business would soon be normal again. "If this is a sustained attack, there's no worry about business moving forward, because there won't be any," he said.

Six months after the attacks, AIReS was "way ahead of the game," Wangler said. "Business bounced back and we were light years ahead of our competitors, who laid off sales and customer service staff and then had to go out months later and try to find people to hire," he said.

In the years following 9/11 and through the Great Recession, the first thing companies would cut is training and development. AIReS, on the other hand, increased training and development initiatives. If they couldn't afford to hire ten people, Wangler said, at least they could invest in their existing employees. "When times are tough, it's really a good time to go for it . . . when other people are shutting down," he said.

As the U.S. comes out of the recession, AIReS is flourishing, Wangler said. But he noted that the state of the economy caused tension between Gen Y workers and Baby Boomers. "Understand why they are like they are," he said of Gen Y.

Wangler, a Boomer, said his father told him to work hard, do what he was told, and work for the same company for his entire life. For the Greatest Generation, that plan worked. "But somewhere in the middle there, people started to get laid off, and

(*continued*)

they told their kids, 'There isn't a job for life. Have some fun, go out and do what you want to do,'" he said.

Wangler said if he had to do it over again, he'd take six months off and travel, just for the experience. "Maybe we're mad because we never got a chance to do it," he said.

But Gen Y took that chance.

And Wangler said if you give Gen Y what they want—"a solid work environment and a little bit of flexibility"—you'll be rewarded with "fun, sharp, and successful" employees. "It can be done," he said; noting some older workers might roll their eyes, he said, "It's just tough."

Conclusion

There will be one *major* difference between the generation who went through the Great Depression and the one who went through the Great Recession as it relates to the desire for job security. Security will not trump everything for Gen Y. The Greatest Generation believed and experienced, possibly for the last time, one job for life. No matter the situation, the Greatest Generation did not even think about quitting their jobs. That *will not* be the case for Gen Y. They will seek job security, but not at any cost. If opportunities to grow are not available, if leadership does not "walk the talk," if they are not given timely feedback, or if they are not assigned meaningful work, they will leave. They will not trade security for their sense of self-worth.

Julie's Gen Y Profile

Name: Julie

Location: Northeast

Age: 27

Background:

- Graduated with a bachelor of science degree in business administration from a large state university

- Worked on several marketing campaigns as part of her undergraduate work
- Worked at a small marketing firm after college
- Now works as a public relations and marketing professional for an international luxury hotel brand

During college, Julie worked on a successful on-campus marketing campaign showcasing a new model of a worldwide automobile brand. After college, Julie went to work for a small marketing firm that was hard-hit by both the recession of 2008 and poor management. She felt she was overworked and underpaid in that position; on occasion, her paychecks didn't come in on time.

Julie left the small firm to work for an international luxury hotel brand, handling public relations, communications, and social media. She said the atmosphere in her workplace is "empowering and colleague-focused."

"The corporate culture is very strongly executed from the top down," she said. "Corporate trainings, resources, and events are provided regularly to reinforce this culture."

Julie said one thing she likes about her job is that it allows her to clearly define work and personal time—she only checks her email once a day on weekends and is usually able to complete all of her work before leaving the office, so she can avoid working from home. Her employer also ensures that, when she does work evenings or weekends, she receives time off later in the week.

One of Julie's biggest challenges when dealing with colleagues of a different generation is explaining her role in managing the company's social media outlets. "This subject often causes communication challenges with older colleagues," she said, noting that, while they understand the importance of social media marketing for businesses, many lack a clear understanding of general social media concepts. This makes it difficult to discuss social media marketing strategy, present new tactics that may require financial investment, and report on successes and failures in this area.

Julie said many of her older colleagues are not active on social media personally. Therefore, she said, they are not familiar with terminology, basic concepts, and emerging technologies that allow for meaningful conversations about social media as a marketing tool.

(*continued*)

For Julie, the characteristics of a good job are

- Opportunities for growth
- Challenging work that "makes you feel like you are doing something worthwhile"
- Strong relationships with managers

Julie is motivated by:

- Hardworking, honest colleagues
- Positive recognition
- Possibility for career growth
- A passion for what she's doing

CHAPTER SIX

KEY SKILLS

Understanding Gen Y's Eight Key Skills

In prior generations, new employees did not bring advanced skills to the job. Much time and money had to be spent training them to do some very basic job-related tasks. New employees did not know more than their future employers, nor did they come equipped with instantly applicable expertise.

None of that is true with Generation Y. For the first time in history, a generation is entering the workforce with skills in certain areas—particularly technology—superior to those of their bosses and current co-workers. We believe one of the major challenges many leaders will face is accepting this reality. Since there is no precedent from which to work, many organizations will be too slow to adjust. By adapting quickly, you can profit from Gen Y's skills and enthusiasm to create a stronger organization.

While we are saying Gen Y brings certain superior skills to the job, we are not saying they are also bringing all of the wisdom and life experience necessary to apply these skills productively. Here is where leadership kicks in.

> "Tell me and I forget, teach me and I may remember, involve me and I learn."
>
> Benjamin Franklin

Leaders need to grasp the implications of this new paradigm and provide support for both the new and current employees. For new employees, leaders must mentor and guide them using the wisdom gained throughout the years. For current employees, leaders must make certain the new Gen Y talent is not dismissed, overlooked, and eventually squashed. And they must find ways for Gen Y skills to spread to experienced employees.

Key Skill 1: Gen Y Is Tech-Savvy

Gen Y is highly educated and many will bring advanced degrees with them to the workplace. Gen Y is extremely tech-savvy and, for the most part, will be far ahead of your existing employees when it comes to the latest technology. They already know about working in the cloud, virtual meetings, Twitter and social networking, where and how to find the most succinct and up-to-date information, what gadget will allow them to be the most productive and flexible, and so on. If you need something researched, chances are excellent that your Gen Yer can find it quickly and efficiently.

Managers around the world generally recognize Gen Y's tech skills. Recognition of the talent is not the issue. The issue is damning it with faint praise. Managers too often dismiss Gen Y's technological skills as a given, thereby diminishing the accomplishments. Worse yet, managers tend to call on Gen Y to fix some minor issue on their computers, often multiple times for the same thing.

> **Key Point**
>
> Don't take Gen Y's tech skills for granted.

Dismissing the skill set and then trivializing it sets the exact wrong leadership tone. First, it shows a lack of appreciation for Gen Y's tech skills. Second, it communicates, however unintentionally, the organization's willingness to accept outdated skill sets in experienced managers. Finally, and again unintentionally, it sends a message that this company is not a learning organization.

When it comes to technology, Gen Y has knowledge and proficiency. Gen Yers should not be taken advantage of as a resource. They will not mind sharing their knowledge, as long as it is not dismissed or taken for granted. They will expect their co-workers to at least attempt to learn the new skills and information. One twenty-two-year-old repeatedly showed older co-workers how to do minor tasks on the computer, patiently taking them step by step through the process and encouraging them to write the steps down. After showing them how to do the same tasks dozens of times over a year, she quit. She did not want to work with people who refused to learn and grow.

Key Skill 2: Gen Y Is Diverse

According to the U.S. Census Bureau, Generation Y is the most ethnically diverse generation in history, with only 61 percent of its members identifying themselves as Caucasian. This generation's social circles are also the most diverse with respect to religion and race. A very small percentage of this generation says that all of their friends are of the same race or religion. Diversity has been demonstrated to be a desirable and healthy workplace component.

In contrast, other generations of employees needed "diversity training." Many came from extremely homogenous backgrounds and were not exposed to different races, cultures, or creeds until they arrived in the workplace. It was a serious challenge to teach these insulated workers how to co-exist and work with people different from themselves. Millions of dollars and hours had to be spent on diversity training to accomplish this goal. Gen Y experiences diversity by simply going to the cafeteria for lunch.

Gen Y is open-minded and accepting of those different from themselves. Working and interacting with people outside of their own ethnic group is the norm. Not only is Gen Y comfortable with the increasingly diverse workforce (and client base), but they can make others feel comfortable. This is a benefit to you and your organization and links very closely with the next skill.

Key Skill 3: Gen Y Understands the Global Marketplace

From the moment Gen Yers could interact with a computer, they learned about the international marketplace. At no point in their lives have they ever been without access to information from around the world. At a very young age this generation connected with peers abroad. This connection has continued throughout their lives to date. While Gen Y may have grown up in neighborhoods segregated in various ways, their worlds are surprisingly integrated, and in many ways they cannot comprehend an environment that is not global.

This generation has never known the Berlin Wall, the USSR, or the Cold War. They have never lived without an international space program. For their entire lives, they have used and purchased goods manufactured outside the United States.

Gen Y Thinks Globally

Once their high school education began, the global economy was further reinforced. Many high schools participate in foreign exchange student programs and Gen Yers have either participated themselves, known a classmate who has, or attended class with someone from another country and culture.

In American colleges and universities it would be nearly impossible for a Gen Y student not to interact with someone from another country, religion, race, or culture. Classmates, professors, and alumni are a constant reminder to nearly all college students in America that they are living in a global community. For example, at Arizona State University, 5,137 international students were enrolled in 2012 representing 118 countries.

Helping to further this awareness is the availability of study abroad programs. According to NAFSA,* in one year there were 273,996 American students studying abroad through credit programs. And it works both ways. According to *USA Today*, there were 764,495 international students enrolled in U.S. colleges. This means that over four years there are millions of international students in U.S. colleges. In other words, U.S. college students have a tremendous amount of exposure to other cultures.

Key Point

Gen Y has always lived in a global community.

Gen Y's attitudes toward diversity and international contact are a bit like their feel for technology. They take it for granted and are comfortable being on the cutting edge. They don't need to be "trained" to appreciate cultures. They'll seek out opportunities to expand their knowledge and contacts. For instance, they love to travel to foreign countries.

Key Skill 4: Gen Yers Have Good Self-Esteem

This generation has very strong self-esteem because they have enjoyed parental support and involvement like no other generation. Gen Y often grew up as the center of their parents' lives, with a sense that they were special and could do anything.

The positive result of Gen Y's self-esteem for your company is that they are eager to take on responsibility and believe they can accomplish anything. The Great Recession has not dimmed their view of what is possible. They have a positive, can-do attitude that can be a huge plus for your organization.

*NAFSA: Association of International Educators is a nonprofit professional organization for professionals in all areas of international education, including education abroad, advising and administration, international student advising, campus internationalization, admissions, outreach, overseas advising, and English as a second language (ESL) administration. As of 2010, it served approximately ten thousand educators worldwide, representing nearly three thousand higher education institutions.

Gen Y enters the workplace and immediately looks for ways to contribute. By and large, this generation is not looking to sit on the sidelines, but to be as productive as possible as quickly as possible. The leader's job is different with this cohort. Previous generations believed they would be assigned meaningful work when the time was right. Gen Y believes now is the right time.

As a leader, your job shifts from "push" to "pull." You will not need to push Gen Y to take on challenging assignments. Your task may be to "pull" them back from tasks they are not yet ready to tackle.

Key Skill 5: Gen Y Has a Sense of Security and Is Ambitious

Because of the support they have enjoyed from their parents, Gen Yers know they are loved and cared for. They have a deep-down sense of security that is healthy. This safe feeling makes the members of Gen Y believe in themselves and feel optimistic about the future. They are less afraid than other generations to ask questions and try new things. They have figured out that it is better and less time-consuming to ask questions than to waste time trying to figure things out. They also like to learn and are willing to do things differently.

Gen Y is ambitious—in a good sense. They can envision a good quality of life and aspire to it. This makes Gen Y hard-driving and motivated when they accept and believe in a goal. They look forward to challenges. Donna Korenich, human resource/career management consultant, says, "This generation, maybe more than any other, are looking for chances to excel for their employers very quickly." After a lifetime of involvement with sports and other activities, they are naturally more competitive than prior generations and want to do things faster and better. All of these traits make for a more motivated and confident worker.

Key Skill 6: Gen Y Has Life Experience in the Marketplace

One of Gen Y's more subtle attributes is their experience as lifelong customers. They have been making buying decisions since they were toddlers, choosing between Burger King and McDonald's, Barbie and American Girl, Nike and Reebok. Their parents have allowed them to make purchasing decisions to a greater degree than any prior generation has. In 1960 kids controlled $5 billion of family purchases, and by 2006 they controlled $192 billion (Institute for Global Labour, n.d.).

Gen Y teens had an average of $100 per week of disposable income, more than any earlier generation, and they have made countless choices throughout their young lives about how to spend it. Over one-third of Gen Y teenagers held a part-time job, working on average eighteen hours per week and earning $483 per month (Institute for Global Labour, n.d.). They pay attention to and understand marketing and advertising. As lifelong customers in the business world, they understand how it works. This real-world experience as a customer can be valuable to a company.

Gen Y Understands the Customer Perspective

Because Gen Yers have been lifelong consumers, they have developed an expectation and understanding regarding customer service. They understand how someone should be treated as a customer. If someone does not receive the kind of service he or she desires, he or she is free to shop elsewhere.

For years, businesses have talked about customer service for external and internal customers. Previous generations have come to accept a certain lack of customer service from fellow employees. Companies have invested millions of dollars to enhance the internal customer experience in order to improve organizational efficiency. This point is extremely relevant to you as a leader.

Your new employee will not simply hope to be treated like a customer. As a worker, Gen Y expects to be treated like a customer. You have to sell the company, its procedures, and yourself to Gen Yers before they will "buy" you. As we will address later, today's leaders must understand this and make sure the organization's support systems are in sync.

"Always treat your employees exactly as you want them to treat your best customers."

Stephen R. Covey

Key Skill 7: Gen Y Is Research-Oriented

For previous generations, research meant a trip to the library and learning the Dewey Decimal System. It took hours of effort to gather information. One needed to comb through hundreds of pages of text or look at microfiche for hours to try to find the desired information. The reality of this kind of research was that, as often as not, the information sought was not found.

This has never been the case for Gen Y. CBSnews.com states, "Young people can find information faster and sort information faster than older people. For example, young people are more likely to use the best tool at the best time. They collaborate on Wiki-type tools with ease." As previously discussed, one of the reasons Gen Y asks questions is for context. This context helps them to find new and more productive ways to attack problems

CBSnews.com goes on to state that Gen Y are "aces with downloading software onto the company laptop to become more productive and efficient." Think about it: younger people don't utter the phrase, "information overload," because they don't feel it. They benefit from the plasticity of the brain, which has adapted over their Internet-based lives to process information faster." This is tied closely with Skill 8.

Key Skill 8: Gen Yers Are Problem Solvers

Given all of our research, we have come to one of many very positive conclusions about Gen Y; when faced with a problem or challenge, they will figure it out. The issue many managers and supervisors have is that they don't agree with *how* they figure it out.

As a leader, your job is to realize Gen Y has *many* tools at its disposal. Many more tools, in fact, than any previous generation. Your challenge is accepting this fact and bringing others you work with on board. Previous generations relied on one major tool—trial and error. Much was learned from failure. Thomas Edison was often quoted and held up as an example. His many failures simply taught him how *not* to invent the light bulb.

As a leader, you will possibly find many folks who resent Gen Y's ability to avoid many failures (and thus, according to previous generations, missing the true satisfaction of success and the learning experience that comes with it). The hard truth is that Gen Y does not *have* to learn everything through trial and error. Rest assured, Gen Y *will* have failures and they *will* learn from them. It is just that they simply do not *have to* for everything. Your job as a leader is to coach and guide them accordingly.

Gen Y is socially connected and collaborative by nature. If a problem arises or they are given a problem to solve, they will get help (as well as research solutions, as discussed in Key Skill 7). The best example we can think of to illustrate this point is the growth of online reviews.

Thirty (or even twenty or ten) years ago, most major life decisions were trial and error. For example, if the family went on vacation (a typical major expense), they either went somewhere known (from past trials) or tried something new. If the new place did not live up to expectations, the vacation was less than successful. Trial and error.

Enter Gen Y. This cohort found a way to collaborate, share expenses, and solve the problem of wasted vacation time.

(We are using vacation as a silly example. This same concept can be applied to some very serious business situations.) Gen Y felt no need to experience the error, so online reviews were born. Today, 72 percent of consumers trust online reviews as much as personal recommendations (www.market-truth.com). *Scientific American* says, "These days if you go to a restaurant with slow service, it's your own darned fault. You could have avoided that by consulting the masses in advance."

A leader's challenge is to recognize that Gen Y will research and solve problems. In fact, one of the methods for research and problem solving is to ask questions. This may well frustrate you and others you lead. There is a tendency for folks to shout, "Figure it out. That's what I had to do." Your job is to manage your frustration and help your co-workers understand the problem-solving nature of Gen Y.

Just a quick question. Come to think of it—isn't saying "That's what I had to do" rather self-serving and selfish?

Conclusion

Gen Y will force you to take your leadership skills to a new level. They are looking for true leadership and for employment opportunities that allow them to leverage their skills. In many cases, Gen Y enters the workplace with certain skills that are better than their experienced co-workers. A leader's job is to blend these talents to the benefit of the entire organization.

Jeff's Gen Y Profile

Name: Jeff

Location: Midwest

Age: 27

Background:

- Graduated with a bachelor's degree in English from a large state university in the Northeast
- Worked as a sports reporter and editor at the university's daily student newspaper
- Worked at several newspapers as an intern, sports reporter, and copy editor before landing a job covering college sports for a major metropolitan daily newspaper

Jeff loves sports and has always wanted to be a sports reporter. He worked hard at it, first in college, writing articles and columns and moving up to a sports editor position by his senior year. After several internships, Jeff landed a job covering sports at a paper in Florida. He was there for several years, producing not only articles and columns but also weekly videos with a colleague, all while maintaining a strong Twitter presence, something considered essential to build his professional identity and communicate with readers.

Jeff said he would only leave the job in Florida for a "better opportunity." He found that when he was offered a position at a newspaper in the Midwest.

Jeff notes that most of his colleagues at all the places he's worked have been "friendly and fun, but there's an undertone of fear, too. Folks in the newspaper business aren't too keen on their future," he said.

Jeff said one of the biggest challenges of working with older generations is their misunderstanding of social media. "Some fear social media. Some think social media is more than it is," he said. "The older people who run our company want us to be everywhere at once while still writing thoughtful articles. It's challenging for a lot of workers to do that."

For Jeff, the characteristics of a good job are

- Being surrounded by smart people with strong work ethics
- Having bosses who are smart, accommodating, and efficient

Jeff is motivated by:

- Charismatic, hard-working colleagues
- The fact that he's doing a job he's dreamed of doing since he was five years old

CHAPTER SEVEN

NEW REALITIES FOR LEADERS

We've already discussed how Generation Y is different. In this chapter we cover ten more general characteristics of Gen Y and how these characteristics can impact your leadership strategies.

As a leader you'll have a tendency to fall back on your normal leadership style. Yet you know that every individual is different. In the case of Gen Y, you can use your knowledge of their attitudes and behaviors to adapt your leadership style for greater effectiveness. Gen Y represents a new reality.

"Leaders are made, not born. . . . You become proficient in your job or skill, and then you become proficient at understanding the motivations and behaviors of [your] people."

Brian Tracy, Author and Speaker

Ten New Realities About Gen Y

The following realities about Gen Y will be discussed in the following sections:

1. Gen Y is delaying marriage and parenthood.
2. There is no stigma associated with moving back home.
3. When Gen Y leaves no one is at fault.
4. Gen Y "leases" a job, not "buys."
5. Multiple jobs are a badge of honor.
6. Your leadership is continually being evaluated.
7. Their circle of influence is also watching.
8. The extended family is coming back for Gen Y.
9. Gen Y has a vision for themselves.
10. There is an "ambition gap" between Gen Y men and women.

You Need to Enforce the New Realities

As a leader, it is hard enough to get followers to act when a *written* rule has changed, let alone when there are new *unwritten* rules. Tremendous time, energy, and money are wasted in organizations because after a new procedure is announced and documented, a significant percentage of the employees still try to do it "the old way."

"Approximately 20 percent of the workforce will fight change. If resisters are left within the team or workplace, they can become the proverbial 'rotten apple that spoils the barrel.' However, many resistors can be changed."

Charles Milofsky and Carl Huffman, in
Thriving on Change in Organizations

Awareness of these differences in Gen Y is important. The differences have implications for everyone in your organization. However, what those implications are will not always be clear. As a leader, you need to be in the forefront of handling these implications. Where they impact people directly, you need to make sure that others are changing to meet the new reality—for instance, in accepting Gen Y without bias.

There is a natural tendency for people to fight change. When people resist rule changes, written or unwritten, it is because they think they can. Deep down, people have a belief or desire that they can continue to do it the old way, without any consequences or repercussions.

> "Leadership is the art of getting someone else to do something you want done because he wants to do it."
>
> Dwight Eisenhower

Reality Change 1: Gen Y Is Delaying Marriage and Parenthood

Many of their differences are a direct result of Gen Y's lack of familial responsibilities. Gen Y is delaying marriage. According to the U.S. Census Bureau, the age at which men and women are getting married is steadily creeping up from year to year. In the 1960s, when some of the oldest Baby Boomers were reaching their twenties, the average age for men to marry was twenty-two and the average age for women was twenty. By the 1980s, the age had increased to twenty-four for men and twenty-two for women. In the 1990s, it was twenty-six for men, twenty-three for women. In 2005 the average age for men to marry was twenty-seven, twenty-five for women. By 2012 those ages had risen to twenty-nine for men and twenty-seven for women.

For both sexes, there is now an extra five to ten years (that Baby Boomers did not typically have) to explore the job market, change jobs, move to different cities, and even return home to live with parents. Without the financial obligation to support another person or the limitation of a spouse's separate career plans, needs, or commitments, Gen Y has much more freedom to take risks and make changes.

It is interesting to also note that, in the past, college-educated women were usually the ones who delayed marriage. Now the trend is identical for all levels of education. Also, regardless of education levels attained, women who marry after the age of thirty earn more than those who marry at younger ages. (*Knot Yet! The Benefits and Costs of Delayed Marriage in America*, http://twentysomethingmarriage.org).

Key Point

Without the responsibilities of supporting a family, Gen Y has the freedom to explore alternatives or leave unsatisfactory jobs.

Similarly, Gen Y is also delaying parenthood. According to the National Center for Health Statistics, the average age for women to have a first baby in the 1970s was twenty-one. By 2010, it was at a record high of 25.7 years. Similarly, men are delaying fatherhood. In 2002 the average age for men was twenty-six and by 2010 that number climbed to 27.4.

Reality Change 2: There Is No Stigma Associated with Moving Back Home

In the past, when a young Baby Boomer or Xer couldn't find a job or a job didn't work out, there was disappointment and embarrassment. These generations were not happy about moving back home with their parents. This is not the case at all with Gen Y. For the most part, Gen Yers have close relationships with their parents and feel extremely comfortable returning home and letting their parents help them—and their parents are often happy to do it. Gen Yers believe that living at home is a smart and logical way to limit their expenses. They certainly do not see moving back home as a failure.

According to Kim Parker, in a report from the Pew Research Center, in 2007 30 percent of eighteen-to-thirty-one-year-olds lived at home. By 2012 that number had grown to 36 percent.

Gen Y is also willing to accept money and other kinds of help from their parents when they have a problem. They see taking help as the efficient use of available resources. This provides a tremendous financial safety net for Gen Y that other generations never had and contributes dramatically to their sense of freedom and willingness to risk change.

Reality Change 3: When Gen Y Leaves, No One Is at Fault

This reality is one that has changed significantly since we wrote the first edition of this book. In the past, when an employee left a company the assumption was that the individual was somehow flawed, found wanting, or not satisfactory to the organization. Perhaps he or she did not have the necessary skills for the job or the right temperament. Future employers would question frequent short job stints. Why couldn't this person hold a job for any length of time? What was wrong with him or her?

When we wrote the first book, if a young worker left, the finger was pointed at the employer—the stigma was on the organization. Why couldn't you retain this young person? What did you do to alienate him or her? Why couldn't you provide challenging work? Why didn't you give the necessary feedback? And the word would spread to other Gen Yers. A company could have very easily received the reputation of being hostile to Gen Y employees.

Coach's Corner: Evolution of Mobility

We've now traveled into the third phase of the evolution of mobility. At one time, if somebody left a program or organization, the immediate reaction might be he or she couldn't cut it, something

(*continued*)

was wrong. Then we went into a long period of time when if someone left an organization or team all fingers pointed toward the organization. They couldn't retain that person. I now think we've traveled into a third phase.

If someone leaves a job or a team, it is no one's fault. It is so common now it has become normal. For example, by the end of their sophomore year 40 percent of all players will transfer to another school.

When the numbers start to get that high, it's almost impossible to take the time or energy to attribute blame.

Since it is not at all unusual for Gen Y to move from place to place, and the work world has become accustomed to such turnover, "blame" is no longer instantly established. If a talented worker leaves your company, it is not your fault *or* his or hers. Blame is not assigned. The answer could be as simple as that the company and the employee were not a good fit. Since there are no longer clear reasons for why a turnover happened (bad employee or bad organization), Gen Y has developed tools to make situations more clear. Websites like Glassdoor.com have been developed to give folks "an inside look at jobs and companies"! Past and present employees, as well as those who may not have even been hired, can find places on the Internet to discuss their experiences. As mentioned in Key Skill 7, your future employees will be researching what is being said about you as an employer.

Key Point
Businesses must manage the information being posted about them as an employer of choice.

Businesses must learn to manage this information flow. Prospective employees will look at what is being said about you during every step of the process—from initial interviews to hiring to ongoing employer/career development. In Chapter 12 we will look at aligning your process for each of these critical steps.

Reality Change 4: Gen Y "Leases" a Job; Not "Buys"

Because of their increased freedom and lack of familial responsibilities, Gen Y has a different mindset about commitment to an organization. They do not sign on for life. They have a much shorter horizon. In contrast, when previous generations took their first jobs they were looking for a greater degree of job security; they could envision working with that company for ten or more years, and possibly even assumed they would retire from that same company.

Gen Y would be happy with a one- or two-year work experience. They are not worried about a long-term commitment. They are leasing the job, not buying it. They are more or less taking a long test drive. They plan to check out the job before they make a serious commitment to it.

Our research found that 74 percent of respondents do not plan on staying in their jobs for more than three years. Think about buying versus leasing a vehicle. Buying is a completely different commitment than a three-year lease. A lease is a limited transaction. You pay X dollars per month for a defined usage and period of time. You are merely paying for what you use, not developing any long-term equity.

This is the exact mindset of Gen Y. A company pays them X dollars a month, and for that payment the organization receives a defined amount of time and energy (work) from the Gen Y employee. Like a car lease, more miles can be used per month, but ultimately, if you exceed your limit, there is an additional charge. Once the lease is up, the consumer is free to move on to another vehicle.

If Gen Y doesn't like a job, they're comfortable quitting and looking for another one. They will accept work at a less demanding job, perhaps one that is not even in their field and bide their time until the right job comes along. They are also comfortable going back to school for graduate degrees or even doing volunteer work.

Gen Y is able to live quite inexpensively. If a Gen Yer does not move back home, he or she can find a reasonably priced rental in almost any city in the country just by going online and checking online ads. Gen Y would rather get by on a shoestring budget than make "big bucks" at a job he or she doesn't really enjoy or care about.

Reality Change 5: Multiple Jobs Are a Badge of Honor

Gen Y seldom signs on with the expectation of being in the same job for a long time. They want to learn something from a job or have an experience. Once that is done—or not available—they expect to move on. In fact, it is almost considered an aberration if Gen Y has had only one or two jobs in the course of five years.

A Gen Yer who leaves a job is viewed by his peers as making a smart move to get out of a bad situation or into a better one. There is also a sort of adventurous, exploratory approach to employment. Why wouldn't you want to try different jobs? If you don't have a spouse or family to support, if you are free to move anywhere in the country, why not try something new? Maybe there is a better job out there just waiting to be discovered.

Consultant's Corner: Career Planning for Gen Y

Be open to the possibility of a Gen Yer having multiple jobs within your company in the course of a few years. Sidewise moves are very acceptable to this group. Gen Y may begin in one department and move to others because they offer more responsibility, experience, or ownership. Get comfortable with the notion that Gen Y needs to feel they are making progress and it is a good thing if that progression takes place within your company instead of elsewhere. Gen Y will eventually find the right fit if you are flexible and open.

To recruit well, you must retain well. Word will spread that Gen Yers can enhance their résumés and experience at your company.

This is where your relationships with your current Gen Y employees becomes key. If you are retaining them effectively, if they are satisfied, they will be a big reason for new Gen Y employees to come on board. They will be the living proof that there are good jobs within your company that are worth staying for. By creating a career lattice instead of a career ladder, you will be able to provide multiple job opportunities within one company. Gen Y will have multiple jobs, but there is no reason they must have multiple employers.

Reality Change 6: Your Leadership Is Continually Being Evaluated

Since past generations of workers stayed at their jobs for years, perhaps even decades, their view of leadership also had a long horizon. Traditional leadership thinking was to focus on the long haul and implement strategies with a five- to ten-year timeline. In this paradigm, leaders were viewed from a distance, and developing a personal leadership style versus an organizational leadership style was rarely considered. Since employees tended to stay for longer periods, leadership flaws were often overlooked, ignored, or simply accepted as commonplace.

Generation Y has shattered this paradigm. The new rule is that leaders need to be there, out front, present, and accessible.

Leadership is about *now*, not what can happen in five or ten years. Today's leaders need to be aware that they are always "on" and there is nowhere to hide. Generation Y is continually critiquing their leaders, closely watching words and actions, accessibility, how they (and others) are being treated, and comparing their leaders to other possible options.

Coach's Corner: Evaluating Leadership

One striking difference I have noticed over the past few years is that players are continually evaluating your leadership. Back in the day, if a coach yelled at a player, that was it. That player didn't say, "When so and so did the exact same thing, nothing was said."

I think now players evaluate leadership, and part of that evaluation includes comparing how they're treated relative to others. I truly believe Gen Y is extremely fair, but also sensitive to how you interact with others. If you treat others poorly, they'll hold you accountable for that just as if you had treated them poorly. If you treat someone better than you treat them, they'll hold you accountable for that, too. They might even hold you accountable if you treat them better than you treat someone else, and they'll wonder why you didn't treat that other person as well as you treated them. They evaluate your leadership and they want to make sure you're giving everybody equal time. And the right amount. Not just equal . . . but the right amount. A major difference in today's players is they evaluate and compare leadership.

Not only is personal leadership being continually monitored, but so is strategic leadership. In the traditional model, strategy development and execution were the domain of the executive team for the benefit of the shareholders. It was rare to see an organization truly link corporate strategy to day-to-day activities.

Gen Y demands otherwise. In fact, Gen Y can choose an employer based upon overall corporate strategy and their own ability to contribute to its execution. Gen Y will research a company's strategy and commitment to their customers, employees, and the environment. Strategies that discuss this "triple bottom line" will intrigue and attract Gen Y talent.

The Triple Bottom Line

In addition to the traditional profit bottom line, the triple bottom line adds social and environmental concerns. These include effects on all stakeholders such as customers and communities, as well as environmental impacts.

"There is no doubt Gen Y is different when it comes to evaluating leadership," says Bob McNeice, an expert on sustainable business practices. "Gen Y is not only constantly evaluating the personal leadership they witness, they are also looking at an organization's strategic plans and how a company exerts its leadership in the environment at large."

"There is no doubt Gen Y is attracted to firms that embrace sustainable business practices," says McNeice. "All of the research I have done shows that more and more of this generation say they want to use their business degrees to contribute to society. Over and over we hear that talent wants to make social responsibility a priority. Having the reputation for sustainable business practices and being socially responsible are important factors for becoming an employer of choice. Nearly three-quarters of all graduates are looking for organizations that have strong social responsibility reputations."

"It is important that business leaders understand the difference between sustainable business practices and 'being green,'" McNeice adds. "I believe Gen Y has become jaded toward the term 'green' and believes it has been grossly misused. Since Gen Y is particularly savvy as consumers, they do realize many green products have overstated their actual performance."

Not only are Gen Yers evaluating individual leaders, but they are also looking to see if the organization is "walking the talk."

Voices of Experience: Chuck Fowler

Fairmount Minerals, a company that mines sand for oil and gas companies to use in hydraulic fracturing, might not seem like the most likely candidate to jump on the "green" bandwagon.

But that's exactly what they did, said Chuck Fowler, who was president and CEO of the company from 1986 to 2013. He retired and now serves as the company's director and chairman of the executive committee.

"We do disturb the earth," Fowler said, but Fairmount tries to go about it in a way that limits environmental impact by focusing on the three P's—people, planet, and prosperity.

Fairmount has a lengthy mission statement, but the short one—and the one employees remember—is "do good, do well." "It's a lot easier to remember, and it's a lot easier to state," Fowler said.

With Fairmount's employees, the motto is carried out every day. Each facility has a sustainable development team that works together to come up with new ideas for how to improve the company's efforts toward a more sustainable business. More than half of the company's workers are involved in a sustainable development team. "And then those ideas progress through the company," Fowler said. The teams work in communities to volunteer and do other good work in the towns near where Fairmount mines, something that has struck a chord with younger workers, Fowler said.

"They like the fact that they can get involved in their communities," he said of Gen Y employees. "They were much quicker to come on board with that." But the Gen Y workers ensure older Fairmount workers understand why sustainability is important. "It's kind of fun to watch," Fowler said. "The typical thought is that the old folks are going to lead the young folks to where the trough is, and that's not happening in the Gen Y group. They're out in front of this, and they're bringing the older workers along with them."

He said recruitment hasn't been a challenge and the company has a very high retention rate. "A lot of the young folks in our company say, 'Fairmount Rocks,'" he said. The good work the company does is recognized by young people who live there, which draws them to work for Fairmount.

In 2012, Fairmount started a program called "SD pays"—for sustainable development. The company records how much the program costs the company and accounts for any baggage created by the program. In its first year, Fairmount spent less than $5.8 million on the program, but recorded more than $11 million in direct savings. "We can definitely say, without any question, that SD pays," Fowler said.

He said he often brings all of his employees together—from executives to hourly workers—for summits to talk about the company and build missions and strategic plans. "The biggest thing that we've done is actually get everybody in the same room and talk about our business and how we want our people to respond and react to our communities," he said. By following what Fowler calls the "ask/listen/respond" credo, Fairmount is able to glean ideas on how to improve the company from every member of its workforce. "We work very hard at giving everyone the opportunity to have his or her input heard, and a lot of companies in the past have done suggestion boxes and that sort of thing, but we do it by bringing people together," Fowler said.

These programs have made Fairmount a successful business, with growth not in 8 or 10 percent increments, but in hundreds of percentage points. Fowler said the company, a billion-dollar business, has grown "exponentially" since 2004, from four hundred employees to more than one thousand in 2013; from twelve mines in 2004 to twenty-eight in 2013.

Reality Change 7: Their Circle of Influence Is Also Watching

When Baby Boomers and most Gen Xers started working, part of their experience was learning how to navigate the business world on their own. Rarely, if ever, did Traditionalists, Boomers, and Xers look to their parents as a sounding board when things were not going well. If they did, chances are they would have received input supporting the employer, not them. Many Traditionalists, Boomers, and Xers have heard, "I'm sure there is a reason why such and such is happening. What are you doing to cause it?"

Traditionalists, Boomers, and Xers learned early that their parents would not automatically take their side. Only in the most egregious situations would parents disregard an outside authority like a coach or teacher and side with their offspring. It was the responsibility of the Traditionalists, Boomers, and Xers to "figure it out."

The new rule is completely different. In most cases, important circles of influence—friends, family, and other Gen Yers—are also evaluating your leadership and how you handle particular situations as they relate to their person of interest. No longer does the authority figure get the benefit of the doubt. Circles of influence almost instantly side with the Gen Yer first, and sort out the facts later.

Circles of influence are putting increasingly greater focus on their persons of interest and are less likely to see (or care about) the bigger picture. In fact, circles of influence may even dig for negative issues. Once such issues are uncovered, the circles of influence can then feel involved and supportive as they comfort their persons of interest.

It is critical that today's leaders recognize this new rule and develop strategies to be proactive. Including the circles of influence in company communications such as newsletters and press releases may help balance their perspective. Also, having HR rules about how you may or may not communicate with them is crucial in the 21st century. If you will not or cannot discuss an employee's job performance with a person of influence, then put this in your employee manual, which will save a lot of grief down the road.

Consultant's Corner: 21st Century Employee Manuals

Having spent the last twenty plus years as a consultant, one thing I have learned over and over is that some of the most difficult issues have some of the simplest solutions. I remember learning about "Ockham's razor" in college. William of Ockham in the early

1300s proposed, in simple terms, that sometimes the easiest answer is the best answer.

We have given this advice to many business leaders who get frustrated with some Gen Y issues. We simply tell them to make sure their employee manual is up-to-date and reflects their 21st century workforce. Update the dress code, and avoid frustration about unprofessional dress. Spell out who you can and cannot talk to about employee performance and avoid the uncomfortable call from a parent wanting to discuss his child's recent appraisal. Write the rules for gadgets at work.

Many of these issues simply did not exist when many employee manuals were written. Only a few years ago smart phones did not exist, nor did an inquiring parent, but they do now. My advice is to be proactive and listen to Ockham. These need not be complex issues, and sometimes simply addressing them in your employee manual will avoid future headaches.

Reality Change 8: The Extended Family Is Coming Back for Gen Y

Extended families are back in new ways for Gen Y that makes their circles of influence even larger. Long ago, for Boomers' parents or before, extended families meant grandparents living in the same house (or on the same farm) with children and grandchildren. Or it meant grandparents moving in for the last year their lives.

Today Gen Y is exposed to extended family in two ...mily they often create their own pseudo-families. Betwe...upport. lings, and half-siblings, Gen Y often creates ar...ly" differ- unit that offers them social, emotional, and e... This is a new reason why Gen Y balances ... elderly grand- ently than previous generations did. ...eir grandparents

Second, Gen Y is more like...
parents when they themsel...

are living longer than past generations did, so they are often active and around beyond Gen Y's childhood. Gen Y would have a natural bond with their grandparents. Grandparents are often more accepting than parents, as well as being a source of resources and advice.

Gen Yers, in turn, act as occasional caregivers. This gives them additional experience and furthers the contact with an extended family. It's also a reason for Gen Y to value flexibility. For instance, one twenty-three-year-old quit working at a boring job to look into starting her own business. In the meantime, she takes one day a week to visit her two grandmothers separately, takes them to appointments, and so on.

Key Point

Gen Y will help you take your leadership to new heights.

Reality Change 9: Gen Y Has a Vision for Themselves

In many cases previous generations began preparing for their life's work in high school. Some students went into college prep courses and some into technical or general studies. This early decision put them on a road that would determine their career decisions for the rest of their lives. After graduation (either from high school or college), previous generations sought employment in "their field" and began to climb the corporate ladder.

During previous generations' college years (or early jobs if they not choose college), if the choice that was made at seventeen hteen began to seem wrong, off track, boring, or "not for arıv changed majors (or quit their jobs to pursue something cision had been made, and Traditionalists, Boomers, switch it out."

a red flag ng-time human resources executive, said that professional eeking employment "out of your field" was sionals as little as ten years ago. "Hiring ing for 'fit' when they interview," said

Perrin. "We wanted to see that what interested you and what you prepared for was what we were offering. We would not even consider someone for certain positions, and I'm not talking technical, specialized positions, if he or she did not major in that field," continued Perrin.

Times have dramatically changed. According to Perrin, "Now HR professionals are looking for 'fit' in different ways. For example, it is not unusual to hire someone with a biology degree to work in a completely non-scientific or non-technical job. We want to know this person is capable, smart, hardworking, and willing to learn. We can teach them the job."

Even Perrin is an example of career changes. Perrin says, "Take me, for example, I spent over thirty years in HR and now am doing something completely different, and I love it. I would say for far too long our old system kept folks locked into positions that they had either outgrown, did not fit in the first place, or simply did not allow for any lateral movement and innovative thinking."

The previous system was designed to present a career ladder, and professionals moved step-by-step on a predetermined and usually well-defined career track. One's "vision" for his or her future was in many ways influenced by what was *available* and not necessarily by what an individual wanted.

That is not to say previous generations did not have goals. In fact, Boomers and Xers were very goal-oriented. What many did not have, at least early on, was a *vision* for their futures. Many Gen Yers have a vision for themselves and it is important for leaders to understand this, learn what the vision is, and then align those efforts to the company/team vision. (More about the importance of having a vision will be discussed in Chapter 10.)

"Effective leaders help others to forge their aspirations into a personal vision."

—John Kotter, Author, Harvard Professor

Identify Gen Y's Personal Vision

Determining a Gen Yer's personal vision can occur during the initial job interview, in a training exercise, during a one-on-one review, during a scheduled feedback session, or in the break room over coffee. But it has to happen. You must identify and understand a Gen Y's personal goals and interests.

In the past, employees may have been asked a question something like: "Where do you see yourself in ten years?" The smart employee (who was usually desperate to please the boss) would enthusiastically spout something along these lines: "Why, doing a good job working here, of course!" Older generations of employees would generally say what they thought the boss wanted to hear. Gen Y will say what they really mean.

Leaders need to be ready to hear very different answers to that same question. A Gen Y candidate or employee may well say something like, "In ten years I hope to have started my own business" or "My goal is to learn as much as I can in my first few for-profit jobs, get my master's of social work, and pursue my dream of working in the nonprofit sector."

> **Key Point**
>
> When you find out what the individual Gen Yer's vision is, you will find out what he or she cares about and is really willing to work for.

Today's leader who is not ready for these types of answers may be caught off guard. In reality, a good leader today should be looking for these answers. By understanding someone's vision, a leader is better equipped to coach, mentor, and guide that person along the "career lattice."

Develop a Shared Vision

Once you have identified a Gen Yer's vision, you must take the final step and link your vision for the organization with the Gen Yer's personal vision. Show the Gen Yer that his or her vision and goals dovetail with yours, that, in fact, not only do they coincide, but they can be achieved together. To be a world-class leader, you must be able to convince a Gen Yer that he or she can achieve his or her personal goals by *staying with your organization and working together with you.*

Reality Change 10: There Is an "Ambition Gap" Between Gen Y Men and Women

There is a very subtle but important shift in career attitudes between Gen Y men and women. This shift will have an impact on how businesses recruit, train, mentor, and develop talent moving forward. It will also require many organizations to address compensation, benefits, and career tracking.

A Pew Research Center survey (Patten & Parker, 2012) found that two-thirds of eighteen- to thirty-four-year-old women rank a successful and high-paying career as "one of the most important" or "very important" things in their lives. Of their male peers, 59 percent feel the same way.

While there is not a huge difference in these recent numbers, there is a big difference since 1997. Women now rank the importance of a successful career a full 10 percent higher than they did in 1997, while men are only 1 percent higher. It is not as if men are becoming less ambitious, but that women are becoming more so.

This trend is even playing out in higher education. Nearly 60 percent of the bachelor's degrees awarded in 2010 went to women, and over 60 percent of the master's degrees were awarded to women (Fast Facts, n.d.). In certain fields, such as law and medicine, women have increased their percentage of enrollment by a full 8 percent in a ten-year span.

Voices of Experience: J. Maureen Henderson

J. Maureen Henderson, a researcher and writer on Millennial culture, believes this shift will continue and that business leaders

(*continued*)

who understand this phenomenon will have the best chance of attracting top talent.

"Women will be looking at the same opportunities as men and will be looking more aggressively," Henderson says. "Gen Y women will not be sitting back and waiting for the opportunities to come to them." Business leaders who are prepared will have a greater chance to recruit this talent.

Attracting the talent is one thing; retaining is another. Henderson believes business leaders who are prepared to coach, mentor, and guide Gen Y woman will retain this talent by displaying strong leadership. Previous generations of professional women had fewer options available to them as they began their families, and many chose the "mommy track" and left the workforce. "Women will be opting out of the labor force less and less to raise their children. If a woman leaves a job, it will more likely be to find a better opportunity and not simply to leave the workforce," believes Henderson.

A world-class leader for Gen Y women will be prepared to coach and offer strong career advice. Henderson sees Gen Y women needing this kind of guidance. "Gen Y women believe they can have it all; family and career without necessarily doing what the previous generations had to do," notes Henderson. "They are not really looking at these 'best practices' and modeling their behaviors accordingly. Gen Y women believe they can have success *and* balance, not either/or."

A good coach will help guide Gen Y women along the career track/lattice. Henderson says Gen Y women "want to achieve but have not necessarily been socialized to this point. I see some things a good mentor would provide. Negotiation skills is a good example. Women may not be as aggressive with salary negotiations as their male counterparts."

"Another area is career self-promotion," observes Henderson. "I find women believe much more deeply in a meritocracy and see less need for self-promotion. It may or may not be naïve to believe results will always trump other career skills." A great leader will help guide Gen Y women as they navigate these unfamiliar challenges.

Henderson finds Gen Y women "to be very open to coaching, mentoring, and guidance. They are sponges of information." Our research validates Henderson's statements about both Gen Y men and Gen Y women. It is important to note that Gen Y women do not show a strong preference one way or another in regard to gender of their mentors.

Consultant's Corner: Mentoring

J. Maureen Henderson has written for publications such as *Forbes* and *The Atlantic*. She has made a career out of researching and writing about Millennial cultures. I found her advice for mentors of Gen Y, particularly Gen Y women, to be extremely insightful.

First and foremost, Henderson believes mentees will look for authenticity from their mentors. Gen Y will want to know "Where are you coming from?" and "Can I see myself doing what you do?"

Gen Y will ask themselves if their mentor is living the life they aspire to, or have they gotten off-track and settled somewhere along the way.

The next question Gen Y mentees will ask themselves is: "Has my mentor achieved success by a means that is replicable and palatable?" In other words, Gen Y will ask themselves:

- Is my mentor authentic?
- Is my mentor achieving his or her vision?
- Is my mentor "walking the talk"?

As discussed in Chapter 5 the Great Recession has impacted Gen Y's view on career and retirement. Since Gen Y believes they may never retire, it is a very wise decision for women to focus more on their own careers and earnings potential. Our guess is that, while life expectancy is not driving this shift, it is a positive move for young women to take more control of their earnings. A thirty-year-old male in 2012 could expect to live to be 76.9, while a thirty-year-old female could live to 82.3.

Conclusion

Gen Y brings many good things to the workplace—advanced degrees, technical skills, diversity, experience as a consumer, and an appreciation of the world market. Gen Y also have innate characteristics like ambition, high self-esteem, and competitiveness that can make them highly motivated, independent, and optimistic workers.

Your challenge as a leader is to craft jobs or frame the situations for Gen Y that tap into these natural talents. Gen Y's natural ambitiousness will turn into motivation only if Gen Y believes in the goal. Gen Y's competitiveness will turn into efficiency only if Gen Y feels the work is meaningful. Gen Y's ability to learn, ask questions, and try new things will turn into productivity only if the work is challenging. Gen Y's independence will turn into new ideas for your organization only if Gen Y feels a sense of responsibility.

Gen Y's work must be linked to a bigger project, or a component of it must be something Gen Y cares about, or there must be some challenging aspect to it, or Gen Y must be able to see something with increased responsibility in the near future.

Your challenge is to recognize and maximize Gen Y's special talents and positive attributes. Expect the most out of them—and then help them achieve it.

Kate's Gen Y Profile

Name: Kate

Location: Northeast

Age: 26

Background:

- Graduated with a bachelor's degree from a large state university

- Served as editor-in-chief of the university's daily student newspaper during her senior year
- Worked as a newspaper reporter before moving into her current position as a TV producer

Kate works hard, but that's not unusual in the large city where she lives and works. While some believe limited hours, good pay, and low stress amount to a good job, Kate said she doesn't mind working fifty to sixty hours a week or on weekends if it means she can contribute to projects, self-direct assignments, and receive criticism and credit when deserved. "Overall," she said, " I seek a feeling of empowerment and value." But, she said, her current job "does not have the characteristics of good quality of life."

"I have to remind myself to balance my personal and professional lives," she said. "This year, I took up running and a few other sports so that I would force myself to unplug, mentally and technologically, for a few hours a week."

Kate notes Gen Y workers have more options than their grandparents did, but they also face more risks. "My grandfather lived in a mid-sized working class town that had steel mills and coal mines, and therefore, he went to work in one," she said. "He never faced the option of leaving town permanently or changing careers. He had a good pension and a big family, so why would he uproot those things?"

For her, the goal was to leave her hometown and work toward a successful career in a large city. "Higher education muddies that straight line from childhood to working adult," she said. "Millennials often move away from home to attend college. Our class stratification rests more on how we execute our lives from high school until shortly after college."

Kate is looking for new work, but said she's "picky" about where she'll go next. Kate said some of her older colleagues and members of upper management "hold grudges against younger employees—as if we could never be as smart or experienced, as if our work is much less important than theirs."

She said some of that is true, noting that a lot of Gen Yers in her industry wind up working on "mindless monkey tasks that involve technology instead of real skill," such as web production and managing social media. Kate said she hopes her next job

(*continued*)

involves more in-depth reporting and writing and managers who support and nurture that kind of work.

For Kate, the characteristics of a good job are

- The ability to work with older colleagues who will mentor and teach
- Managers who "create an environment where talent can thrive" and set challenging expectations

Kate is motivated by:

- A desire to "be more successful than the people I grew up with"
- Constructive criticism
- Contributing to big projects

CHAPTER EIGHT

YOU HAVE A PERSONAL BRAND

Brand (n., bran(d)•
Having a well-known and usually highly regarded or marketable name, image, or reputation.

The next major building block for a winning recruiting and retention culture is awareness of your personal leadership brand. Talk about brands has become almost passé for marketing products and services. We all are aware of product brands and the tremendous investments that are made to create household names like Apple, Coke, or Welch's.

It is rare when leaders even think about, let alone actually take the time to analyze their own personal leadership brands. In fact, it is rare when leaders even realize they *have* a leadership brand, whether they think about their brands or not. A leader who takes the time to develop a desirable personal brand will attract and retain the best of Gen Y.

In sports and most other areas, your "pedigree" includes where you've worked and who you've worked for. However, the reverse is also true: leaders are judged by the managers they've developed.

For instance, basketball and football coaches have been rated by how successful the coaches who've worked for them have become.

Almost every definition of branding you'll see talks about making a clear brand promise. This is generally a benefit that the buyer will receive from purchasing your product or service. When you fulfill the brand promise repeatedly, you build brand value. For instance, if a soft drink promises "cool and refreshing" and delivers it, you may begin to value that drink over others. Conceptually speaking, the idea of brand is similar to earlier concepts in marketing such as unique selling proposition (USP) (Reeves, 1961) and positioning (Ries & Trout, 1981).

More recently, brand concepts have been applied to leadership. However, most of these applications have simply extended an organization's brand promise to the leaders and managers in it. If a company promises great service, then leaders must train and support employees in delivering great service (cf. Ulrich & Smallwood, 2007).

The New Leadership Brand Promise

> "It's clear that today's celebrities are becoming brands unto themselves. But now even middle managers can get into the act. So if you see your VP of finance in the gossip pages next to J. Lo, don't be surprised."
>
> *Fortune* Magazine

We don't expect you to appear in the style pages with Jennifer Lopez, but your personal leadership brand is far more relevant than you think. Just as some coaches are celebrities who attract top athletes and fans to a program, some managers and leaders are stars others want to work for and with. This is because they create a positive atmosphere. Their units might be known as places where merit rather than politics dominates, as fun places to work, as punching a ticket that opens more opportunities, and so forth. The "star" leader offers some benefits that others do not offer.

Interestingly for our collaboration in writing this book, a number of practices in sports coaching apply to the leadership of Gen Y, but not because college athletes are part of Gen Y. Some of these practices can help you become a better leader of any age employees. In this chapter, we deal with personal leadership brand promise. By this we mean something different from "traditional" leader styles like authoritarian or democratic. We'll show you how your more personal leadership style impacts Gen Y—and others you lead.

The average fan may not realize it, but college coaches deal with two brand promises—the first is fulfilling the university's image, but the second is their personal coaching style.

Of course, a great coach—and leader—can provide a personalized style for each player/worker. For example, some people respond best to pushing and some to supportiveness. But each coach/leader has a general personal style that projects to employees. If that style is a brand promise that provides clear benefits to employees, the leader will be more successful.

Some Examples

What kind of leader was a role model for you? Who did you borrow styles from to develop your own? Think of the different managers or leaders you've known. Following are some examples of different styles:

- Task masters only care about getting the job done. They might be authoritarian, democratic, or even charismatic in how they motivate workers.
- The people-oriented leader wants everyone to get along and might use personal charm to get things done.
- The trainer helps workers develop their skills to do the job.
- The motivator uses positive encouragement to motivate people.

Your own leadership style is your leadership brand and brand promise to employees. Now look at the list again. Which ones would Gen Y and other employees see as benefiting them? Styles that simply get the task done are the price of admission for them, but don't help them grow as people and leaders themselves.

In addition to your own task and people skills, we're saying that, to be a great leader, there are things you can incorporate into your style that will become an attractive brand promise for employees. For example, some leaders work within the organization to obtain the resources their people need to do their jobs. They protect their people from internal politics. They go to bat to get employees promotions and raises.

Mentors help develop workers. They advise them. They reassure them. They might help them with networking connections. They may even guide them to new and better jobs in or out of the organization. Servant leaders (as discussed later in this chapter) don't treat workers as underlings, but as valued people they support in any way possible.

How can you set working for you apart from working for other leaders in your field? Is your area a launching pad where, once people put in a couple of years, they have their choice of other jobs? Is it part of a growing company where stock options will make employees wealthy? You may not have the organization or the control to promise these things. They are just samples. What brand promise can you make that will attract Gen Y and others?

What Is Your Leadership Brand?

Your leadership brand has traditionally been looked at as the style or manner in which you provide direction, implement plans, and motivate or inspire people who work for you. In other words, how you act as a leader or manager to accomplish tasks. Looked at this way, three main styles of leadership have been studied by Lewin and others: *authoritarian*, *collaborative*, and *delegative*.

Authoritarian leaders do not seek outside input or advice and generally make all decisions independently. They give very specific directions in expectation of a standard response.

Collaborative (democratic) leaders take more of a team approach, seek input from employees whose skills and expertise they value, and give more open-ended direction, allowing for individual adaptation and modification.

Delegative (laissez faire) leaders, although ultimately responsible for the decisions made, give others virtually complete power to make decisions, place the highest trust and confidence in them, or defer to their superior knowledge.

Research shows that there are particular circumstances where each of these styles is most effective. For instance, when time is short and the leader is the expert, an authoritative style often works best. Great leaders normally use a combination of these styles, tailoring their use to the particular circumstances and individuals.

Key Point

Being aware of your own leadership brand is the first step to better results.

Coach's Corner: Know Your Leadership Brand

In my first year of coaching at North Carolina State, we were playing at home against the University of North Carolina, coached by the legendary Dean Smith. Our stadium, Bayne Reynolds Coliseum, was approximately fifty years old.

It had been a warm day and, typical of the coliseum, there wasn't a lot of air flow; in fact, it was downright uncomfortable, hot, and sticky. As the players competed, their fingers would turn prune-like, similar to when you stay in the water too long. As the game progressed, our fans were in the faces of the

(*continued*)

Tar Heels players. Our fans were on their feet screaming nonstop. It was an unbelievable environment, almost threatening for the opponents. Dean Smith had a team, as was typical for North Carolina, filled with tremendously talented players—great players. We were clearly outmanned in terms of talent, yet our fans were doing everything they could to help us.

I noticed that, as the game progressed, as hot and uncomfortable as it was, Dean Smith never took his coat off, never loosened his tie. I think he was trying to convey to his team that they were the more talented team, that even under these threatening conditions, this hostile environment, all they had to do was perform with poise and composure. So he didn't sweat, he didn't flinch, he didn't loosen his tie, he didn't take his sport coat off. He portrayed to his team that he was going to be unaffected by the environment. That they were going to do what they do; they were the better team, and if they did that, they would be successful.

Dean Smith knew his leadership brand.

John Chaney at Temple University, another legendary coach, also knew his brand. At Temple, Coach Chaney took a lot of kids who in many ways were underdogs. So when he coached, even before the jump ball occurred, his tie was off and loosened, sometimes all the way down to his sternum. His shirtsleeves were rolled up above his elbows. He didn't wear a sport coat. It seemed to me he was subtly conveying to his team that, as underdogs, "I'm in this fight with you and I'm ready to scratch and claw, bite and kick, do whatever it takes to help us be successful." He didn't have the same kind of team that Dean Smith had; he had a different brand—he was more of an underdog—whereas Coach Smith had great talent year in and year out. Both coached masterfully knowing their different brands.

It is important that you identify your leadership brand in two directions. Looked at traditionally, as above, it will determine how you communicate with your Gen Y employees and the type of work you are willing to entrust to them. Gen Y wants and needs to communicate with you. They need feedback about what they have already done and they want input into what they will do. Gen Y also wants very much to be a participant in decision making, to have responsibility, and to have at least some control over the work they are doing.

If your leadership brand is too authoritarian, you will repel Gen Y. Authoritarian leaders are the antithesis of the boss they are looking for. These leaders will have to modify their styles to become more Gen Y–compatible. On the other hand, if your leadership brand is naturally collaborative or delegative, you should be able to work well with Gen Y.

Consultant's Corner: Leadership of People Is the Point

In nearly every organization in which we have ever worked, we have encountered managers who were promoted because of their proficiency at the task at hand. Whether it is accounting managers, IT managers, shop floor supervisors, or any other kind of manager, they were promoted because they were good accountants, programmers, or machinists. More rare are the managers who were promoted because they had superior *people* skills and reasonable knowledge of the task at hand. In other words, people who were promoted because of their *leadership* skills.

In today's environment, technical skills are the price of admission. But overreliance on them may be counterproductive. We've all known cases where the best salesperson was promoted and

(*continued*)

was a lousy sales manager. Simply being the best at a function is not a reason to be promoted. It is critical for everyone who supervises *people* to understand *people*. As good leaders know, the job is to get things done *through* others. Their own skills at the work they supervise become irrelevant except for training and evaluation.

Take the time and make the investment to develop your leadership skills. Learning finance, programming, or the way a machine operates may be difficult, but many people master these skills. A good manager who wants to become a leader works just as hard, if not harder, at the people skills as he or she ever did at mastering technical skills.

What You Do for Employees

Up to this point, the discussion of leadership styles has followed traditional lines: how you deal with employees to get the work done. But as the introduction indicated, most leaders have ignored how their brands look from the point of view of how they help employees develop. That is, if you have a good leader, often you will learn and adapt his or her style. But what about things a leader can do to more directly help employees?

The "new" direction we're focusing on here is sometimes contained in the first, but often overlooked. How will you develop the people under you? What do you offer them outside of how you get tasks done? Will you be known as a leader who mentors, who advocates for employees, who uses contacts to help advance employees, and so on. For instance, is there a long history of "servant leadership"?

Robert Greenleaf first contrasted servant leadership with traditional approaches in the 1970s. He suggested that, although traditional leadership generally involves the accumulation and exercise of power by one at the "top of the pyramid," the servant-leader shares power, puts the needs of others first, and helps people develop and perform as well as possible. (See Greenleaf.org for more details.)

In broader lists of leadership styles, many factors are included that more directly impact employees' self- and career development. For instance, a *coaching* style works at teaching and training. A *situational* style adapts to each individual being led. A *transformational* style helps create change in individuals, and so on.

Better Leadership Works for Everyone

If you adapt your leadership style to increase what you offer Gen Y for their development, you will also become a better leader for all generations. In research in New Zealand at Massey University, Kristin Murray found that all four generations (Traditionalists, Boomers, X, and Y) were similar on many dimensions. They all rated job dimensions like satisfaction and fulfillment highest, along with social dimensions like supportiveness and rapport with colleagues. She added that organizations "will get the best results from staff if they look at needs on an individual basis."

> "Create customized career paths: This will create a sense of control that Gen Y desires and will give them a measure of their progress in the organization. . . . If you want them to do something, tell them why."
>
> NAS Recruitment, Communications

Communication Fundamentals

As in any sport, or most activities for that matter, there are a series of fundamentals that must be mastered before someone can move on to more advanced levels. Even if a performer is an all-star, his or her coaches usually take time to revisit every fundamental.

Legendary football coach Vince Lombardi used to start his preseason camps by saying, "Gentlemen, this is a football." Even the great Green Bay Packers teams needed to refocus themselves on fundamentals and be *aware* not to overlook the obvious.

There are three key communication fundamentals we need to revisit before moving to the next level (choose your words, nonverbal, listening). While these may seem obvious at first, please do not overlook their importance. In many ways, nothing else can be successfully implemented unless the leader is *aware* of these distinctions between how the generations see the world; see Table 8.1.

TABLE 8.1. Then and Now

Gen X/Boomer	Gen Y
Conditioning	Wellness
"Tree hugger"	Green/sustainable
Job jumping	Leveraging opportunities
Telephone	Smart phone
Walkman	iPod
Encyclopedia	Google
Mid-life crisis	Quarter-life crisis

Choose Your Words

You must choose your words with care when you communicate with Gen Y. Words that mean one thing to a Baby Boomer or Gen Xer may mean something completely different to Gen Y. Also, Gen Y is much less formal than prior generations. The way they communicate with you can be very different.

Even the words we use to describe your leadership role vis-à-vis Gen Y mean something. You aren't going to "deal with," "handle," or "train" Gen Yers as if they were a problem or an animal you were working with. You are going to collaborate with, communicate with, and lead Gen Yers. That's what today's leadership is.

Coach's Corner: Welcome Gen Y

When I was coaching at North Carolina State, I visited Jerry Wainwright's office at the University of North Carolina, Wilmington, where he was the head men's basketball coach.

When I walked into Jerry's office, I was immediately amazed at what I saw. This didn't look like any other office I had ever been in. Every nook and cranny, every wall space, was filled with a fun or interesting object. He had race cars, cartoon characters, sports figurines, stuffed animals, bobble-heads, and characters from the TV show *Family Guy* cluttering his office and making it impossible to see it all at once.

Curious, I asked him what the purpose of all this stuff was. Why was his office decorated in this fashion? His reasoning was ingenious. He wanted his office to be inviting and welcoming to his players. He wanted to make it easy for them to want to go and see him. He wanted to encourage casual drop-bys.

We always talk about spending quality time with our children and families, but some of the best stuff happens when we're simply hanging out. It seems like when we're just hanging out spending time is the time when our kid takes his first steps. It's hard to plan for that. Jerry understood this, as he cultivated relationships with his players. That's why his office was decorated in this unique and brilliant fashion. And it worked.

Nonverbal Communication Counts

Some research suggests that people often understand more about your attitudes from your nonverbal cues than from what you say. How do you walk around the office? What is your posture like when you meet and greet employees? Where do you stand or sit when you talk to someone individually? Facial expressions, posture, and body positioning all matter. Also, be conscious of the physical environment at your organization. How is your office decorated? What does it say about you? How is your lobby area decorated? What does it say about your organization? Gen Y is very observant and will respond to nonverbal cues, even subtle ones.

As a leader, your body language must align to your message. Often we are not conscious of times when our words and our appearance are misaligned, and we send the exact opposite message we intended to send.

Key Point

Gen Y may be especially anxious to give you input when they are first hired. They are seeing things from a fresh perspective and have new ideas. This is a very important time to listen. If you squelch Gen Y now, you may *never* get their enthusiastic input for your organization.

The first step in aligning your spoken and body language is to really be *aware* of your prejudices toward Gen Y. If you are harboring too many negative feelings, they will notice, and it will be a distraction to your spoken words.

Make yourself *aware* of your physical presence. Conduct a self-audit of how you (and your physical space) may be communicating without your even knowing it.

Communication Involves Listening

As with most fundamentals, this is an obvious communication principle, but one that cannot be overstated with Gen Y. They want to be heard. They want to talk to you. They want to give you their perspective. You need to listen to them!

It takes multiple positive reinforcements to equal the impact of one negative comment, so you need to be very positive with Gen Yers early. If you show Gen Y that you can listen, are interested in their ideas, and actually will consider implementing what they suggest, you will earn their respect and attention. You will also profit from their increased interest and commitment to your mission. If you tell Gen Y to hold their ideas until they understand "how things are done around here," you may lose them. At all costs, avoid the ubiquitous "We thought about that, but . . ." response.

Conclusion

Despite the fact that there have been books on leadership brands (cf. Ulrich & Smallwood, 2007), little attention has been given to employees' views of leaders on more personal dimensions. Most leaders and managers are less aware of their personal brands than you might expect. Most of us have done what we do so long that we often operate automatically without much self-analysis. In addition to *how* you get work done through others, greater focus on *what you offer others* will improve your leadership. Because Gen Yers respond best to personalized styles, they can help you become more aware of your own leadership brand. As many mentors of Gen Y say, they learn as much as their mentees because of the fresh view Gen Y brings. Gen Y will be particularly useful to you as they come onboard. Gen Y (and any newcomer) sees things with fresh eyes. As you listen to them you'll gain, and their loyalty to the job will increase.

Kim's Gen Y Profile

Name: Kim

Location: Northeast

Age: 27

Background:

- Graduated with a bachelor of science in education degree with a minor in English before heading to graduate school, where she earned a master's of fine arts degree in creative nonfiction

(*continued*)

- Currently working as a high school teacher in a large suburban school district near her hometown
- Contemplating going back to school to earn a doctorate of education degree in curriculum and instruction

After obtaining an MFA, Kim went to work as a high school teacher in a large city school district in the Northeast. She said that job met her expectations of a "good job"—it was intellectually challenging, and she looked forward to going to work every day.

She said she left only because "the district kept freezing the pay and messing with benefits and insurance, and it didn't look like it was going to get any better."

In her new job as a high school teacher for a large suburban district near her hometown, her situation has improved—she said she is well-compensated, and the district administration treats teachers well.

That said, she still faces the challenges of working in education. "The nature of education is that it takes a long time to have a 'changing of the guard,'" she said. "Most people get a job and stay put, and there also tends to be a lot of negativity in school systems. Basically, older teachers are set in their ways and don't want to bother with professional development, creating an environment that can easily breed negativity."

She said some of her older colleagues aren't interested in learning about new research or modern trends in education. "I think some, but not all, teachers of the older generations think that they are finished growing as professionals," Kim said. "They write off district initiatives and wait out retirement."

For Kim, the characteristics of a good job are

- A positive and fun environment
- A focus on professional development
- Intellectually challenging work

Kim is motivated by:

- Supervisors who challenge her and are willing to have "philosophical conversations about educational theory"
- Desire to see her students succeed

CHAPTER NINE

WORLD-CLASS PERFORMERS

Our research into world-class performers is an ongoing process. We use both formal and informal methods to gain input from world-class actors, actresses, athletes, business executives, musicians, nonprofit pioneers, policemen, and just about every other area where we find and can document excellence. Over the years we have been fascinated by the similar reactions and responses we receive from all walks of life and all world-class performers. A decorated policeman tends to say the same things as a multiple Stanley Cup winner, or Super Bowl champion, or even an Emmy Award–winning actress. We would like to make two very important points. First, there are certain things the truly "world class" do that sets them apart. Second, one need not be famous to be world class. World-class performers are all around us. You may even be one, or chances are you know one.

Since our first edition of this book, we have found at least three characteristics to add to our list. Our guess is they have been there all along and we just missed the nuance of the discussions. Or maybe some of the additions are because of the "mental side" of the game. Business leaders, as well as top athletes, have recognized the need to put in time on the "mental game." Many folks we have talked to lately have referred more often than in the past to their "coaches," and we are not just talking about athletes.

Our goal in sharing our research about what sets the truly world class apart from the merely average is to help leaders everywhere look in the mirror and see areas for improvement. If one wants to be world class, it stands to reason that one could get there faster and easier by adopting what the world class do to set themselves apart. If one is already world class, then even he or she can continue to get better. We love the John Wooden* quote, " It's what you learn after you know it all that counts."

Although we will talk about nine characteristics of those who are world class, there are two elementary aspects that they share. All possess a certain amount of talent in their fields. They may not be the most talented, and in some cases had to work hard to develop their skills, but they do possess talent.

Over the past ten years or so, we have seen one additional universal truism: the "world class" work on their "people skills." It is not enough to simply be talented. That will get you only so far. Being world class is relative, since there is always someone seeking to become better and redefine world class. Folks who work to get on top, and stay on top, realize they need to work on their "people skills." This used to be considered a "soft skill." Now the best of the best realize its importance, how very difficult it can be, and how important it is to success.

World-class performers and leaders:

1. Use performance feedback or "game film."
2. Turn unconscious, negative tendencies into conscious, positive choices.

---

*John Robert Wooden was an American basketball player and coach. Nicknamed the "Wizard of Westwood," he won ten NCAA national championships in a twelve-year period—seven in a row—as head coach at UCLA, an unprecedented feat.

3. Practice energy management.
4. Realize that what is required for improvement may be counterintuitive.
5. Develop a clear vision.
6. Seek out coaches/mentors.
7. Develop tactical and measurable action plans.
8. Recover from losses quickly.
9. Use positive self-talk.

Skill 1: World-Class Performers and Leaders Use Performance Feedback or "Game Film"

In every profession, people who desire to improve their performance know they must reflect on what they have done in the past in order to do it better in the future. Athletes review game film; actors study film clips; and musicians listen to recordings of themselves. Teachers are observed and evaluated by their supervisors; doctors have peer reviews; police film themselves while taking firearms practice; lawyers read transcripts of depositions and trials. Every world-class performer has a tool that enables him or her to examine and evaluate his or her behavior, to see what is being done well or poorly, and to pinpoint areas for improvement or growth. World-class performers then make the conscious decision to address their areas for improvement.

While you may not have actual game film to analyze, some tools can help you identify your strengths and weaknesses. These tools are personality profiles, 360-degree evaluations, and employee surveys. (We will refer to a 360-degree tool in Chapter 10.) These types of tools can provide you with the "game film" you need to become a better leader.

One of the best tools we know of to increase your awareness is personality profiles. Personality profiles identify behavioral tendencies, personality traits, and types. These tools help in two ways. First, they help you understand yourself, and, second, they help you recognize behavior patterns in other people so that you can understand them better. As a leader, you need to work with a variety of people, on a variety of levels. It will help you do your job better if you can identify how different employees think, react, and want to be treated as you supervise and reward each one. This is especially true of Gen Y employees, who are particularly sensitive to how you interact with them (and others!), the words you use, and your management style. Gen Y thrives on feedback and communication. The better you understand your own behavioral tendencies and those of Gen Y, the better you can communicate.

Perhaps you unknowingly dominate conversations, ask questions without listening to the answers, or have little patience. Perhaps you are too critical, uncomfortable with change, or overly concerned about details. Everyone has blind spots—areas where they need to improve. But these blind spots can be particularly detrimental when interacting with Gen Y.

> "The communication style of leaders helps us distinguish great leaders from the wannabes. When facing a problem, the great leader says, 'Let's find out,' while the wannabe says that 'nobody knows.' . . . Great leaders have the capacity to listen while wannabes can't wait for their turn to talk."
>
> —Reed Markham, Ph.D., American educator

Key Point
The best of the best study "game film."

Chapter 10 has an extensive discussion of DiSC, one of the most widely used personality-profiling programs. DiSC will give you "game film" to uncover the behavioral tendencies that you need to work on in yourself.

Skill 2: World-Class Performers and Leaders Turn Unconscious, Negative Tendencies into Conscious, Positive Choices

Studies show that 90 percent of what we do is rote. We have routines, habits, and familiar practices that are more or less automatic. But great leadership is not a passive, unthinking activity. It is the opposite of routine and rote. It is thoughtful, dynamic, and proactive.

As discussed above, some of our unconscious habits, routines, and tendencies can be negative. The little things we don't even realize we're doing can have a disproportionately large impact, especially with respect to Gen Y.

For example, one of the more common tendencies we see is multi-tasking. In today's busy world everyone tries to accomplish multiple things at once. If this becomes an unconscious habit when you are interacting with others, then you are in a danger zone. Every employee, particularly Gen Y employees, will begin to believe their input is not valued if you are not fully attentive.

World-class performers seek to uncover these unconscious tendencies and develop conscious triggers that control or direct them. Particularly when dealing with Gen Y, we need to be sensitive to the ways we communicate and interact. The DiSC profile discussed in Chapter 10 will help you understand and identify your tendencies and turn them into conscious, positive actions.

Consultant's Corner: Five Most Important Things Today

Here is a tip we give to folks we work with to help them manage their time and their energy. We advise folks to start their day with their calendar and a list of the "five most important things today." This in *not* a "to do" lists. Those can be defeating. "To do" lists

(*continued*)

seem to always grow, not shrink. At the end of the day, if you manage by "to do" lists you will usually feel like not much has been accomplished. Instead, we ask folks to write the five most important things they need to do that day . . . in order! With some practice, this can be accomplished over the first cup of coffee.

If one of the most important things today is to get to your child's soccer game, then put it on the list. If it is *the* most important thing, then make it number 1. This will force you to work your schedule to make it happen.

By working with a "Five Most Important Things Today" list, instead of the traditional "to do" list, priorities become clearer and energy is managed better. In addition, at the end of the day, you have a real scoreboard to measure the day's success. This list has been done and checked off. A "to do" list just keep growing.

Skill 3: World-Class Performers and Leaders Practice Energy Management

Every world-class performer we have ever met practices some sort of energy management in addition to time management. At some point during our careers we all are exposed to a time management course. We learn there are only so many hours in the day and to prioritize our tasks accordingly. Time, we learn, is a finite resource.

World-class performers further learn that energy is also a finite resource. How to spend that energy is a critical decision, and it is not taken lightly. Maximum energy is invested in areas that can improve performance, and little or no energy is wasted on events or situations beyond their control. As a leader, it is critical not to waste energy on events beyond your control. It is equally important not to continually rehash the same old issue or try to wish a challenge away. Wishing is not a strategy!

We see three consistent energy wasters business leaders repeat in regard to Gen Y.

Energy Waster 1: Why Can't They Be Like We Were?

Every older generation has probably said this same thing. Why isn't today's generation like we were? It's time to accept and adapt to reality: "What is, is." Don't waste energy wishing that Gen Y was like prior generations of employees. They're not and, as discussed earlier, they're not playing by the same set of rules that prior generations did either. They certainly have different interests and needs. They are looking for very different things in the workplace, and they are going to require you to do some very different things to attract and retain them. As discussed earlier, they're different, not wrong. They may even be better. Don't stew over who they are, embrace it. Work with it.

Energy Waster 2: Why Do We Have to Change . . . Why Can't They Change?

Many of us had to "pay our dues," perhaps by working for a lousy boss at a mediocre job for many years. We "toughed it out," so why can't Gen Yers do the same? The fact is that Gen Y has figured out that they don't have to tough it out when work conditions are poor. They realize that they have the option of leaving and finding fulfilling employment elsewhere. They are keenly aware that a whole generation of Baby Boomers will be retiring and Gen Y will be in demand. They have delayed marriage and parenting and are free of familial responsibilities. They do not need to spend time in a bad situation and simply hope it changes. They can be, and are, action-oriented.

Other generations, Traditionalists, Baby Boomers, and Gen X, did not have the freedom or the mind-set to leave. We had to "grin and bear it." We had families to support, mortgages to pay, and we could not count on our parents to foot the bill. Fortunately, for most of us, the wait paid off. We survived the poor bosses, the menial tasks, the lack of feedback, and so forth. Gen Y is not so patient and is keenly aware of many alternatives. The sooner we accept this new reality the better.

Energy Waster 3: Defensiveness

World-class performers do not waste their energy on being defensive about situations. If a coach, director, conductor, or mentor offers challenging advice, world-class performers stop and listen.

Likewise, when faced with new members on the team, members who ultimately want to contribute and maybe even take their jobs, world-class performers waste no energy being insecure or defensive. They know it is a drain on precious resources. They up their game. They don't sabotage the new person. They accept his or her presence as a challenge and strive to get better. Improvement is not a zero sum game. One does not get better when a teammate gets worse. Both can improve at the same time.

As a leader, it is important to manage your (and your team's) defensiveness. As discussed earlier, Gen Y is very educated and tech-savvy. They generally bring superior skills to the job in one area or another. They will know more than you about some things. You may have to ask them about something or have them explain something to you or your other employees. Don't be defensive about this. It doesn't mean you cannot lead or manage this bright generation. You have other superior skills and knowledge, and your experience is irreplaceable. Be happy Gen Y has skills to add to your organization, so never lose faith in yourself as a leader.

Energy Waster 4: Judging the Messenger

World-class performers know their coaches are not perfect. In fact, many world-class performers, on a personal level, do not even like their coaches. It is a fantasy to believe that all players and coaches see eye-to-eye all of the time.

What sets the best of the best apart from others, however, is that they realize it is a waste of energy to sit in judgment of the messenger (coach) and allow that judgment to obscure the message. Many folks, when given input from others, take too much time and spend too much energy determining whether the *messenger* is someone worth listening to. What happens then is that the messenger becomes the critical input, and not the *message*.

World-class performers waste little to no time thinking about the messenger and put all of their energy into determining whether the message is valid. It becomes about the input and feedback and not about who is giving the input. Many times, world-class performers receive some of their best input from their biggest critics. By not wasting energy sitting in judgment of the sender, the receiver can spend his or her energy on what is important, getting better. Judging the messenger is a waste of precious and finite energy.

Skill 4: World-Class Performers and Leaders Realize That What Is Required for Improvement May Be Counterintuitive

World-class performers are able to think outside the box and force themselves to rethink and change their game plans in order to improve. The saying "you can't teach an old dog new tricks" does not apply to successful people because that is exactly what they do—they "learn new tricks."

World-class performers know that everything is not going to come to them naturally and that there will be many times when they will need to do things counterintuitively. The simplest example is basketball. Every player, just like everyone else, is either left-handed or right-handed. Even with years of practice each one will *always* have a dominant hand. When playing the game there are always times when a player must "counterintuitively" go against his natural tendency. He will need to succeed using his "off" hand. Granted, players will have practiced this for years, but even the best player in the world has a dominant hand and will intuitively use it in most situations (writing and eating, for example). However, world-class performers know there are times when success depends on being counterintuitive.

Some research shows that managers tend to learn one style when they are younger and continue to apply it throughout their careers. They always use their "dominant hand." Because of this, managers often fail when facing new challenges. Leaders, however, are much more adaptive. Leaders know, deep down, "that one size does not fit all." Gen Y can help you and others develop more leadership tools and adaptability. Particularly when dealing with Gen Y employees, doing what you always did, or what comes naturally or what is comfortable, may be the opposite of what you should be doing. This generation sees and interprets things differently. They have much different expectations and needs. What you did instinctively for Traditionalists, Baby Boomers, and Gen Xers may not work for Gen Yers.

For example, it used to be that getting called into the boss's office was akin to being sent to the principal's office when you were a kid. In the past, the boss was fairly isolated and unapproachable. He or she didn't really rub shoulders with the average employee and rarely talked casually to new, young employees. Being called in meant you had made a mistake or were in trouble and the boss was going to confront you with the mess you made. It was usually embarrassing and uncomfortable to see the boss. In fact, the boss only seemed to be interested in you when you were in trouble.

Gen Y Wants Feedback

Today, Gen Y wants and expects to be called in by the boss, and not because they are "in trouble." Gen Y wants to talk to the boss to share ideas, receive face-to-face feedback, and ask questions. In fact, Gen Y will be upset if they do not get to talk with the boss.

You may be operating under the old system and think that communication is only for correction. You may think intuitively that it is not "normal" to talk to new, young employees and it could somehow diminish your position. Yet, in order to be a world-class leader, you must do what is counterintuitive. Gen Y's need for communication is actually a good thing because it will give you an opportunity to reinforce your mutual vision and keep your finger on Gen Y's pulse.

The way you communicate is only one example of the counterintuitive behavior you must now adopt. The reality is, you will have to do things in almost every area of recruiting, interviewing, on-boarding, and interacting with Gen Y that are different and not "what you always did." Be prepared to stretch your comfort zone and adapt. Be prepared to master your "off hand."

> "I am convinced that nothing we do is more important than hiring and developing people. At the end of the day you bet on people, not on strategies."
>
> Larry Bossidy, Businessman, Author, *Execution: The Discipline of Getting Things Done*

Skill 5: World-Class Performers and Leaders Develop a Clear Vision

Perhaps the most important attribute of world-class performers is they have a vision. They can see what others can't, long before it happens.

In our first edition we discussed the importance of world-class performers (WCP) and having vision. Then we glossed right over it and proceeded to talk about Gen Y's vision and the importance of a leader knowing, nurturing, and linking Gen Y's vision to the company. In our ignorance we said, "Countless books and articles have been written about vision and we will not attempt to reinvent the wheel here. You know what vision is, how critical it is to your success as a leader, and to the success of your organization."

Since that time three things have happened. First, we have come to realize how *dramatically* important this WCP concept is for leaders. Second, we have learned how difficult it is for many leaders to develop and cascade a vision. Finally, a remarkable tool has been developed to help leaders understand the strengths and challenges they may have with developing and implementing a vision. (More in Chapter 10.)

It was true what we said before that most leaders know how important it is to their and their organization's success to cast a powerful vision. What we overlooked was how many leaders fail to do it and why so many find it difficult. We began using a tool, *The Work of Leaders* (Straw, Scullard, Kukkonen, & Davis, 2013), that has helped us understand much more about the importance of casting a powerful vision and why all world-class performers do it.

We have come to understand that, while developing a vision has always been important, it now is *critically* important for leaders at *all* levels of an organization. This is where three key concepts converge. Gen Y has a vision for themselves (and you have to link it to the corporate vision). All world-class performers have a vision, and research shows overwhelmingly that crafting a vision is what the best-rated leaders do to drive their organizations forward. After all, leaders lead, and that means taking people from one place to another. Most, if not all, employees want to know where they are going.

How visions are crafted and how employees look at corporate visions has evolved dramatically over the years. Traditionalists, Baby Boomers, and Gen X, for the most part, felt no real need to develop a personal vision, or even their department's vision. An overarching corporate vision was enough.

In *The Work of Leaders*, the authors attempt to address the myth of "crafting vision." They point out that, in the past, most employees believed crafting a vision was the sole responsibility of the C-Suite. The executives, or more often the president and CEO, sat "high atop a mountain, deep in contemplation until inspiration hits, and bam, the vision appears." This concept was in practice for many years. As time went on, a select few organizations were able to create a compelling vision that drove real results. Most places, at least in our experience, developed fairly meaningless statements that were put on plaques on the wall, often ignored or even made fun of by the "rank and file."

The practice of crafting a vision, and the need to do it collaboratively, is now critical for an organization's and a leader's success. People want to have a say in where they are going and will not blindly follow a "plaque on the wall." As we discussed in Chapter 7 under "Reality Change 9," Gen Y has a vision for themselves and a leader's role is to link that vision to the larger vision. Also, research indicates that leaders at all levels must craft a vision for their teams, departments, work groups, shifts, and so on. It is not just the C-Suite's job. Every leader needs to have a vision for his or her work group that links that group's efforts to the corporate vision.

The Reticular Activating System

Part of the problem with people's ability to learn and retain information is physical and hereditary. It is because of a switch in your brain called the reticular activating system (RAS), and most people are unaware it even exists. The reticular activating system controls and dominates everyone in different ways and on different levels.

It plays a significant role in determining whether a person can learn and remember well or not and also whether he or she is highly motivated or bored easily. It is a loose network of neurons and neural fiber that is connected at its base to the spinal cord and runs up through the brain stem to the mid-brain. It is the center of control for other parts of the brain involved in learning, self-control or inhibitions, and motivation. In short, it is the attention center of the brain, and it is the switch that turns your brain on and off. When functioning properly, it provides the connections that are needed for the processing and learning of information, plus the ability to stay focused on the correct task.

If the reticular activating system doesn't stimulate the neurons of the brain as much as it should, that is, when people have difficulty learning, poor memory, lack of attention or self-control. If the RAS over-stimulates the brain, people become hyperactive, talk too much, and become too restless. It must be activated to normal levels for the rest of the brain to function as it should.

The reticular activating system is best known as a filter because it sorts out what is important that needs to be paid attention to and what is unimportant and can be ignored. Without this filter, we would all be over-stimulated and distracted by noises from our environment around us. As an example, let's just say you were a mother who has a baby sleeping in the next room, and you live right next to a busy airport with lots of loud noise from jets taking off and landing. Despite the constant roar of the jets and other noise, you will hear your baby if it makes even the smallest noise in the next room. The RAS filters out the airport noise, which is unimportant to you and keeps you focused on your baby, which is the "most important" thing to you. The RAS is a filter between your conscious mind and your subconscious mind. It takes instructions from your conscious mind (like "I need to hear my baby") and passes it on to your subconscious mind, which becomes diligent and alert to your request.

(*continued*)

In the world of learning, the RAS is a switch that turns on and off based on how much telling tension or self-talk you have going on inside your head. If the switch is open, you can retain information easily, and if the switch is closed, you cannot. If you are sitting in a seminar bored because the person speaking is not engaging enough (your brain is not stimulated enough), your RAS will turn off and treat the person as irritating background noise, just like the noisy airport. You see the person speaking and hear her voice, but do not retain the information.

Now that you are aware of your RAS, you can control it. If you are sitting in a room listening to a speaker and feel yourself daydreaming or self-talking, take a deep breath and become present with the person's words. Staying present is the most important part of keeping your RAS open and absorbing what is being said. I believe that awareness brings change, and this awareness can have dramatic impacts on being a great student, leader, employee, parent, friend, or spouse.

Excerpted from www.thriveinlife.ca/thrive/wp-content/uploads/2011/03/The-Reticular-Activating-System1.pdf

---

World-class performers have known this, perhaps even unconsciously, for years. New research on brain function, as well as research done on the most effective business leaders, confirms the need for all leaders to craft a strong vision. Having a strong vision opens one's mind to information that would otherwise have been filtered out as noise. If one does not open his or her RAS and, by cascading a strong vision, open the collective RAS of employees, important and possible game-changing information will be filtered out by their brains. It is simply how the brain works.

Consultant's Corner: Quiet Time

Genesis 2:2—On the seventh day God rested.

There are nearly unlimited distractions for today's business leader. We live in a 24/7/365 world. Twenty-four-hour news cycles, global competitors, and ever more demanding shareholders and stakeholders makes it a real challenge for people to slow down and find some quiet time. This may be one of the more counterintuitive things a leader needs to do. When the world is speeding up, slow down.

We have had the good fortune of consulting with some of the best business leaders one could know. They have found a way to create enormous shareholder, stakeholder, and personal wealth. Some have started businesses on card tables in the garage that now are worth a billion dollars, some have rescued a dying firm and turned it into a global force . . . and everything in between.

One thing these folks have in common is the wisdom to slow down. It seems the faster the world around them moves, the more they focus on slowing down and seeing the whole picture. Much can be accomplished when you slow down and make quiet time. Strategies become clearer and options become more abundant. Every single successful leader we have worked with has found a way to make time to just think.

As a leader it is critical for you to find the "think time." Turn off your gadgets, schedule some strategic thinking time, or just take a walk. Find a way to make time to "just be." More importantly, also coach your folks to find some time to think and strategize. Ask them about it. Talk to them about how they carve out strategic thinking time. Wars are won with the strategy forged behind the lines as much as they are during the heat of the battle.

Coach and mentor your folks to find some time to "just be."

Skill 6: World-Class Performers and Leaders Seek Out Coaches/Mentors

Many times when we are working with groups we ask folks to list some world-class performers who come to mind. More times than not, the lists contain several athletes from team sports. Team sports, unlike most other places one can find world-class performers, has a built-in advantage. Team sports have coaches.

However, most other activities do not have a *built-in* coach. Professionals in many areas need to hire a coach. Actors and actresses, golfers, tennis players, and business leaders, to name a few, do not have a built-in coach and need to acquire one from time to time.

Our research has found a few interesting things about acquiring a coach. First, the coach's role is to make his players better. Pure and simple. The coach's job is *not to be better than the player,* but to make the player better.

In business we find this to be a challenge. Many successful business people think they need even more successful business folks to mentor or coach them. Can we learn from others who have achieved success? Of course we can. However, not every coach is, or ever was, better than the players they coach. The job is to *make the player better.* In fact, some great coaches never actually did well at the task at all. They were not talented enough to perform the task, but they were masters in helping others perform it.

Good coaches also stay on top of the latest and greatest trends and tools that can help their players. They study other winners and adapt winning tools and techniques for their charges. They provide the all-important "outside eyes" that can spot small things before they become major issues. A good coach deploys a toolbox that makes his or her players better.

The next key thing about those who are world class is that they do not become defensive when a coach provides feedback. To become defensive is counterproductive. World-class performers seek out a coach, and then they *listen.* They may not always implement the advice because they lack the skill to pull it off, or their instincts tell them to do something else, or they flat-out disagree with the input. No matter the reason, world-class performers find a coach or mentor and then thoughtfully consider the advice they receive.

Coach's Corner: Leadership Is Key

Jeff Van Gundy played Division III college basketball at Nazareth College. He joined our coaching staff at Providence College, and we immediately recognized his brilliant mind and passion for the game.

Eventually, Jeff became one of the most respected coaches in the NBA as head coach for the New York Knicks and later for the Houston Rockets. Great players like Patrick Ewing and Mark Jackson were quick to praise him.

It did not matter that Jeff himself played small-college basketball. It didn't matter that these NBA players knew that Jeff wasn't nearly as gifted or skilled at basketball as they were. Instead, they looked to Jeff with respect because of his leadership, vast knowledge of the game, and passion. In short, they knew that, because of his work ethic and expertise, he could help them improve as players and win. Jeff's ability as a coach could help them achieve their goals.

Skill 7: World-Class Performers and Leaders Develop Tactical and Measurable Action Plans

World-class performers not only set goals, but break each goal into measurable, bite-size chunks that are committed to a plan. They do not hope to get better. They break everything down into action steps that have a timeline and can be measured. When they practice, it's meaningful. The old adage "practice makes perfect" really is "perfect practice makes perfect." By breaking everything down into bite-size chunks, world-class performers can measure their progress.

World-class performers create their own personal development plans and choose areas for improvement. Using their "game films," they pick a few areas to develop and create actionable tactics. Here is where coaches help. Often, world-class performers cannot actually *see* what has to be addressed, even with game film. Most times things *look* and *feel* correct, so finding ways to improve is impossible if one believes he is already doing it correctly.

What then happens, in the absence of game film and a coach, is that people will actually perfect the wrong things! Since it felt correct and they did not know their technique was flawed, although they may be practicing, they are flawed in their approach. A coach, using game film, can help world-class performers take a step-by-step approach to continuous improvement.

The same can be applied to leaders. Game film, a "coach," and a personal development plan help even the best leader get better. Everyone has techniques that can be improved.

Skill 8: World-Class Performers and Leaders Recover from Losses Quickly

World-class performers can be some of the most competitive people on Earth. They want to win and work hard to achieve results. A loss is an affront to all they have worked and prepared for. It hurts.

Key Point

Think of a professional golfer or even a Broadway actress. The performance is in real time. If a mistake is made, there is no room to dwell on the error. Recognize it, acknowledge it, and move on.

With that said, the best of the best recover quickly and move on. There is something to be learned from a loss. The lesson can be applied in the future. There is little time to sulk. There is another game to play, or deal to make, or audition to attend. There simply is not time to dwell on a loss. They move on quickly.

This also links directly to energy management. It is a waste of energy to dwell on *what was*. It is far more productive to look at what is and, even better, *what can be*. Nothing can be done about what was, but everything can be done about what can be.

As this relates to leadership and Gen Y, it is amazing to us how much energy is wasted dwelling on what was versus what can be. Leaders need to look to the future and drive their followers to a better outcome, not dwell on what is uncontrollable. The past is most definitely uncontrollable. Gen Y will never be like the previous generations. Gen Y is Gen Y. Leaders must focus on the task at hand and not waste time and energy wishing things were different.

Skill 9: World-Class Performers and Leaders Use Positive Self-Talk

Our research into world-class performers is an ongoing endeavor. When we have the opportunity, we interview folks who meet the criteria. Lately, we have been hearing something a bit different in our conversations. World-class performers have been telling us about their "self-talk." Reviewing our previous notes, we found that similar points had been made, but mentioned differently. In the past we heard things like "optimism" or "self-confidence" or "strong belief in myself" or "I am always reminding myself of XXX." Now we realize this was another way of discussing "self-talk." The concept of positive "self-talk" also links directly to opening one's reticular activating system.

World-class performers know that their actions tend to follow their thoughts. Negative thoughts produce negative outcomes. Positive thoughts produce positive outcomes. What we "see" in our minds sets the stage for what actually happens. Visualization is a form of "self-talk." Most professional golfers interviewed talk about "visualizing the shot" and setting their brains on course for implementing the vision.

Most of us have heard at one time or another how athletes are able to "stay in the moment." Again, golfers are a great example. The best of the best concentrate on one shot at a time and forget the previous shot; whether it was good or bad is irrelevant to the next shot. World-class performers work at the messages they send themselves. Not only does this produce better results, but research shows it can even make one happier. WebMD says, "You can learn a lot about your own worldview by paying attention to 'self-talk'—the conversation you have in your head about yourself and the world around you. Even more important, changing how you talk to yourself can actually help shift your perspective" (The Power of Positive Thinking—http://www.webmd.com/balance/express-yourself-13/positive-self-talk?page=2).

The Mayo Clinic defines "self-talk" as "the endless stream of unspoken thoughts that run through your head every day." *Psychology Today* tells us that "those inner voices talk incessantly. And we should be paying attention, because what we say to ourselves has a direct impact on our success—or failure. Plenty of research indicates positive self-talk creates positive results. Now an analysis of thirty-two different studies of self-talk in sports indicates the specific words we use when talking to ourselves also play a role in how well we perform" (Positive thinking: Reduce stress by eliminating negative self-talk—MayoClinic.com—http://www.mayoclinic.com/health/positive-thinking/SR00009/NSECTIONGROUP=2).

Among the many disciplines world-class performers develop, work out, practice, study, stay current on latest trends, develop people skills, and so on, they *work* on developing the discipline of "self-talk." It is one of those things in life that is simple, but in no way easy. It takes work and discipline.

WebMD says, "The process of shifting your language is a lot like getting in shape." If you have not worked out in some time, you will need to get your muscles in shape. It makes sense that developing this key skill would take work and discipline. It is a simple concept, but if it were easy, more folks would be world-class.

The Mayo Clinic has one of the best tips we have ever seen to help people build these "self-talk" muscles. They suggest: "Start by following one simple rule: Don't say anything to yourself you wouldn't say to anyone else. Be gentle and encouraging with yourself. If a negative thought enters your mind, evaluate it rationally and respond with affirmations of what is good about you."

We know there will be those out there who look at this as being "soft" and not real-world. Our challenge is this: it is what world-class performers do, and often the "soft" things are the *hardest* to master.

> "Whether you think you can, or you think you can't—you're right."
>
> Henry Ford

Conclusion

We've outlined the results of our research on what makes world-class performers. Other research suggests that most leaders and managers develop their own personal styles (or brands) of leadership early in their careers and then stick with that style. Thus, they can fail because they don't adjust when the situation changes. Generation Y is a major change in the workplace and provides you the opportunity to adapt your style for the better. If you'll accept the challenge, you'll come out ahead because world-class approaches not only work with Gen Y, but they work with all your staff.

Liz's Gen Y Profile

Name: Liz

Location: Northeast

Age: 30

Background:

- Earned bachelor's and master's degrees from a large state university in the Northeast, where she is currently working as a graduate student researcher while pursuing a Ph.D. in psychology

After earning her bachelor's degree, Liz took a marketing job for an organization affiliated with her alma mater. She opted to

(*continued*)

continue her education because she felt like she was "going nowhere and not doing something meaningful" in that position.

While her current work as a graduate student researcher makes her situation somewhat unusual, Liz still faces challenges when dealing with professional peers from other generations. "As a result of the recession and the general economic climate, I think most people my age are fairly cynical when it comes to their relationship with a company; we don't expect that the company feels a lot of loyalty to us, and we don't feel a lot of loyalty to the company," she said. "I've occasionally had high-ranking professionals from older generations talk about working my way up in a company in ways that don't feel realistic to me."

Liz said she faces communication challenges with both younger students and older colleagues. She discourages undergraduate students from texting her when they need help with their schoolwork, instead steering them toward email or, if urgent, a phone call. "I know some colleagues from older generations who would much rather talk on the phone about things that I think are really better communicated through email," she said. "I realize we're both working to accept each other's preferences, though, so I try to be patient on the phone with the understanding that the other person is being patient when I'm sending emails."

For Liz, the characteristics of a good job are

- The ability to capitalize on her strengths while developing new skills
- Finding meaning and value in her work

Liz is motivated by:

- A desire to help others
- Having a satisfying, fulfilling professional life

CHAPTER TEN

STUDY YOUR GAME FILM

Knowing Personality Types

Mary, twenty-four, is happy with her new job but somewhat worried that her boss, Tim, doesn't like her. He has never said that her work is poor nor has he ever criticized anything, but neither has he ever complimented her on her work. This makes her very nervous. More importantly, one morning she saw him in the elevator and he barely acknowledged her, only grunting a terse "Hello." He generally strides through the office with a stern, preoccupied look on his face.

Tim always keeps his door closed and has never stopped by Mary's office to talk. Furthermore, when she approached him to ask a few questions about a project, he seemed annoyed with her for worrying so much about the details. He kept cutting her off and twice changed the topic. Mary wishes Tim would just tell her what she is doing wrong and why he doesn't like her. She doesn't know how much more of this tension she can take.

What went wrong? The sad thing about our case study is that Tim actually does like Mary. He just doesn't show his approval or acceptance in a way that Mary understands. Tim is a Baby Boomer who believes in minimal communication. He will let Mary know when something is wrong. If he doesn't say anything, she is doing well. He would "call her on the carpet" when something is unacceptable, and he assumes Mary knows this. He never talks to his older employees, and they are fine with that.

Tim will only go to someone's office if there is an urgent problem. He doesn't believe in making small talk with subordinates, especially not with new hires. He would have been alarmed and uncomfortable if his boss had talked to him when he was starting out. Tim is not really a "morning person." He doesn't say more than a few words, even to his wife, in the morning. There is no way he could be chatty with employees early in the day.

Tim is a "bottom line" guy. As we will discuss shortly in relation to the DiSC profile, he is a "High D." He is not really concerned about the details or socializing with employees. He is happy to let employees manage the little stuff and just present him with the final facts. He gets impatient with endless, detailed questions and discussions. If he cuts people off, it's just because he has all the information he needs and he doesn't want to waste time—his or theirs. It certainly doesn't mean the work is not good or he doesn't like the employees.

A Lack of Self-Awareness

The above case study is a classic example of poor communication between people with different expectations, communication styles, and personality profiles. Mary is interpreting Tim's actions to mean something that they don't mean. Tim is insensitive to what he is doing and the message he is projecting to this Gen Y employee. He is not tuned into her need for feedback, her sensitivity to unconscious behavioral tendencies, or his need to adapt. Tim would be stunned to learn that Mary thinks he doesn't like her. He is oblivious to the subtle signals he is sending her.

Tim is not alone. Many people are not meeting the communication needs of Gen Y—or their other employees for that matter. As we have said throughout this book, Gen Yers are extreme communicators. They are in touch with each other and the world.

Gen Y is so tuned in to communication and feedback that when you don't communicate with them it is a negative communication.

It's All Communication

As we learned in our case study, a closed door is interpreted by Gen Yers as meaning you don't want to talk to them. The failure to engage in casual conversation means you don't like them. A failure to compliment them on a job means you didn't think it was well done.

Leadership Is Communication

You must be able to communicate effectively with Gen Y at every point of your employment interaction: recruiting, interviewing, orienting, training, and managing. Your ability to communicate will directly affect your ability to retain Gen Y. You must also be able to recognize the subtle, unconscious things you are saying or doing that might alienate Gen Yers at any stage of your interaction with them.

Fortunately, there is an excellent tool, a personality profile, which will help you do this. We discussed the use of "game film" by world-class leaders in Chapter 9 Now we will explore it in detail.

People Are Different!

We make three main points in this chapter that are obvious in general but important in the details of their application.

- First, people are different.
- Second, it's useful for leaders to know about those differences and how to relate to them.
- Third, you can use knowledge of individual differences to improve performance.

Despite the fact that everyone knows intellectually that we are all different, at a primitive level we judge others by ourselves. We expect others to be like us. We manage others the way we want to be managed. When someone doesn't respond the way we would, we are uncomfortable.

Styles, Personality Profile, and the Four Generations

As we said early in the book, for the first time in history, there are four distinct generations in the workforce. We do not see this changing any time soon. By the time the Traditionalists will be leaving the workforce and Baby Boomers will be retiring en masse, an entirely new generation will be entering. This next generation is still in elementary school, but they are on their way.

Just as there are distinct differences in each generation, there are unique and distinct differences between individual styles. While this certainly makes communicating across generations a challenge for leaders, we do have some good news.

Communicating effectively with various personality styles has not changed in decades, probably ever. Each *individual* within each generation has his or her own communication style. There is no "one size fits all," and it is irrelevant, for purposes of communication, which generation one represents.

For leaders trying to communicate effectively, this means you *do not* need to calculate style *and* generation into every communication. The generational information is a separate issue. As for styles and personal profile distinction, we have found no difference between generations.

As a leader, you need to work with a variety of people on a variety of levels across four generations. It will help you do your job if you can identify how different employees think, react, and want to be treated as you supervise and reward each one. The better you understand and communicate with each individual, the better the results you'll produce. This is particularly true for Gen Y.

As we have discussed, Gen Y has different wants and needs, cares about different things, and is motivated in different ways. Gen Y is also the most diverse group in history. They are very different—from their managers, from other employees, and from each other. Thus, it is even more important to treat them as individuals. The easiest way to do this is to become aware of their personal styles and give them a little undivided attention.

While *every* generation will appreciate a leader who adapts, other generations, in many ways, have grown used to bosses who are not the best communicators. Gen Y will not be as patient, nor as forgiving. In the 21st century, for a 21st century workplace, leaders who clearly understand the need to communicate with *every* style will attract and retain the best talent.

Coach's Corner: Don't Peek!

Sometimes during practice I go over and talk to a player on the sidelines and give him my undivided attention, even though practice continues to take place on the floor. I will purposely turn my back on the rest of practice so I am only focused on a single player. This sends a strong message to the player that he is, at this moment, the most important person and has my undivided attention.

The key, for me, is not to peek at what else is going on around me. I am confident the other coaches have the rest of practice handled. If my focus strays from this individual player, it would send the exact opposite message from the one I intend.

Business leaders need to find opportunities to turn their backs on some day-to-day minutiae and give their Gen Y "players" some undivided attention. Put the phone on "do not disturb," ignore the email for a few moments, and show your players that, in this moment, the one you are speaking to is the most important person in the organization. No matter what the temptation, don't peek.

Personality Theory

The classic way to categorize profiles and understand different people has been through the use of personality theories. Personality is the study of individual differences. You can also consider personality to be a collection of habit patterns or personal styles. It is how you differ from others. Some of your personality depends on your experiences in life. Different people learn different things and are exposed to different events. However, much of your basic personality comes from your genes. Studies from the University of Minnesota show that identical twins raised apart will usually end up with very similar personalities.

A personality profiling system you trust will help you read people and communicate better with them. By gaining an understanding of personality styles, you'll be better at accepting and appreciating others. As a bonus, when you study personality, you will also understand yourself better.

The DiSC™ Personal Profile

There are many well-established and valid personality profiles. We recommend and use DiSC, the oldest, most recognized, and most widely used commercial personality profiling program. It was developed more than seventy-five years ago by Dr. William Moulton Marston.

DiSC stands for Dominance, Influence, Steadiness, and Conscientiousness, the key personality traits. We will describe the four primary styles, but most people have a blend of two or even three behavioral styles.

We strongly encourage leaders to obtain this "game film." If you have completed a Personal Profile in the past, pull it out and study it again. If you have not, you will find it to be one of the most useful leadership tools you can have. It is your "game film," and in our opinion is the single best tool available for leaders who are serious about becoming better.

All world-class performers (Chapter 9) study performance feedback or game film. Unfortunately, in business there is very little opportunity to study game film. Business leaders are always "live" and not "practicing" for a future "performance." Every day is a "performance." Results and decisions are due *now*, not at some future point. In business there are not four days of practice and conditioning in preparation of "game day."

The DiSC system provides business leaders with invaluable "game film." One can uncover one's unconscious tendencies and become more aware of intuitive behaviors that *feel* right. What "feels right" may well be exactly the *wrong* action, decision, or strategy. "Game film" allows world-class performers to uncover even the smallest developmental issue, as well as highlight strengths to be leveraged. DiSC is "game film."

We will talk about DiSC profiles in two ways. First is the high-level understanding of the tool and the four DiSC styles. Next, we will delve much deeper into how this tool can be applied specifically to leaders.

Primary DiSC Styles

Dominance

People who score high in this area are Direct, Drivers, Demanding, Determined, Decisive, and Doers. They are goal-oriented rather than people-oriented. They're not shy about telling others what to do. They tend to move fast, talk fast, and think fast.

High "D" Behavioral Tendencies:

- Action is critical.
- Demand results.
- Know what needs to be done, not necessarily how to do it.
- May miss emotional cues from others.
- Not known for their patience or listening skills.

Influence

People who score high in this area are Inspiring, Impressive, and Interactive. They are people-oriented rather than task-oriented. They are socially skilled, persuasive, and friendly. They make people comfortable and are imaginative, optimistic, and easily distracted.

High "i" Behavioral Tendencies:

- People interaction is critical.
- Want to be around others and are outgoing.
- Social recognition is important.
- May prioritize socializing over task completion.
- Are not the best time managers.
- Enjoy many types of social interactions.

Steadiness

People who score high in this area are Stable, Supportive, Steady, and Structured. They are people-oriented, but tend to have a few close friends rather than being outgoing. They are accommodating and peace seeking. They like stability and supporting others.

High "S" Behavioral Tendencies:

- Task completion and process is critical.
- Want to be a part of a team.
- Change is to be feared. "If it ain't broke, don't fix it."
- Work step by step.
- Want to know how to move a project forward.
- Are known for their patience and listening skills.

Conscientiousness

People who score high in this area are Cautious, Calculating, Careful, and Contemplative. They are task-oriented. They tend to be careful thinkers and perfectionists. They are logical, organized, and follow rules.

High "C" Behavioral Tendencies:

- Details are critical.
- Want to have all the facts and data.
- Motivated by being "right."
- May not handle criticism well.
- Known to be logical and not emotional.
- "If a job's worth doing, it's worth doing right."

Remember, this is just a summary overview of the four primary DiSC types. Most people are a combination of types, and their behavioral tendencies are more complex. However, most readers will be able to identify themselves as predominantly one of these four types.

In our case study at the beginning of the chapter, Tim was a High D. His style was to be direct, concise, and to the point. It is common for a High D to cut people off and grow weary of details. High D styles are not particularly chatty or warm. Mary, on the other hand, had many i and S tendencies. She was looking for warmth and conversation. She talks freely with co-workers and would love to talk to Tim as well. To her, Tim's one-word greeting was negative. It meant Tim didn't like her. Mary also had some "C" characteristics in that she was very interested in details. If Tim had reviewed DiSC profiles of himself and Mary, he could have handled everything much better.

Knowledge about yourself and others through DiSC is only meaningful if you adapt your behavior in response to it. Once you recognize the personality styles and behavior patterns of yourself and others, you must take the next step. You must adapt your behavior. Knowing someone's personality type is useful only to the extent that you tailor your behavior to communicate with people based on their individual profiles!

Consultant's Corner: Miscommunication

When we are working with leaders we will often ask, "Is it more important what is said, or what is heard and understood?" We have yet to have anyone tell us what is said is more important than what is heard and understood.

We will then follow up and ask, "Have you ever said something like:

- But I said. . . .
- I told you to. . . .
- Didn't you read the email?
- We talked about. . . .
- Didn't we discuss. . . ?"

The point I am trying to make is, people often put *more* credibility and importance on what was said versus what was heard and understood. What was said, most times, is irrelevant.

When miscommunications occur, too often the *sender* blames the *receiver* for not understanding. In our travels as consultants, we often find the issue is the exact opposite. The *sender* is to blame more times than not. Most people don't want to believe that. Good leaders, however, accept this responsibility and work to improve their communication styles and techniques.

The challenge is that most times leaders are communicating in the style in which they like to *receive* information. In other words, leaders often do not adapt to the listener's style. Therefore, what was *said* becomes the focal point, not what was heard.

Different styles communicate differently, both in sending and receiving information. That sounds very basic and simple. Good leaders not only *understand* this truism, they also *adapt* their message so the listener is receiving the information in a way that allows him or her to "hear and understand" the communication.

The best leaders we have worked with practice this in all communications, whether face-to-face, email, or in groups. Knowing and adapting to your audience is key to "being heard and understood."

Leaders Communicate Effectively

If you still treat everyone the same, the value of DiSC is lost. However, if you adapt your communication approach to match the needs of different people based on DiSC, you are more likely to get the responses you want from each one.

Adapting your communication strategies to the audience is obviously a good idea for all of your interactions. It is especially critical for retaining Gen Y. Gen Y must know you are listening, care about them, and respect their ideas.

Let's look at how the DiSC profile can be a guide for basic communication. You will need to pay attention to whoever you are talking to and adapt your approach to that person.

If the person you are communicating with is Dominance (High D):

- Avoid small talk. Get to the point quickly.
- Don't react to his or her impatience.
- Don't give details unless asked. State what you want or need.
- Present facts; list benefits.
- Be decisive.
- Don't tell the person what to do; ask for an opinion.
- Ask "what" questions and give "what" answers. (*What are your thoughts on this? Here's what we'd like to do with this issue.*)

If the person you are communicating with is Influence (High i):

- Be friendly and interested in him or her.
- Take time to socialize.
- Avoid details of the task; follow up in writing.
- Build the relationship.
- Ask for input.
- Use emotional appeals.
- Suggest courses of action.
- Ask "who" questions and use inclusive pronouns. (*Who do you know who might help us with this? We would like to work on this together with you.*)

If the person you are communicating with is Steadiness (High S):

- Be patient with him or her.
- Listen to him or her.
- Take time to explain things.
- Show an interest in the person.
- Give details.
- Project calm, including in your body language.
- Don't hard sell an idea.
- Listen more than you talk.
- Ask "how" questions and explain the process. (*How can we get this project started? This is how our process works.*)

If the person you are communicating with is Conscientiousness (High C):

- Provide details.
- Don't be loud or overly expressive.
- Show that risk is low.

- Don't open with new or unusual ideas.
- Answer questions clearly and directly.
- Don't criticize.
- Don't be blunt.
- Ask "why" questions and explain your reasoning. (*Why do you need this information? This is why we're handling this in this way.*)

The Accuracy of DiSC Profiles

There is a lot of research to support the reliability and validity of the DiSC system. Reliability means that scores are consistent over time or within the test instrument. Validity means that the test predicts something accurately. Test scores within the dimensions and over a six-month period are very stable ($r = .90$) for DiSC.

In our experience, DiSC results are extremely valid overall. However, they certainly can be wrong in some areas. One good way to test the validity of your own DiSC profile is to ask someone close to you whether it seems to reflect your personality. Ask someone you trust if your DiSC results seem to be "you."

Game Film for Leaders

Being self-aware is one of the greatest skills a leader can develop. Our new research into world-class performers (Chapter 9) showed a direct correlation between self-awareness (people skills, being counterintuitive, and recognizing unconscious tendencies) and success. It seems the more open one is to feedback and personal development (coaching/mentors), the greater the chances for success. Of course, one must take this feedback, manage defensiveness, and create an actionable game plan. Knowing is not enough; knowing plus action creates results.

Many times very self-aware people are also thought to be highly emotionally intelligent (more about emotional intelligence in Chapter 11). All of our research about Gen Y, both formal and informal, points to this fact: Gen Y values emotionally intelligent and self-aware leaders. Being "authentic" is critical to Gen Y.

By extension, Gen Y respects authentic leaders. Being a self-aware leader means one knows both the person's strengths and areas for development. One knows what comes naturally and what must be developed. A self-aware, authentic leader does not *pretend* he or she has no areas for development. Good leaders do not pretend their weaknesses do not exist or are not important. Most of all, authentic and self-aware leaders *do not* have an attitude that says, "I know I do X, but I'm the boss; deal with it."

Gen Y will move from position to position in order to find authentic leadership. They realize no one is perfect, and pretending to be is not being authentic. Gen Y actually admires leaders who recognize their weaknesses and are working on developmental areas. This is why game film is so important.

Patrick Lencioni, in his book *The Five Dysfunctions of a Team*, lists the "absence of trust" as the first dysfunction. One of the areas Lencioni points out that can create mistrust is the leader's (and the team member's) unwillingness to be vulnerable within the group. Lencioni has his fictional team complete personal profiles so everyone can have "game film" in order to understand themselves and each other better.

Every generation appreciates a leader who is willing to be vulnerable and not be a "know it all." Gen Y even more so. In their quest for authentic leadership, Gen Y will disengage very quickly from organizations whose leaders are not authentic, show some vulnerability, and display the willingness to learn and grow.

Gen Y is always asking, "What's next?" and looking for learning and growth opportunities. When leaders display and model the behavior, Gen Y is more likely to find that leader, and by association, that organization, authentic. Leaders must continually work on their own skills and then coach others along the way. It is certainly easier to coach and mentor other leaders when one has accepted and acknowledged his or her own vulnerabilities and developmental areas.

Consultant's Corner: Preparing the Next Generation

Much of our work as consultants revolves around preparing the current leadership for ever-expanding challenges as well as preparing the next generation of leaders to move up. We use "game film" in both cases. *Work of Leader* profiles and *360-degree* evaluations are powerful tools.

In our work with executives, it is quite useful for them to get a solid view of where they are currently so they can build an action plan to continually improve. All world-class performers have step-by-step plans for improvement. This also goes for business leaders. We help our clients see where they are currently by looking at their unknown tendencies.

This holds true for future leaders, as well. Many times Gen Y leaders are unknowingly modeling behaviors they have seen other leaders use, whether correct or not. In fact, their immediate bosses may not even be able to help coach them, since they are the ones modeling the unproductive behaviors. Game film helps uncover these unconscious tendencies and allows them to prepare their action plans accordingly.

The challenge with leadership "game film" is that the term "leader" can mean different things to different people. Sometimes a leader must be decisive and take control, while at other times he or she must be empowering and collaborative. There are times when leaders need to gather data, while at other times "gut and experience" is all that are needed. Leaders must be able to motivate others to see a brighter future, while also maintaining a focus on executing the daily operations. In short, leadership is not easily defined, and many times can require two *completely opposite* mindsets.

It would be virtually impossible for a leader to *naturally* possess the variety of skills and styles required in all situations. Natural strengths must be leveraged while developmental areas are uncovered and addressed. To make a leader's work even more challenging, Gen Y is watching. They are evaluating their leaders constantly.

Coach's Corner: Everyone Is a Leader

It all starts during the recruiting process. I tell players and their circles of influence that we want to help develop each and every one of them as leaders. Every one of our players wants to be a leader. There isn't a prospect who wants to come into our program and allow the leadership to come from the other guys. Although leadership may take different forms, we want everybody to be aware of the unique opportunities to use their personalities and their gifts to be leaders. A freshman, a newcomer, may have a different leadership role than a senior co-captain, but nonetheless, through the course of our season, through the course of the year, there will be opportunities when he has a personality or a gift or the insight to offer leadership. Leadership is constantly growing and evolving. You can't wait until there's an opening to allow someone to start becoming a leader; it's an ongoing continuum.

We still have a senior member or someone with tenure and experience to be the captain of our team, but that doesn't displace the need for everyone else to be aware of opportunities to lend their own leadership. At any one time, everyone is a leader, and everyone else is a follower or listener. Different situations call for different team leaders, depending on what gifts and talents may be needed and the opportunities that may present themselves. To the extent that you see yourself as a leader, I believe, the more likely you are to take ownership. If you see yourself simply as a follower, then you're far less likely to take ownership at a deep and meaningful level. Your mindset is more likely to be: "Well, when it's my turn to be captain, here's what I'll do."

In a traditional top-down leadership paradigm, where the cables only run north-south, those cables are easily severed. The leadership chain can easily be broken. When it's more circular, more matrix-like, and the cables run in every direction, it's very difficult to break the leadership chain.

Gen Y is looking for leaders who can clearly show what the future can be . . . who can cast a strong vision. Not only is it important for a leader to cast a powerful vision, but he or she must also understand Gen Y's vision for themselves. By finding where these two visions intersect, a leader can most effectively mentor Gen Y.

Leadership, of course, is a lot more than casting a strong vision. Successful people must also be able to gather the right resources and then execute on the strategy. In the book *The Work of Leaders* (2013), Julie Straw, Mark Sculland, Susie Kukkonen, and Barry Davis have written what we believe may be the ideal leadership book for attracting and retaining Gen Y.

The Work of Leaders distills a leader's job into three very distinct areas: vision, alignment, and execution. Each of these areas requires quite different skills and mindset. Some folks are naturally better at one than the other. *The Work of Leaders* also has a DiSC-based companion leadership profile to help leaders understand their natural tendencies in each of these key areas. The profile shows leaders what may come more naturally and what may need to be developed. Every area can be developed; it just may take more energy and effort on the leader's part.

Let's look at the importance of all three (vision, alignment, and execution) paying special attention to how critical each area is to Gen Y.

Vision

Most leaders would not argue the importance of crafting a vision for their organization. If people are to be led, they will usually want to know where they are going. For the most part, leaders understand this truism.

The issue is not that leaders fail to *intellectually* understand the importance of creating a vision. Many times the issue is truly understanding the importance of the task. Creating a vision is *not just* for the CEO. *All* leaders within the organization should have a vision of where they are leading their teams. These visions should align with the larger vision, *and* this vision should help to align Gen Y's vision for themselves.

There are three key elements to vision. First, where is the organization as a whole headed (corporate vision)? Second, what is the individual leader's vision for his or her team (team vision)? And finally, what is the vision of the Gen Y employees for themselves (individual vision)? In the 21st century, the leader who understands how critical these three visions are and works to bring them into congruence will attract, retain, and engage the best Gen Y talent.

We need to think about the importance of casting a strong vision through a 21st century lens and through the eyes of an ambitious and talented Gen Yer. The Gen Yer has taken the time and energy to think about the future. Gen Yers have thought about where they are going, what they want to accomplish, and how they want to contribute to society and the workplace. For many, this has been a challenging process. But they felt it was critical to success.

Now these talented and ambitious Gen Yers are deciding where they want to work and who they want to lead them. One of the *first* things they want to understand is the corporate vision. What is it, really? Is it a strong statement or a meaningless plaque on the wall? Is it powerful, motivating, and authentic? Or is it empty . . . or even worse, nonexistent?

This will be the first decision point. If the organization a Gen Yer is about to join cannot take the time to envision its future, how will it be able to help him or her achieve his or her goals? The challenge here is that the Gen Y candidate may still join the organization as a temporary solution to gain experience. However, this is a very temporary "short-term lease."

The second decision point for Gen Y, assuming there is a strong and compelling corporate vision, is: "Does my manager have a vision?" Has my manager taken the time to understand the corporate vision and how the team's efforts help drive results? If so, then perhaps the manager is actually a leader, too. Since creating a strong vision is every leader's job, Gen Y will begin to look at that manager as a leader. Respect, buy-in, and engagement will increase accordingly.

Finally, does the direct manager take the time to understand the Gen Y employee's vision? And if so, does he or she try to align all three visions (corporate, team, and Gen Yer) and try to help employees achieve their goals? If an attempt is made by the manager to do this, then the Gen Yer will *know* he or she is working for a true leader. Again, respect, buy-in, and engagement will increase accordingly.

Alignment

There is a very simple process we believe all leaders should embrace when dealing with their employees: "ask, listen, and respond." Every generation wants to be heard and know their input is valuable. This is especially true for Gen Y. In order to create alignment, leaders have to ask questions, listen to the input, and then respond appropriately. It is not enough to simply have a powerful vision. Good leaders must create buy-in for the vision and align all of the resources at their disposal. Resources include human and otherwise. We are always surprised, although by now we shouldn't be, at how much time is spent on "budgeting." Businesses spend hundreds of hours determining how the *financial* resources will be spent and invested. Too many times there is little to no discussion on how the "human capital" will be invested.

History is riddled with businesses that started out with very strong financial positions, great concepts, and willing markets, only to fail in the end because too little attention was paid to alignment. No one bothered to make sure the *people* were brought into the vision. We believe this is why so many mergers and acquisitions struggle.

Gen Y *must* buy in to the bigger picture. They have a strong desire to contribute and to work for "something bigger than themselves." A misaligned workforce is a challenge. A misaligned Gen Y workforce is a certain failure.

In *The Work of Leaders* the authors point out three important reasons to build alignment. The first is that "alignment conserves time and energy." When leaders are looking to "budget" resources, there tends to be an inherent understanding that money is a finite resource. However, time and energy are also finite resources. In fact, we would argue that time and energy are two of the more important elements workers have to "spend" on a task.

As discussed in Chapter 9, world-class performers learn energy management. Energy, like time and money, is a precious resource. World-class performers learn to spend their energy wisely. Successful business leaders, by building alignment, will waste less energy, a very precious resource.

Second, *The Work of Leaders* points out that "alignment provides a forum for questions and concerns." Gen Y, and all employees for that matter, are not engaged by a "do as I say" atmosphere. Some people will work in those environments, for sure. However, study after study shows that when workers are not engaged productivity suffers.

Leaders who work to build alignment will be very attractive to Gen Y. The very nature of aligning one's human capital means attention is being paid to the *humans*! When leaders are paying attention to their folks, there is more real-time feedback and collaboration. Perhaps most importantly, leaders driving alignment "ask, listen, and respond." Not only is a better sense of "team" established in these situations, but people also feel more connected to the goal.

Finally, in *The Work of Leaders*, the authors establish that "alignment unites and excites people around a vision." Gen Y wants to feel a sense of ownership to the vision and the results.

In some of the best, most functional teams we have seen, the *team* polices itself. A leader leads and does not have to monitor (wasting time, money, and energy) the individual players' actions and motivations. A united and aligned team, with an understanding of the vision, will not allow any individual to block success. Gen Y is quite used to "calling each other out."

Coach's Corner: Self-Policing Teams

The best teams, the teams with the best leaders, self-police. They really take care of a lot of things on their own. To take it one step further, a concept we took from the legendary coach, Don Meyer, is that, even in practice, we encourage our players to "buddy coach." Our players are encouraged to instruct each other. They may even go so far as to stop practicing and make a point. That's rare and unusual, but it highlights how much we encourage our players to take an active role in instructing and teaching each other. "Buddy coaching" is another form of ownership and leadership.

Self-policing is important, but that is more about governance. Good teams do that as part of their culture. Great teams care about each other and have a commitment to continually improve and help each other out.

Social media, the diversity of Gen Y, the willingness to express their opinions, as well as their commitment and belief that they can change the world, has made Gen Y very open to challenging each other and the status quo. A well-led Gen Y team will not hesitate to address performance and attitude issues within the team. A self-policing team means the culture is on track. In our experience, these kinds of teams will outperform much more talented teams that are not aligned to a common goal.

Execution

In Jim Collins' best-selling book, *Good to Great*, he talked about the concept of the "flywheel." Collins uses the flywheel to illustrate how important momentum is to the success of any project, venture, or business. Sometimes it takes great energy to get a flywheel started. Once started, however, at a certain point it becomes difficult to stop and nearly impossible to reverse its direction.

Gen Y is motivated by being a part of something bigger than themselves. They want to contribute and know that what they are doing benefits the "greater good." Gen Y is team-oriented and wants to collaborate and associate with other like-minded peers. In short, Gen Y wants to contribute to building and maintaining positive momentum. They want to know that their efforts are making a difference.

In *The Work of Leaders* the authors break execution into three points, all with a very direct link to what motivates and excites Gen Y. In order to execute, the authors say, a leader needs to create momentum, develop and maintain structure, and provide feedback along the way. We want to look at two of these key points as they relate to Gen Y—momentum and feedback.

Building and Maintaining Momentum

A leader's role is to create momentum to "get the ball rolling." As anyone who has ever needed to push a stalled car knows, it is difficult to get it rolling. A great deal of energy is expended just to move it a few inches. However, once it is going, keeping it rolling is fairly easy.

The same holds true for business. It is a leader's job to "push the organization" forward. A great deal of energy is expended along the way. Difficult decisions must be made, and it is the leader's job to be accountable for the final outcomes.

Gen Y wants to work for and learn from good leaders. Gen Y employees will be motivated by a leader who *thoughtfully* makes tough decisions and pushes the team forward. The difference for Gen Y versus other generations is that word "thoughtfully." We mean that all decisions are not knee-jerk reactions nor are they presented in a "do as I say" way.

Twenty-first century leaders, those who will be successful leading Gen Y, will still be required to make difficult and unpopular decisions. Leadership for Gen Y is still like Harry Truman's "the buck stops here." When a challenging decision is to be made, it is the leader's job, and the buck stops there.

Today's successful leader, however, must add a skill to his or her repertoire. Previous generations would have accepted, not liked but accepted, having a final decision announced without question or explanation. Gen Y will not blindly accept a decision if they do not agree with or understand the reasoning for it.

In order to lead Gen Y, one must be prepared to "explain the why" of decisions. Gen Y is looking for context and wants to understand why things are done the way they are done. A strong leader will explain the rationale for a decision while not apologizing or sugar-coating it.

Building momentum is critical to successful execution. With Gen Y there are a few things that, if not handled appropriately, can derail momentum. For example, Gen Y will question decisions they do not understand, thus slowing productivity.

Leaders who want to be successful with Gen Y may need to add some new tools to their toolboxes. One timeless leadership tool, being willing and able to make the tough decisions when appropriate, has not changed. What has changed is that today's leaders must be open to input, be able to "explain the why," and provide context for their decisions.

On the day-to-day management level, don't just give orders, give the reasoning behind them. If you want your Gen Y employees to do something, tell them why in a way that lets them know the importance of the task to the company. Show them how their work will contribute to the bottom line and the big picture. They need to know they are making an impact, and details are also educational for them.

Let us be very clear. We are *not* telling leaders that, in order to be successful with Gen Y, one must have their permission to make a decision. Leadership at times is the farthest thing from democracy. Many times it is a single vote that counts . . . the leader's vote. We are saying that momentum can continue to build . . . even in the face of difficult and possibly unpopular decisions. For Gen Y it is not necessarily the decision itself that can slow momentum, but not understanding *why* that decision was made.

Our research has indicated that Gen Y, much like every previous generation, will question unpopular decisions. The main difference is this: Gen Y will question these decisions *out loud* and *in front of* the decision-maker. Gen Y is far less likely than other generations to have "the meeting after the meeting" and question decisions behind the decision-maker's back.

Thus, openness should be embraced by leadership and not be viewed as "questioning one's authority" or being "disloyal." Quite the opposite. Openness to question decisions is Gen Y's being *extremely* loyal and authentic by giving the decision-maker a chance to address issues in real time. This allows the decision-maker to maintain momentum and not lose precious time and energy with "back room" conversations that slow momentum.

Twenty-first century leaders will still be required to make unpopular decisions from time to time. The difference is that Gen Y will follow those leaders who provide some context for the decision and are secure enough to explain the why.

Coach's Corner: Team Momentum

Building and maintaining momentum is critical. It is far easier to "keep it going" than it is to "get it started." Jim Collins, in *Good to Great*, refers to the flywheel concept. Coaches are keenly aware of this concept.

That's why coaches use timeouts to stop the momentum of their opponents. What we like to do is divide the forty-minute game into ten four-minute games. We actually keep a record of each of those ten segments. Specifically, we talk about winning four key spurts—the start of the game, the end of the first half, the start of the second half, and the end of the second half. Those four four-minute games are really critical when it comes to momentum and to finishing. We talk about our record after a game: we just played ten four-minute games. What was our record? Were we six and four? Were we four and six? Were we eight and two? What did we do in those four highlighted games that I just mentioned?

Another concept from coach Don Meyer is knowing that basketball is a game of runs and momentum. We keep track of things like: How many times in the game did we have three consecutive stops? How many times in a game did we score on three consecutive possessions? How many times did we get a stop, a score, and a stop?

We challenge our guys to string together those kinds of successful possessions in a row to build momentum and take advantage of the fact that basketball is ultimately a game of runs.

Of course, the opposing team will try to break our momentum if we are on a run. They will call a timeout to slow us down. During the timeout, more than anything, we talk about having to be ready to match and exceed the other team's response. For example, if our opponent calls a timeout to stop our momentum, we talk about the

(*continued*)

fact that right now they're down in that huddle galvanizing, getting ready to come out and throw a punch. We need to respond by matching their energy, matching their effort, if not exceeding it. We talk about the things that are allowing us to be successful right now. We reinforce why we do have momentum. Last, we always talk about the next play. It's important to win possession out of the timeout in order to regain the momentum that might have been curtailed by the opponent's timeout.

Providing Real-Time Feedback

As we addressed in Chapter 4, there is a myth that Gen Y wants instant gratification and a trophy for just showing up. What Gen Y really wants is real-time feedback, guidance, and leadership. For this to happen, two elements of 20th century leadership must be changed. First is the annual performance appraisal. Gen Y will simply not work long for an organization that provides feedback irregularly. The annual review must be a *part of* a performance management system, not the system.

The second element that must change is the old adage, "No news is good news." Previous generations were taught that, if I don't hear anything from the boss, then everything must be OK. Gen Y simply will not thrive in that kind of an environment. The point for leaders is to provide *feedback* to their folks. The challenge for leaders is threefold. First, there is a gross misinterpretation of what feedback really is as it relates to anyone, especially Gen Y.

Voices of Experience: Tom Grealish

Instead of an annual review, Henderson Brothers Inc. President Tom Grealish and the company's managers and supervisors conduct a minimum of four and as many as a dozen performance management meetings with employees every year.

The employee arrives for the one-hour meeting with his or her manager or supervisor and goes through an agenda of things the manager and employee want to discuss. Minutes of the meetings are recorded. That might sound like a time-consuming process, but Grealish said it's what keeps the insurance and financial services firm running smoothly. "We're somewhat relentless in communicating with all of our people," he said. The performance reviews are "consistent, in the same format, and both sides have their say."

While annual performance reviews can be an "awful, climactic event," doing the reviews several times a year ensures it's not an event—it's just part of the job. And that's the best way to develop workers' skills, Grealish said.

He said he spends approximately twelve hours a month on his reviews, which might seem like a lot, but it ensures that relatively minor problems can wait until the routine meetings. "I can't tell you how much that cuts down on interruptions," he said.

While Gen Y is known for craving positive and constructive feedback in the workplace, Grealish says the system Henderson Brothers uses works across generations—performers of all ages love it, while non-performers dislike it. "It never goes away," he said. "People can hide behind an annual review, in my opinion."

Grealish also regularly communicates the "state of the union" in quarterly meetings with the whole staff: everyone gathers in the lobby for fifteen minutes to discuss operations, and new business is announced via email weekly. "People need to know they're part of something, and what they're doing is important to what's going on and is part of the company's success," he said.

Henderson Brothers also takes time to identify the results of employees' hard work, as opposed to celebrating tenure. New business results are posted in the lobby, and if someone receives a designation or promotion, that's an occasion to be marked, Grealish said.

"We were stuck in a position that we were just celebrating the fact that someone had been here ten, twenty, thirty years," he said, "and that didn't separate performers from non-performers."

"Look, if you want to stay here and do well, you have to keep getting better, I don't care if you're twenty-five or fifty-five," Grealish said.

When we talk to leaders around the world about providing "feedback" to Gen Y, often their interpretation is: "Gen Y wants constant pats on the back" (or even worse—undeserved pats on the back!). Gen Y's desire for real-time feedback is often interpreted as a need for undeserved and constant praise.

Consultant's Corner: Not Searching for Compliments

One challenge many leaders have is giving real-time recognition. In our research we have found leaders *think* they give out praise significantly more often and significantly more specifically than they do.

I believe this is an issue because most Gen X and older leaders never really had this modeled for them, so they did not learn how to do it. Early in their careers an occasional "nice job" was offered from time to time. This "high praise" had to suffice. Our research also points out something very interesting about Gen X and older managers. They began to turn a deaf ear to this kind of praise since it was given for both minor *and* major accomplishments. Even though this was the case for many managers, they still do the same thing, because that was all that has been modeled for them.

Employees of all ages are crying out for earned, genuine recognition. Many feel they are noticed only when they've made a mistake. Many organizations don't have a culture of rewarding employees. Others have complicated, ineffective, and expensive programs to motivate workers. Many assume that employees will be motivated by regular raises. Yet the best reward techniques are immediate and personal, particularly with respect to Gen Y. Better still, most of them are free. The reality is, it does not take much to reward employees, mainly just thoughtfulness. (For many examples, see Bob Nelson's book, *1001 Ways to Reward Employees*.)

Do not just say "Thank you" or "Good job"—tie the praise to a specific project, idea, or accomplishment. This shows Gen Y that you actually know what they are working on and that you understand their personal role in the achievement or accomplishment.

Reinforcement is most effective when it is immediate. When a bonus is presented at the end of the quarter, employees have often forgotten what they are being rewarded for. Act promptly to praise achievements.

Our research reinforces the fact that an employee's favorite reward is an immediate, personal pat on the back. In other words, do not wait for a predetermined date nor do it as part of a planned program.

Webster's Dictionary defines feedback as "helpful information or criticism that is given to someone to see what can be done to improve a performance, product, etc." This is *exactly* what Gen Y is looking for: helpful information. It doesn't matter whether it is positive or challenging, as long as it is helpful and can improve performance.

The second challenge for leaders providing feedback is that many times it was never modeled for them. Therefore, they don't really know how to do it effectively. Since many current leaders grew up in a "no news is good news" culture, the only thing they had modeled was how to deliver bad news!

Providing feedback means a leader can give both positive and constructive input and guidance. Giving feedback means addressing problems *and* offering praise in real time. Since many leaders have never had the "praise" part modeled, they have only learned how to address problems.

We also believe many leaders have an unconscious tendency to dismiss the need to offer praise. We believe this is an unconscious defense mechanism. "I didn't need to be told I was doing a good job, and I've done OK" is a common refrain we hear. This unconscious mechanism offers a defense against "I never got it" and "I don't really know how to give it."

We believe leaders should look at all of this a little differently. We think they should ask themselves: "How might I have been able to do better if I had received solid feedback along the way?"

The third and final challenge for leaders is that only the criticism side of feedback was modeled. Most supervisors, managers, and leaders over the age of forty experienced, to some degree, a "no news is good news" culture. At some point, whether it was at work or being called to the principal's office, people over forty learned that being summoned meant nothing but trouble. We believe this has unconsciously taught leaders to devote more time, words, energy, and focus to *problems* instead of to victories. Granted, our research on this is informal, but in our travels we see leaders go on and on about problems to address and take very little time on praising victories. Somehow, spending twenty minutes pointing out someone's mistakes is OK, but when something great happens, saying "nice job" is adequate. This, of course, is if someone even says "nice job."

Gen Y wants real-time *feedback* equally between good and bad. Great 21st century leaders will realize, and Gen Y will demand, a new equation, equal (or greater) parts praise and constructive criticism. A simple "nice job" every now and then will not be enough for Gen Y, nor was it enough for previous generations either. The fact that other generations did not receive their due is no reason to say they did not deserve it! Certainly, people learn from their mistakes. They also learn a great deal from their successes. Learning to repeat winning ways leads to more winning.

More winning builds confidence and momentum. Confidence and momentum lead to more winning. Real-time feedback is a critical component of 21st century leadership. If leaders want to execute on their plans and drive results, learning how to (and thus helping others learn how to) give meaningful feedback will be crucial. Gen Y wants and needs it, *and* it is a critical ingredient to organizational and leadership success.

"Ambition moves with comfort gained by success."

Raf Decaluwe of JENSEN Group

Consultant's Corner: Timeless Leadership

During a trip to meet with one of our clients, The Jensen Group, I had the good fortune of reconnecting with their chairman, Raf Decaluwe. Decaluwe is "NonExecutive Independent Chairman of the Board," representing GOBES c.v. of JENSEN Group NV. He is the former chief executive officer of the Bekaert Group. He held senior positions at Black & Decker and Fisher-Price prior to joining the Bekaert Group. To say Decaluwe has held several leadership positions is an understatement.

Decaluwe is someone who "gets it." Much of his career was spent leading other generations, not Gen Y. However, he is the perfect example of "timeless leadership." His concepts were learned working with very different generations, but his leadership would be embraced today by Gen Y. I believe the reason he has proven to be a "timeless leader" is because he truly and deeply understands that leaders must engage employees from the heart as well as the head.

While he was speaking, I could not take notes fast enough. Decaluwe believes deeply that success, ambition, and confidence are intertwined. He also believes people will gain more confidence when their leaders help them to understand their successes more regularly.

Real-time feedback. Timeless leadership.

Self-Assessment

Logically speaking, you'll want to understand yourself before you apply a system to others. Of course, you know yourself well, but thinking about yourself with a particular framework like the DiSC can give you a different perspective. For example, High Ds pride themselves on getting things done. However, they can come to realize that, in dealing with others, a greater reliance on social skills may be important for getting the tasks done. Focusing on the goal is not always as important as knowing how to persuade other people to share your goal. Self-assessment will not only help you be more flexible, but it will help you understand others. The DiSC/Work of Leaders Profile will be useful in several areas.

Hiring

Hiring the next generation of workers means utilizing new recruitment methods. Eric Chester, author of *Getting Them to Give a Damn: How to Get Your Front Line to Care About Your Bottom Line*, suggests that employers should not focus on hiring the "best" people, but on hiring the "right" people. In professional football, some coaches draft "the best talent on the board," others "the best fit for our needs." Sometimes it's best to bring in a person who is strongest in a particular position or who fits well with your team, not the best general athlete.

> "Hiring people is an art, not a science, and résumés can't tell you whether someone will fit into a company's culture."
>
> Howard Schultz, Starbucks CEO

A job may be more suited for a particular personality type. For instance, an impatient person shouldn't be put in a position to deal with slow, repetitive work. People who are more social and outgoing relate better to customers, and so on. Capacity to do the job is not enough for a good fit in an organization. A new hire also has to fit the corporate culture and want to do the job. DiSC will not precisely determine job fit, job fitness, or success. What it will do, however, is describe a person's work behavior patterns, style, traits, and "type." You're looking for the behavioral patterns that fit your job and organization. Your goal is to find a good fit by matching personality inclinations to your specific situation.

Career Planning

You can also use profiles for the career development of existing employees. Helping people analyze their styles and skills can be valuable for them and for the organization. Using DiSC and other tools, you can develop employees, as well as help them determine their best positions. When you are coaching an employee, a profile can serve as "game film" to be reviewed.

The Work of Leaders Profile has proven to be particularly useful in developing succession candidates and Gen Y leaders. The tool requires participants to create actionable game plans, much like all world-class performers do. By using this game films to develop leadership skills, an organization can match skills to developmental tendencies. Positive habits can be created before bad habits become irreversibly ingrained.

Team Building

When forming work teams, you need to include a variety of skills and personalities. If everyone in a team likes to be in charge—or if everyone is a follower—your team won't function well. If everyone on the team has the same style, you may end up with conformity of thought from the lack of diverse opinions or approaches.

Depending on the task, you may need big-idea thinkers, detail-oriented workers, devil's advocates, and so on. For instance, a typical team needs both a task leader and a social leader. Superior teams require a certain chemistry. Understanding personality can help you create chemistry that leads to great teams. With an awareness of different personality styles, you can teach employees how to understand, communicate, and interact more effectively with each other. Even if these tendencies do not naturally occur on teams, being aware of any gaps will help a team succeed. Understanding styles when building teams can uncover the team's need to be "counterintuitive" at times.

Flexible Leadership Style

The "best" leadership style depends on the situation and the people you lead. You'll need to adapt your style to the situation and people involved. Different personalities respond differently in the same situation. For instance, people handle stress differently. As a leader, it is your job to get the most out of your employees. That's why we have emphasized ways in which Generation Y is different from previous generations. Depending on their personalities, you can adapt your behavior as you reward and interact with your employees. For example, social types (i and S) like to have more contact and discussion during a job, while task types (D and C) want to focus on the job.

Preventing or Resolving Conflicts

When you understand people, you are more tolerant and less likely to become upset. You can communicate about problems better and avoid or resolve them. When conflict arises, you are better able to deal with the issues without being distracted by personality and style differences. You don't assume that the other person is wrong because he or she is different from you. The Work of Leaders Profile actually has a "comparison" component whereby individuals can compare styles and see where they may need to focus more energy. Sometimes just recognizing a "style" conflict can go a long way in improving interactions.

Game Film

Having a DiSC or Work of Leaders profile of yourself, will help you to better attract and retain Gen Y employees. In every profession, people who desire to improve know they must reflect on what they have done in the past in order to do things better in the future. As we've mentioned, every world-class performer has a tool that enables him or her to examine and evaluate his or her own behavior, to see what is being done well or poorly, and to pinpoint areas for improvement or growth. World-class performers then make the conscious decision to correct their own weaknesses.

Key Point

Twenty-first century leaders will embrace the use of game film, use it for their own development, and then use it to coach others.

Consultant's Corner: Manage Your Film Clips

We tell leaders that their actions and decisions are like a full-length movie. Ultimately, their success depends on directing a quality production. We challenge leaders to be aware that they are always being judged on the film clips, not on the full production.

Most leaders tend to focus on the full movie and do not manage their film clips. Leaders may rationalize away an action,

(*continued*)

decision, or inaccessibility on their part because they are focused on, and judge themselves by, the entire movie.

Generation Y is judging leaders on what they can see and experience, not what is happening behind closed doors. When a leader is "out there," he or she must be aware that the audience does not know what may have happened before this scene or what is happening afterward. The audience only sees this short clip. Today's leader must be aware of this new rule and always manage his or her film clips.

Game film is particularly helpful because it allows the viewer to slow things down, study execution, and become aware of mistakes, omitted opportunities, and what was done well. While you do not have actual game film in the world of business, the personality profile you obtain from DiSC can serve this purpose.

DiSC allows you to take a snapshot of your behavioral tendencies, unconscious actions, and traits. Your profile can help you see your strengths and weaknesses as well as your style of communicating. This will help you at every point as you interact with Gen Y and other employees.

Your DiSC profile will alert you to your tendency to unknowingly dominate conversations, to ask questions without listening to the answers, or to cut people off. Perhaps you are too critical, uncomfortable with change, or overly concerned about details. Maybe you are too analytical or antisocial. These unconscious characteristics could alienate Gen Y. DiSC helps you see them so you can control or eliminate them.

On the flip side, DiSC will show you what your strong suits are in dealing with Gen Y so that you can focus on utilizing your positive traits. Vision, alignment, and execution are all critical to leaders. Knowing one's strengths and developmental areas, then building an actionable plan to improve, will be highly attractive leadership traits for your Gen Y employees.

Coach's Corner: Overlooking the Fundamentals

In my experience, when our team isn't playing well or we're struggling, we have a great need to return to the basics, to review the fundamentals. There's not a practice that should go by without a real emphasis on and review of the fundamentals. That's what we focus on. Any time we move away from those, that's when we tend to struggle. It's not the elaborate plays or the tricky schemes that make the difference; it's always fundamentals.

Sometimes leaders tend to get ahead of themselves. There is a tendency to think, "I am beyond that now" and to look for a fancy play to succeed while overlooking the simple things. If leaders stopped to review the fundamentals, they could spot when they weren't listening, saying thank you, or being available, to name a few fundamentals of leadership.

Conclusion

As a leader, you have to work with a variety of people, on a variety of levels. It will help you do your job if you can identify how different employees think, react, and want to be led. This is especially true of Gen Y employees, who are quite sensitive to how you interact with them, the words you use, and your management style. Gen Y thrives on feedback and communication. The better you understand your own unconscious behavioral tendencies and those of Gen Y, the better you can communicate and work with them.

Once the behavioral traits and tendencies of employees are understood, a great leader adapts his or her behavior accordingly and leads each employee differently. A leader has to respond to the current situation by adapting his or her communication style to the audience. When you're aware of both the need for communication and your own style, you are in a strong position to relate better to your workers.

Think about the successful, world-class people you know personally. Are they successful with just technical skills, or do they succeed with a combination of technical skills and social intelligence? Think of how you feel when you interact with these people, and think about their bottom-line performance. The combination of technical skills and self-awareness works!

Mallory's Gen Y Profile

Name: Mallory

Location: Northeast

Age: 27

Background:

- Graduated with a bachelor of science degree in biochemistry from a small private college in the Northeast
- Earned an M.D. from a large state university in the Northeast
- Works as a resident physician for a large hospital system in the Northeast

Because Mallory is still technically in a training program, she has to stay in her current job until she becomes a board-certified physician. Her current work isn't what she would call a "good job," but she recognizes that staying with this organization means she will ultimately land in a position with flexible hours and better pay.

Like a lot of Gen Yers, Mallory would like to have more control over her time and a better work/life balance, but that isn't feasible with her current work load of about eighty hours a week.

"It's hard," she said. "My husband is very accommodating, and we try to be flexible with each other's schedules."

Mallory said one of the biggest challenges in her work as a physician is older doctors' belief that work comes first. While Mallory enjoys her work, is passionate about what she does, and cares about her patients, she values her personal life. "Supervisors who act as though this job should be my life are out of touch with my generation," she said.

For Mallory, the characteristics of a good job are

- Flexible schedules
- Ability to affect change in the organization and take on leadership roles
- Intellectually stimulating work
- Appropriate compensation and paid time off

Mallory is motivated by:

- Having control over her work schedule and her time
- The ability to take on meaningful projects
- Straightforward communication and positive feedback from her supervisors
- A desire to help others

CHAPTER ELEVEN

EMOTIONAL INTELLIGENCE

EQ can be defined roughly as emotional awareness and control that translates into strong people skills. "Understanding emotion in oneself and others is at the root of good people skills," observes Dr. Vanessa Urch Druskat, associate professor of organizational behavior and management at the Peter T. Paul College of Business and Economics at the University of New Hampshire. "EQ helps you to recognize how your own emotions impact the people with whom you interact." While aspects of EQ had been studied sporadically for years, it was Daniel Goleman's 1995 book, *Emotional Intelligence*, and a *Time* magazine article on the book, that popularized the concept.

Dr. Druskat, whose award-winning research has examined how teams and leaders effectively manage complex interpersonal challenges, explains, "Emotion is present in *every* interaction we have with another human being. Stopping this emotion is harder than stopping a sneeze. The passing back-and-forth of emotion conveys subtle messages such as when a conversation should begin and when it should stop. Emotionally intelligent people are more aware of emotion and the signals it sends. They treat it as information, which allows them to manage the conversation in a way that produces mutually positive outcomes. This all happens so quickly that it isn't always fully under our conscious awareness. Building one's emotional intelligence requires slowing down the process and making it more conscious. Our research shows that people are capable of increasing these skills if they want to work at them."

Why the Interest in EQ?

One of the reasons emotional intelligence attracts so much attention is that many people believe it explains why some people who are very successful in their careers don't have the traditional "smarts" indicated by IQ tests. When everyone in a company is fairly intelligent, IQ may not predict success. In that case emotional intelligence—particularly as it pertains to people skills—is a better predictor of success. A way to think about this is that a "high enough IQ gets you in the game." It gets you educated and hired. But if your job involves working with people, it doesn't necessarily lead to career success.

Some people have all the MBA smarts you'd want, but don't work well with others or make good leaders. On the other side are the people who aren't brilliant but who work well with others and know how to inspire their teams. They make good leaders. You probably know of many cases like this yourself—on both sides. If those with low social-emotional skills have strong technical skills, they can do well in "back-office" jobs. On the other side are the people who aren't always the most technically proficient, but they connect well with others and are inspirational leaders.

Consultant's Corner: Listen to Yourself Listen

Everyone readily recognizes the importance of being a good listener. But as you listen it's important to listen to yourself listen so that you're aware of any preconceived notions, prejudices, or bias you may have. As you listen to someone, if you find yourself immediately reacting, responding, or judging, I think it's good to listen to yourself listen to be aware of it. You can pollute the message. You're not really listening. You're listening with a preconceived interpretation or notion. I guess we all do that to some degree: bring your own background to everything you hear. But to the extent you could be aware of it, and not jump to conclusions, nor let your biases unduly influence your thinking, I think it will benefit you as a leader.

In a Gen Y sphere, a boss may give himself great credit for listening to the ideas of his Gen Y employees. However, if he's immediately, in his own mind, discounting what they say and he's not aware he's doing that, is he even really listening? If he's dismissive because of his preconceived notions or his immediate judgments, does his listening have any value? But if he's aware that he has some of those biases going into the conversation, he may catch himself and be able to keep an open mind while hearing the conversation through. Now he's listening to himself listen.

In Dr. Druskat's view:

> "Emotionally intelligent leaders know how to ignite the kinds of emotions that make our work meaningful. Inspiration involves stirring positive emotions. A strangely little known fact is that motivation requires emotion. . . . Without emotion, motivation does not exist! It is emotion that gets you out of bed in the morning. One can get out of bed because of fear or because of 'inspired excitement.'"

The concept of emotional intelligence (EQ) caught on in a big way without actually being precisely defined. Organizations have always been interested in how to measure talent. You want to hire the best and invest your training dollars in those who will benefit the most. The EQ concept has grown popular, in part, because it explains why and how people can be successful despite lacking "book smarts."

Until EQ came along, most non-job-specific measurement looked at IQ and achievement tests that focus on verbal and mathematical skills as general intelligence indicators. However, it's been known for a hundred years that people had *different kinds* of intelligence. Howard Gardner and others have discussed up to nine types of intelligence, and there are probably more. For instance, mechanical intelligence, is seldom listed—that hands-on ability some people have that gives them the ability to fix any piece of machinery. (Some of the other noted types of intelligence include musical, spatial, and kinesthetic.)

Three Ways to Define EQ

Because EQ is a relatively new concept, there is not full agreement on how to define it. In fact, most people don't know that there still isn't full agreement about how to measure EQ. What is important is that how you define EQ determines how you measure it, and even whether you believe it can be taught (the same is true for IQ). Different researchers describe it as a form of intelligence, a personality trait, or a learned skill. Of all the research groups who have defined and studied EQ, three stand out as most influential. We describe these below. Depending on whether EQ is a kind of intelligence, a personality trait, or a skill, you would measure it differently.

Peter Salovey and John D. Mayer (2003) were the first to define and formally discuss EQ. They presented their ideas in a 1990 journal publication. They defined EQ as: "The ability to perceive emotion, integrate emotion to facilitate thought, understand emotions, and to regulate emotions to promote personal growth."

They set out to define EQ as a form of intelligence, but one that focused on emotional skills. Their model presents four related emotional abilities:

1. Perceiving or recognizing emotions—your own and others—this represents the basis for emotional intelligence.
2. The ability to use emotions to facilitate one's own and others' performance.
3. The most complicated ability is to understand emotion, its subtle cues, and the information and knowledge it provides.
4. The last point is the ability to manage or affect emotions in both ourselves and in others.

Two other psychologists, Daniel Goleman and Richard Boyatzis, developed a slightly different model of EQ that focuses on four emotion-focused workplace competencies:

1. Self-awareness about your own emotions and the ability to use gut feelings in decision making.
2. The ability to control your own emotions and to deal with change.
3. The ability to understand others' emotions and emotional relationships.
4. The ability to emotionally inspire and influence others.

The third research approach comes from Reuven Bar-On (Bar-On & Parker, 2000), another social scientist, who developed one of the first measures of EQ that used the term "Emotion Quotient." His definition of EQ has been criticized because it also describes general maturity or competence. Bar-On defines emotional intelligence as understanding oneself and others, relating well to people, and adapting to and coping with your environment.

For our purposes, it seems clear that the ability to understand and manage our own emotions, and to understand and manage others' emotions, is at the core of relating to and connecting successfully with other people. Dr. Druskat believes that "recognizing and managing our own emotions is one of the most critical elements of EQ. It doesn't do us much good to understand our emotions if we can't use that understanding to behave effectively in a given situation."

Gen Y and EQ

Research by Travis Bradberry and Jean Greaves (2005) on more than 500,000 people showed that EQ tends to increase with age. Gen Ys would have less self-awareness and practice understanding and managing their emotions than would older workers. On the other hand, the well-adjusted Gen Yers you want to hire are emotionally mature and very group-oriented. There are plenty of Gen Yers who demonstrate these characteristics. They can be easily identified by their willingness to have stepped into emotionally challenging situations (for example, emotionally difficult volunteer opportunities or jobs) and through their effective listening abilities and social skills.

A Good Manager Needs to Have High EQ Social Skills

One area of EQ-related research shows that first impressions strongly influence judgments. As we've mentioned earlier, to deal with Gen Y, you need to set aside any prejudices against the young and project positive emotions yourself. Your "natural" first inclination is possibly to be cool to Gen Y, especially people with piercings, tattoos, or other visible differences. You need to suspend any negative impressions you form and make an effort to project a warm first impression to your young workers. Mature Gen Yers are often independent thinkers when it comes to dress, but creative thinkers and hard workers when their positive energy and attention are emotionally engaged.

Gen Yers Are Group-Oriented

Goleman's research and the research of many educators in the area of emotions and emotional intelligence have had a large impact in school systems. Thus, many Gen Yers who came through school systems in the 1990s were exposed to EQ training. Also, colleges and universities have been pressured by companies who hire their undergraduates to do much more team learning and teamwork in their classrooms so that graduates are more ready to work in teams than previous generations were. According to Dr. Druskat, who teaches undergraduates and MBAs at the University of New Hampshire, "Business schools have learned that one of the top skills companies want job applicants to hold is the ability to work effectively in a team. Thus, most schools today place students in teams throughout their four years and present them with group projects. However, experience matters, and translating EQ skills, like conflict management, as it develops from school into work organizations, is not a simple matter. Thus, the greatest application for EQ in the Gen Y work situation is the necessity for managers and leaders of Gen Y employees to demonstrate EQ in their interactions with these employees."

Because Gen Y employees are likely to be very different from their managers, all aspects of EQ are relevant to managing Gen Y. A good example is the Gen Y employee who, because of his or her good work, unrealistically expects to be promoted quickly. Recognizing and managing such expectations is the first step. The second step is working to understand more about this expectation and what it means (for example, what kind of developmental experience is the person looking or hoping for). Finally, it is necessary to manage this person's emotions by behaving in a way that doesn't snuff out the person's motivation, but channels it into more accurate expectations and, if the person can handle it, more challenging work.

Self-Awareness

This is the cornerstone of EQ. Leaders need to recognize their own unique personalities, skills, values, and tendencies. They need to understand how they are different from others and to understand the various dimensions on which people differ (see Chapter 10 on DiSC). It naturally follows that it is the leader's job to get to know and understand the unique traits, skills, and tendencies of individual employees. This helps a leader to understand the tasks that will most interest and suit each employee and the way an employee must be treated in order to bring the best out of that individual.

"Analyzing" Yourself

To communicate effectively with today's workforce, *you* must have emotional intelligence about yourself. Tomorrow take fifteen minutes to review the following tips to practice your people skills:

Reflect on your personal style: What are your tendencies, both conscious and unconscious? Think about ways you need to adapt to successfully communicate today.

Who will you see today? What are their tendencies? What type of interaction will they prefer to maximize communication?

Put your antenna up! If you expect to enter into new relationships today, be conscious of your EQ and people-reading skills. Look for behavior that may vary from dynamic to discerning, and prepare to monitor your emotions and adapt your style to communicate effectively and build trust in the relationship.

What are the primary goals of your meetings today? Record the primary goals of your major interactions today. What do you want to accomplish? Whether the meetings are with clients, bosses, subordinates, or co-workers, a review of your primary goals will drastically increase your chances for success.

Understand your emotions and mood (moods last longer than fleeting emotions)! How do you feel today? If you don't know, your clients, co-workers, and subordinates soon will. Your emotions and moods spread like viruses. Get in touch with your mood early in the day and adapt if you want to communicate effectively.

Focus on listening, not telling! Prepare open-ended questions and listen to the responses. If you have lunch with someone and he or she finishes eating before you, you're doing all the talking!

Self-Management

Managing oneself is a critical skill for successful interactions and for effectively influencing others. Some employees may be best influenced using a directive command; others may need a more empathic influence style. Managing one's own tendencies so that one is optimally effective in different situations and with different employees is indicative of those with high EQ. It is a skill that can be learned. Look for behavior that may vary from dynamic to discerning and prepare to adapt your style to communicate effectively and build trust in the relationship.

Managing Others' Emotions

Once a leader understands his or her own unique tendencies (including emotions), values, and skills, it is easier to know what to look for when seeking to more fully understand the tendencies, values, and skills of others.

Leaders who are practiced and skilled at interpreting the emotions of others will find it fairly easy to become practiced and skilled at reading or interpreting the emotions of people in groups. The next step is managing those emotions. For example, one can calm a nervous group by providing information in a confident, calm, and clear way. You can increase tension in a group that is too relaxed and calm by demonstrating tension. Increasing the motivation of a group usually involves communicating a message in an inspirational way. Many of the most admired leaders of our times studied inspiration so that they would know what it looked and felt like to audiences. This isn't always intuitive—it requires knowing, understanding, and empathizing with your audience and authentically inspiring them.

Emotional intelligence is seen in organizations or groups with cultures or climates that support EQ. Your goal should be to create an emotionally intelligent climate so that even non–emotionally intelligent people have a chance of behaving in an emotionally intelligent way. Some of the dimensions that can create this climate, as identified by Dr. Druskat, include:

1. Interpersonal understanding: People understand what they need to know about each other to work together effectively.
2. Confronting members who break norms.
3. Addressing counterproductive behavior: People address counterproductive behaviors that hurt team or organizational performance.
4. Caring behavior: People value, respect, and support each other.
5. Team self-evaluation: People and teams consistently evaluate how well they are doing.
6. Creating resources for working with emotion: People and teams create the time and language needed to discuss difficult issues and feelings.
7. Creating an optimistic environment (oriented toward a hopeful future): People maintain a "can do" attitude.
8. Proactive problem solving: People are proactive about solving and preventing problems and avoiding a "victim" mentality.
9. Organizational awareness: People understand the priorities in the organization and are aware of the priorities of those who affect their performance.
10. Building external relationships: People build relationships that can help their performance.

Conclusion

Emotional intelligence is a concept that calls your attention to a fact you already knew—that raw technical ability does not always translate well to a job. The ability to manage your own and others' emotions is valuable in managers and leaders, as well as Gen Y hires. For most jobs, you're looking for people who can work well with others and who have good emotional maturity. Being aware of EQ should help you be a better leader, choose more capable managers and interviewers, and select new employees who fit best in your company.

Meghan's Gen Y Profile

Name: Meghan

Location: South

Age: 27

Background:

- Graduated with a bachelor's degree from a large state university in the South
- Currently completing an M.B.A. while working in media relations for the medical center of a large state university in the South

After graduating with a bachelor's degree in journalism in 2008, Meghan—like many Gen Yers during the recession—struggled to find work in her chosen profession, ultimately leading her to seek positions in communications and media relations. That led her to the university where she currently works and attends classes part-time.

Meghan said she's typical of Gen Y workers in that she wants to "redefine success by increasingly focusing on and valuing creativity." But, she said, that doesn't mean she wants her supervisors to be completely hands-off, noting that she looks for "a combination of structure and freedom. I want to be sure the company can thrive and I can have some time and space to be

(*continued*)

creative," she said. "You have to be sure there's a box before you can think outside of it."

Meghan said she tries to "shut off completely for the weekend," but is willing to respond to calls or emails in an emergency, adding that her personal and professional lives are equally important. "I don't like to think of them as separate pursuits," she said. "To do my job well I have to feel supported at home, and to be a happy person I have to feel like I'm doing fulfilling work."

Meghan said one of her biggest frustrations in working with older colleagues, particularly because she's in the field of media relations and communications, is their inability to adapt to technology. She said colleagues are either overenthusiastic—"Facebook isn't your personal diary"—or very leery and reluctant to adapt—"Twitter isn't spying on you. I've found that most of my colleagues are willing to take on new challenges regardless of the technology involved, but can cling to outdated ideas about that technology once a workflow has been established," she said.

For Meghan, the characteristics of a good job are

- Supervisors with clear expectations of themselves and their employees
- Opportunities to learn new skills
- Being part of the company's larger vision

Meghan is motivated by:

- Structure with the ability to be creative when necessary

CHAPTER TWELVE

ADDRESSING THE BURNING PLATFORM
Change Management

"No company can escape the need to reskill its people. . ."

—Gary Hamel & C.K. Prahalad,
Competing for the Future

This chapter gives you a general outline of how to both implement change *and* keep change going. Here we give you a brief overview within the context of dealing with Gen Y. Many change programs are started, but few are successful over the long term. Gen Y can be both a source of change for you and a powerful tool to accomplish it. When you work with Gen Y effectively, you'll be able to implement changes more easily and be more in touch with the changing times.

Consultant's Corner: What Is Change Management?

"Change management is a systematic approach to dealing with change, both from the perspective of an organization and on the

(*continued*)

individual level. For an organization, change management means defining and implementing procedures and technologies to deal with changes in the business environment and to profit from changing opportunities" (*Webster's Dictionary*).

Any major adaptation within an organization requires a great deal of effort to be successful, and that includes changing the culture of your organization. Change is one of the hardest things to accomplish in any company. Many efforts, such as reengineering, total quality management (TQM), or Six Sigma, have failed as often as they've succeeded.

Gen Yers *are* different than older generations were. Many managers see their job as "training" Gen Y to fit into the current organizational mold. But what we need are leaders (not managers) who see the broader picture. Gen Y is only one factor in the constant change around us. Leaders know the organization must deal with changes that are happening, and they want to ride those changes to greater success. Rather than being a disruptive influence, Gen Y can actually help you achieve constructive overall change.

Improving Your Organization

There will be many challenges as you try to lead your organization into the new Gen Y era. Just as world-class performers study game film of themselves to uncover tendencies, leaders must study "game film" of their organizations to find team tendencies. Once tendencies are uncovered, a game plan must be put in place to address any issues.

Every coach knows that it is not enough to simply develop a solid game plan. A great game plan, poorly executed, will result in a loss. Execution is critical. We believe every leader or manager must take three key steps in order to uncover team tendencies, prepare the team for success, and coach effectively for change:

1. Conduct an organizational/team assessment.
2. Develop effective change management strategies and tactics.
3. Sustain the change.

Your Organizational Assessment

Business leaders worth their salt know it is important to understand how engaged and satisfied their employees are. Surveying tools, used mainly by HR (employee surveys) and marketing (customer surveys) have provided invaluable data to drive an organization's strategy. Based on the feedback, new employee programs are developed to increase morale, and new products and programs are implemented to secure customer loyalty.

For years businesses have conducted employee and customer satisfaction surveys to understand the current environment. Completed surveys are *game film*. Data can then be reviewed to uncover strengths, weaknesses, opportunities, threats, and *tendencies*. Surveys do not need to be limited to simply employee and customer satisfaction instruments. Over forty aspects of organizational "climate" have been measured in the last fifty years, from attitudes toward co-workers to attitudes toward advancement.

Before you can prepare the team to implement your game plan, you must know your starting point. Surveys can be used to gather a wide range of feedback. There is no reason why these successful tools should be limited to HR and marketing. As a leader, you can develop your own surveys that allow you to gain insights into your organization. Once your game plan to attract and retain Gen Y is in place, surveys can provide you with just-in-time data to make the adjustments necessary for increased success.

We strongly recommend that leaders conduct some sort of "attitudes toward Gen Y" audit or survey in order to take the pulse of the current management team, from top to bottom. We also urge organizations to survey their current Gen Y population (if the population is large enough to create an anonymous and statistically valid survey).

Survey Two Gen Y Issues

Before you can prepare the team to implement your game plan, you must know your starting point. Surveys can be used to gather a wide range of feedback. Regarding Gen Y/Millennials, you can take either of two directions:

1. Survey Gen Y in your organization to understand how to attract and support these young workers. You'll probably be surprised to hear what Gen Y has to tell you about how they're treated and how they see your setting.
2. Related to the first goal, survey all of your employees on how they see (and treat) Gen Y.

Gathering input from your people will provide tremendous insight into your teams' attitudes, hiring, and management practices. Once you have received the information, it is critical for you to take the time to:

- Thank everyone.
- Analyze the data quickly.
- Communicate the results.
- Link every change you make to the team input.

This final point is critical. One consistent mistake we see made by leaders is the failure to *continually* link change programs to team feedback. You can never tell the team enough times, "We are doing ABC because you said it was important." That encourages ownership and buy-in.

Gen Y presents a unique and exciting leadership challenge. They are indisputably bright and talented, yet they think differently, have very different needs, and will require a very different style of leadership. In comparison to previous generations, Gen Y may seem to be high maintenance. You will have to do many things in a new and different way to attract and retain them.

Most important, Gen Y will force you to take your leadership skills to a new level, which will help you with all your employees. You have a lot less room for error. You will have to do things better and quicker. Why? Because this group has more freedom and job options than any other group in history. If they see things they don't like in you, your employees, or your organization, they are going to leave. They do not think they have to tough it out or pay their dues the way other generations did. They have a shorter horizon.

Most of your team will find these challenges disturbing. Many of your managers will feel no change is necessary. They believe that eventually Gen Y will conform to the current way of doing things. In talking with leaders around the country, many feel they can "fix" Gen Y.

Your Change Efforts

Gen Y is not a problem to be fixed. They are not broken. As the leader, it is your job to take your organization to the next level. You must lead a change management effort.

Your Gen X, Baby Boomer, and Traditionalist managers and supervisors who have come up through the ranks have learned a set of employment rules that no longer exist. This old reality has been deeply ingrained over the years. They are very comfortable with how they currently manage new employees.

As you begin to transition your organizational culture, you must understand and accept the anxiety and natural pushback that will occur as you move to your desired future situation.

People respond differently to change, and it is important to understand how the various DiSC styles respond to this challenge.

Voices of Experience: Sue Ross, Maurices

For many of the employees at Maurices, a nationwide chain of stores that sells clothes for twenty-something women, their first experience with the stores was as a shopper. Many of the store managers have "grown up from being our best customers," said Sue Ross, Maurices' executive vice president of human resources.

Longevity is common in the corporate offices, too. Company President George Goldfarb, for example, worked in a variety of roles with Maurices before he took the top job, Ross said. "He got a good bird's eye view of the company before he ascended into that role," noting that path is typical for people who have been at Maurices for twenty or so years.

Maurices, headquartered in Duluth, Minnesota, has opened the specialty retail stores in small towns across the United States since 1931. In 2003, Maurices had approximately 450 stores, when they were bought out by the Ascena Retail Group. The chain now boasts nearly nine hundred stores in forty-six states and in Canada. When the stores were privately held, Ross said, growth was more conservative, but the chain has always had a solid business model and a great culture for employees. "We had all the ingredients there to make things happen," she said, but the fast growth brought a lot of newness to an older retailer.

Because the store markets to Gen Y women, it employs a lot of Gen Y women in sales associate and store manager positions, Ross said. But in the corporate offices, it's a slightly different story. Ross calls it "the barbell"—on one side of the bell, about half of the employees are in their forties and fifties and have been in the business for twenty-plus years. The other side is all workers under thirty. The expansion, including a recently developed website and mobile site, meant Maurices had to hire people for more specialized positions, such as digital marketing jobs. To draw and retain Gen Y workers, Maurices worked on updating its culture a bit.

The corporate office now focuses on wellness—there's a gym and meditation room, stand-up desks are available, and classes like Zumba and yoga are offered throughout the day. Ross said flexible work arrangements, including the ability to work from home, add a "component of care." "We want you to have time to go to your kid's play," she said.

When those changes started moving into Maurices' corporate offices in the early 2000s, Ross said, there was some pushback from older workers. "We had a good culture at the time, but it was a more traditional culture," she said, noting some workers would "get a scowl" if another employee left at noon to work from home. "This is the new reality," she said. "This is the way the world is going to work moving forward."

Getting everyone used to the new normal is a challenge, Ross said, but some older workers have welcomed the changes, with more working from home and taking advantage of breaks. They "see the beauty . . . and the positive influences that the Millennials have helped us embrace." Instead of assigning older mentors to younger workers, Maurices tried a bit of "reverse mentoring," giving older associates an opportunity to learn from younger workers. That program is "less of, 'I'm Yoda the wise mentor who's going to meet with the young person here and impart my wisdom,'" Ross said. "It's more of a partnership."

Five Steps to Sustaining Change

Most change efforts fail after being introduced. Resistance, inertia, and other forces swamp changes that are not vigorously followed through by champions from above and below. If you take the premise of this book seriously and understand that you *are* transitioning to a Gen Y workforce, then dealing with that demographic change is crucial for your organization.

Key Point

Sustaining change is harder than implementing it.

Five things you can do to make change efforts work in your organization are discussed below. They also apply to your integration of Gen Y.

1. Keep score on the actions you want from managers.
2. Link to your front line, who implement day to day.

3. Recognize and reward progress.
4. Use this progress in your performance management system.
5. Give people peer support for the change.

Keep Score

There is an old saying that "People respect what you inspect." Similarly, people do what you reward. In your organization, what are the key metrics or performance indicators that you reward? If you want to sustain changes that you implement, determine what to count, then count it! Do you want more Gen Y in charge of projects? Hired? On task forces? Mentored? Post concrete goals where your team can see them and track their performance. A scoreboard tells everyone who's winning and is often enough to motivate increased performance.

Consultant's Corner: Scoreboards

We have used a variety of metrics over the years for our clients. The key is to pick *meaningful* targets and to review them often. One such scoreboard is modeled after a sign I used to see as a child outside the entrance gate at the steel mill.

Posted for all to see was a sign telling the world how long the plant had operated since a "lost time injury."

Several of our clients have taken this idea and used it at their management meetings. A sign that says, "We have gone___ days without an unplanned turnover" is posted for all to see (an unplanned turnover is a resignation versus a termination).

Another scoreboard is modeled after the deficit clock.

Some of our clients keep track of the *cost to replace* lost talent. These numbers are posted at the management meetings as a way to track the financial impact of turnover.

Link the Front Line

Create clear communications to your front-line managers and supervisors. These are the folks who will be *critical* to your recruiting and retention efforts. Their "informal" behavior can make or break the acceptance of Gen Y. Link every positive improvement to their initial input and their ongoing efforts.

Make sure your managers and supervisors are trained to support your efforts. If you have revamped one of your hiring and management systems, make sure everyone knows how to use the system. Give them tools to encourage and support Gen Y. We are always amazed at how often this step is overlooked. Nearly every company makes sure training occurs when a mechanical or technological change occurs. Management wants to ensure they receive the desired ROI for their investment. However, when a *human system* is changed, training is often omitted or skipped over.

Rewards and Recognition

Who in your organization is demonstrating the best practices? Has the best numbers? Who is, in other words, winning? Showcase their success. Reward their behavior and thank them for their accomplishments.

These folks should also be rewarded with *time*. Spend time with these winners. Find out how and why they have been successful. Ask these folks to help craft and analyze your next efforts. Like attracts like—these folks are what you need to be a winner.

Consultant's Corner: Lottery Ticket Winners

Our observation over the years leads us to believe most organizations are broken down into three types of folks: Teamers (20 percent), Fence-Sitters (60 percent), and Lottery Ticket Winners (20 percent).

(*continued*)

"Teamers" are the loyal and dedicated employees who always give their best. They tend to be positive folks who trust their leaders and always strive to do their part. Unfortunately, since these folks require little "maintenance," managers and leaders tend to ignore them and do not give them much time or energy.

The second group, "Fence-Sitters," usually make up the majority of an organization's employees. These folks tend to be the silent majority. They are not overtly negative *or* positive. Their attitude is "wait and see what develops." Again, since Fence-Sitters are usually "silent," managers do not spend much time with them either.

The final group, the "Lottery Ticket Winners," are the "squeaky wheels." To them, nothing is ever right. They are, so they think (and say), smarter, more qualified, and more talented than their bosses (or anyone else for that matter). Seldom do they offer any proactive ideas, but they *always* are the first to point out the negatives.

Since this group is most vocal and demanding of attention, managers tend to spend the overwhelming majority of their time and energy with this group. Teamers tend to just shrug the lack of attention off, while the fence-sitters quickly learn that, in order to be noticed, you need to be negative.

Managers convince themselves that, if they could just win over these negative folks, everyone else will follow. Therefore, managers *waste* countless hours and enormous amounts of energy trying to motivate employees who are frequently a lost cause.

Don't Coddle the Negative People

When we are working with leaders, we tell them a story to help identify an organization's lost causes. We call it the "Lottery Ticket" story.

A husband and wife wake up one Sunday morning, check the newspaper, and discover they have just won the lottery, a $45 million jackpot! The paper says there are two other winners, so their take will be $15 million.

The couple is immediately overwhelmed. They have a wonderful life now. Happy, healthy, and not wanting for anything. Both of them are afraid this windfall will change everything, and not for the better. In fact, they believe their lives couldn't get much better. They have read countless stories about how lives were ruined after just such a windfall.

After hours of discussion and soul searching, the couple decides they do not want the money. They flip a coin and the husband wins the toss. What he wins is that on Monday, as he walks into work, he is to hand the ticket to the first person he sees.

On Monday morning our generous husband sees Joe, the office naysayer. True to his promise, he approaches Joe, explains the situation, and hands him one of the three winning $45 million lottery tickets.

Joe takes the ticket, puts it in his pocket, and says, "Oh sure, you give me the ticket I have to split," and walks away.

That's a "Lottery Ticket Winner."

Our story elicits uncomfortable laughter from the audience when we tell it. Everyone knows the point we are making. For some folks, even being *given* a winning lottery ticket is not enough. Yet it is just this type of person who demands our time and energy. The regrettable mistake is, we give it to them.

The result of our misplaced efforts is that we are not leading. We are ignoring the "Teamers" and teaching the "Fence-Sitters" that inappropriate attitudes are rewarded with time and attention.

Our *very* strong advice is that, if you have folks who would respond negatively to a winning lottery ticket, *stop giving them*

(*continued*)

your time and attention. Start giving your time to the "Teamers." They deserve it, and you will be teaching the "Fence-Sitters" the correct leadership lesson.

Your goal for the Lottery Ticket Winners is simple. They can

- Start pretending to be positive,
- Start being positive,
- Shut up altogether, or
- Leave.

If you have lottery ticket winners who will undermine your change management efforts toward Gen Y, address it now . . . and head on. Gen Y doesn't like naysayers either. When you've enlisted Gen Y, they'll help you focus on change rather than the complainers.

Performance Management

The final *traditional* step to sustaining your change plan is to incorporate the desired behaviors and outcomes into your performance management system. If you are monitoring the results in your annual, quarterly, and monthly reviews, you will see positive results.

A regular one-on-one meeting is not just for Gen Y. Everyone wants real-time feedback. Leaders need to incorporate the process into their performance management systems for everyone. Gen Y wants real-time feedback, and real-time feedback is critical to sustain change.

To sustain change, leaders should meet with the members of their team regularly and monitor the results for every critical business metric, including retention. Once this is a "standard operating procedure," the change effort will have been sustained.

Consultant's Corner: One-on-One Process

With our clients around the world, we have helped many implement a "one-on-one" process. These are thirty- to sixty-minute meetings, every month, with every direct report. There is a set agenda, which is different for each company and industry. There are a few basics, no matter the industry or position. These meetings always cover results, next month's targets/projects, and feedback (both positive and constructive). Depending on the company, there are other agenda items, but these three are constants. A few times per year career development is also added to the list.

After these meetings, a follow-up note is generated that documents the conversation. These notes provide documentation every month so every employee knows exactly where he or she stands. At the end of the year, these notes provide the basis for a meaningful annual appraisal and career development discussion.

Tom Grealish, president and CEO of Henderson Brothers, has been using this system for the past several years. "Every single employee in our business has a one-on-one meeting with the manager on a regular basis," says Grealish. "Depending on the role, these meetings may be monthly or quarterly. The point is, everyone receives real-time feedback and coaching, and folks always know where they stand."

Almost universally, when we first introduce the idea, our clients protest the amount of time that needs to be dedicated to one-on-one meetings. We usually hear, "Where am I going to find the time for monthly or quarterly face-to-face meetings?"

While it is normally not a good idea to speak in absolutes, in this case we will make an exception. *Every* company that has implemented this process has found it *saves* time. Issues are discussed in real time, problems are solved, and proactive actions (rather than constant firefighting) are taken. This is a real-time feedback mechanism that allows leaders to lead. Providing real-time feedback is appreciated by all of the winners in any organization, regardless of what generation they represent.

Implementing Change

Many change management methodologies are available, but in the end they all contain the four essential components of any good change plan: vision and strategy, organizational alignment, workforce enablement, and sustainability. Or in short, vision, alignment, and execution. Where are we going and why? Are the resources available and pulling in the same direction? When it is clear where the company is headed and everyone is pulling in the same direction, it is time to execute and take action.

Vision and Strategy

Your first job is choosing your vision and staying focused on it. A good leader paints a vision of where the company is headed so that employees have a clear line of sight to the future and the part they play in it. As a leader in your organization, your vision is critical to your organization's long-term success. Without it, employees don't understand where the company is headed or how they fit into the organization.

The challenge is that, over time, situations change. Market conditions, new products, emerging technologies, and a changing workforce (Gen Y) will have an impact on the direction in which your organization heads. Having a clear vision keeps everyone focused and pulling in the same direction, even when conditions fluctuate.

So how do you keep a multigenerational organization engaged and committed in an ever-changing business landscape? You develop the company's internal capacity for change. Just as a coach conditions his athletes, so can you condition your employees to embrace change. It all starts with a clear vision and open, honest communication.

Your senior leadership must be committed to bringing the vision to realization and must actively play a role in supporting it. This is critical to employees buying into any proposed change.

Without leadership support, employees will label your new vision as just the "flavor of the month." How Gen Y is seen by your organization—and vise versa—is now the "burning platform" that you must deal with.

A consistent framework with executive support also addresses a critical need, not just for your Gen Yers, but for all generations within your company. It allows them to be actively involved in shaping the changes that will occur. This is absolutely critical to your success and brings us to the second component of a change plan: organizational alignment.

Organizational Alignment

As for any change effort, you need to look at your "alignment." Your first challenge in preparing your company to benefit from Gen Y might be the stereotypes and prejudice toward them that exist in your company. This might include your own misgivings about Gen Y. Other problems with respect to attracting and retaining Gen Y will be revealed through environmental scans. These will show you the gaps in your organization, the areas you need to change, and your blind spots.

You need consistency with respect to Gen Y. If any step of the recruiting, interviewing, hiring, training, on-boarding, rewarding, or managing process is out of sync, Gen Y will notice and be put off. This is where operational leadership is critical. You must oversee a consistent, unswerving, in-step, organization-wide effort to be Gen Y–friendly and Gen Y–compatible.

Once you have determined what areas need to be improved or corrected, you must take action at every level, by every employee, at all times. Your decisions and policies must be in alignment with your goals three hundred and sixty-five days a year. Likewise, your employees must be consistently on board with your game plan and strategies.

In order for employees to be engaged and committed to any change effort, leaders must develop a comprehensive communication plan that provides the answers to the following "big six" questions:

1. Where are we heading?
2. Why are we doing this?
3. How will I be impacted?
4. How do you know this will work?
5. What is expected of me?
6. What training and support will be put in place so I can be successful?

Addressing these questions throughout the change effort in a thorough, honest manner—with an emphasis on *honesty*—will go a long way toward gaining trust and support. Having grown up in the digital age, Gen Yers are bombarded with marketing and sales messages every day in a variety of formats. As a result, they are particularly adept at identifying communication that is less than truthful. Bottom line: If you try to "spin" information to cover up or downplay something that is less than desirable, they'll be able to tell. Transparency is highly valued by Gen Y and highly respected by every generation.

A missing piece in many communication plans is an involvement strategy. How can you involve your employees in the change? Their voices need to be heard. By allowing them to participate in crafting the solution and assist in implementing the change, employee engagement will rise and the amount of resistance you face will decline. If you do this correctly, it will also help to bridge the different generations in your organization and build trust.

Workforce Enablement

For many people, a major reason for resistance to change is a perceived loss of control. In their current jobs, they have some level of comfort. They can do their jobs fairly well, know where and to whom they can turn for help, and have built up some level of expertise. Their work has, to some degree, become routine. Introducing a culture change may disrupt this routine, and the possibility of disruption can lead to uncertainty and fear.

As mentioned above, one of the critical questions employees ask during any change effort is: "What training and support will I have?" The answer, regardless of the program being undertaken, should include both training on what has changed in the business processes and systems training. Many companies focus solely on the systems or "how" training. Enter "xyz" into field 1, select option C in your pull-down menu, et cetera. While "how training" is a necessary component to any change, it fails to answer the question, "Why?" That's where the business process training comes in; it provides the larger context. Employees understanding the "why" in your cultural change effort is critical to its long-term sustainability.

How you deliver training across generations is also important to maintaining employee engagement. Whether or not you agree with the list in Table 12.1, there are differences between Gen Y and other generations in what styles of training they prefer. Gen Yers are often called "digital natives." They've grown up with technology and are particularly skilled at picking up information quickly through electronic media. Technology is at the center of their personal and professional lives. The rest of us are sometimes referred to as "digital immigrants"—those who have learned to use technology as we've progressed through our careers, but that technology is not part of us. This is a critical difference that must be addressed when delivering training. Offering multiple training

TABLE 12.1. Old vs. New Training

Boomer Habits	Young Learner Needs
Use a leisurely, even pace	Pick up the pace
Use telling, text-oriented methods	Increase interaction
Focus on the content	Link to the learner
Take a linear approach	Offer options
Employ a prudent amount of fun	Make learning fun

From Susan El-Shamy, *How to Design and Deliver Training for the New and Emerging Generations*, 2004.

options, at least one electronic and one instructor-led, provides the greatest chance for broad engagement across all the generations within your company.

While much of the focus of this book is on the need to adapt your organization to Gen Y, you have a more complex situation. You also need to adapt your standard training to help Gen Y become part of your company. At the same time you need to train all of the generations—those over thirty-six as of 2014—to adapt to Gen Y. It used to be enough to gradually change procedures to recruit and assimilate Gen Y. As the whole generation enters the workforce—and then *becomes* your workforce—the evolution has to happen quickly. It needs to become more of a revolution. It is not uncommon for an employee who knows all office procedures to be sixty-four, but his or her boss is thirty-four. You need to thread the difficult path of giving Gen Y opportunities that may put them over previous generations without breaking the morale of the Traditionalists, Boomers, and Xers. The other generations need to become "facilitators," rather than bosses.

Sustainability

Sustainability is the final but most overlooked component to successful change because it is by far the most difficult to achieve. Many companies that initially alter their cultures find that things have regressed within six months. The key here is discipline. In today's fast-paced business environment, once a change is implemented it is off to the "next big thing," and it is assumed that new programs will automatically carry forward.

Before change will really take hold, it has to be embedded into the organization and be perceived as the natural way of doing things. This takes time and focused effort *after* the implementation. Repeatedly coaching individuals, consistently recognizing and rewarding desired behaviors, and providing support tools (posters, reference guides, email reminders, and the like) well beyond the implementation phase are all critical to maintaining any change long term.

Coach's Corner: Making Change Stick

Over my career there have been many times when we had to adapt our plan to the talent available. In the middle of December of my first year at Arizona State, it became increasingly apparent that we would have a very difficult time defending any of our opponents man-to-man. The problem was that, up to that point in my coaching career, I had never coached anything other than man-to-man. We played zone here and there, either under an assistant's direction or simply for a quick change of pace, but it wasn't our deal. To win, we had to move away from man-to-man. By the end of the season the change allowed us to be much more competitive. We continued to play zone into the next season, when we had the single greatest improvement in college basketball from one season to the next.

The change didn't come easy. When you change horses you often get worse before you get better. The leadership team's conviction is critical. If we had vacillated, it would have been more difficult for the team to believe in what we were doing. It was important once we made the decision to change that we commit to making it work. It wasn't the kind of situation in which we had the luxury of experimenting, dangling one foot in the water to see if it was warm enough, so to speak. It was one of those decisions that, once you made it, you do not have the luxury of turning around.

My four points for change success are

1. Make sure you and your leadership team show a united front.
2. No second-guessing the decision (not even in "private" conversations).
3. Show your commitment to success; burn the boats—there's no turning back.
4. Manage the leader's communication, both verbal and nonverbal.

Make sure that your management team demonstrates the conviction and commitment to what you're doing. If you want others to believe in it, you can't waffle yourself. No one must ever see a lack of commitment on your part.

Conclusion

Implementing change is one of the most difficult things to do in an organization. Improving attitudes toward Generation Y in your company is a good place to start. This is an important issue that is both focused and has broad long-term implications for your success.

The Chinese characters for change combine "danger" and "opportunity." As Gen Y becomes your workforce, it is your job to take advantage of the opportunity they bring while managing the danger.

Be continually aware that improving Gen Y integration and retention requires a proactive effort on your part. Assess the situation in your organization and design the change you need. Conduct a survey, then use the results to align your organization with your true values. Most important, commit wholeheartedly and focus on the sustainability of any new program.

Sustaining change is harder than creating it. Measure and record what you want to happen and it *will* happen. When your organization is walking the talk, the climate will be improved for Gen Y *and* for everyone else.

Sarah's Gen Y Profile

Name: Sarah

Location: South

Age: 29

Background:

- Graduated with a bachelor's degree in history from a large state university in the Northeast
- Works as an archivist at a government record repository in a small Mid-Atlantic state
- Will soon enter a master of library science program

After graduating from college shortly after the beginning of the recession, Sarah found herself with few opportunities for gainful employment, working first as an office administrator in a division of her alma mater before going to work as a researcher for an organization that conducts background checks.

Sarah and her husband left the Northeast after he found a job in his field in a small Mid-Atlantic state. She found a job as an archivist, in which she organizes and preserves records with historical value. Sarah said she likes that her job offers her fair pay, a reasonable schedule, and opportunities for professional development. She is frustrated, however, that her colleagues don't seem to share her enthusiasm and desire to learn. "My supervisors are not educated professionals in the field we work in—most were folded into the organization because of consolidation in other agencies—so it's sometimes frustrating to balance their lack of understanding of the profession with a desire to follow accepted, current archival practices," she said.

She said some of her older colleagues express resentment toward her because she is ambitious. "Many of my older co-workers treat their jobs as if it's an entitlement," she said. "They don't try to be good at their jobs, and they often do just enough to get by. They do not fear losing their jobs since we work in a system that protects their employment."

Sarah said she enjoys her work and the challenges it presents, which is why she plans to go back to school to earn a master of library science degree to further her career goals as an archivist. She said she currently enjoys a healthy work/life balance, another reason she plans to continue in this career.

"I'm hard-working at work and focused on my relationships and life when I'm not at work," she said. "I work to live, not live to work. The success I achieve at work enhances my sense of self-worth and makes me a happier person at home."

(*continued*)

For Sarah, the characteristics of a good job are

- Managers who communicate with her about her work performance
- Fair pay and reasonable flexibility
- Opportunities for advancement
- Professional development and continuing education

Sarah motivated by:

- Feeling like she's contributing to society
- Opportunities to learn new things while working

CHAPTER THIRTEEN

ATTRACTING AND RETAINING THE TALENT YOU WANT

In our first edition, we detailed the steps we felt were needed to recruit and retain talent. This may be one of the areas that has changed the most, and we are not talking about the use of technology for recruiting. Finding the right folks for your business and then *keeping them* is a far different challenge as we move forward in the 21st century. This is true for all businesses, big or small. It is particularly true for small- to medium-sized organizations.

Most businesses, large or small, historically have thought of recruiting as one task and retention as another. These two important strategic tasks are no longer separate. Previous strategies dealt with recruiting and retention much like a relay race. Once the baton was handed off, it was someone else's task to complete the next leg of the race. While a relay race is a team endeavor, success depends on individual performances.

Recruiting and retention in the 21st century are most certainly a team endeavor, but not a relay race. Every team member has to be involved throughout the process. Obviously, there will be degrees of involvement, but moving forward, the companies that have achieved the greatest alignment in recruiting and retention have a significant advantage in attracting the best talent.

This will be true whether a business is looking to hire one or ten thousand folks. In fact, we might argue that small- to medium-sized businesses will have an advantage for attracting talent. Smaller organizations may be able to adapt to the recruiting challenge faster, provide Gen Y with more of what motivates them, keep the key hiring folks in the process longer, provide more real-time feedback, and provide Gen Y with more direct access to the business leaders/owners.

Larger companies may have a harder time evolving their processes to meet the demands of Gen Y. One area in particular is granting direct access to the most senior leadership. In large organizations this will be difficult, but necessary. Big companies must find a way to get top management to interface with their new talent. It may not be possible to meet as regularly as it would be in a small company, but it will be critical.

This scenario provides a competitive advantage for all businesses. The small company that "gets it" will be able to attract a far higher level of talent than they could have in the past, giving them a key advantage over any size competitor. In fact, we believe smaller organizations should begin looking at what they can offer as equal, or even better, than Fortune 500s can. Gen Y is motivated by different things, and a company that adapts the quickest will have an advantage, regardless of size.

Larger companies that do evolve their processes will have the best of both worlds. They will be able to attract talent that outpaces similar sized organizations *and* compete for talent that might have been attracted to a small company. This also applies to retention. Many studies show that Gen Y is attracted to larger companies for the initial experience and then look to leave for another opportunity after two or three years. The larger organizations that retain talent longer will maximize their recruiting ROI, save money, and improve productivity.

The Human Investment

For the most part, and at the risk of oversimplifying, recruiting strategies start with sourcing candidates, while retention strategies start with on-boarding. These are both still important steps, but they are not where it all starts. It all starts in the 21st century with having leaders think differently about what it means to hire an employee. In fact, even the word "hiring" may be outdated. We may need to think "investment."

Let's use a story to illustrate what needs to be done in the 21st century.

The Story

ACME Manufacturing is a fifty-year-old company that employs one thousand people in various locations around the world. They have done quite well as a business and can see growth opportunities on the horizon. Their products are first-rate, their customers like them, and their employees are engaged and provide great customer service. All in all, ACME Manufacturing is doing OK.

The one area they know they need to look at is improving their equipment and taking advantage of several technological advancements that have occurred since their last update. This would not only increase productivity, but would also allow them to attack new markets, decrease waste, and sell product at a higher profit margin. The initial investment required is $1 million. This would be financed over several years and would pay for itself and allow ACME to make additional investments, once the equipment was fully integrated.

Senior management has had several meetings about this decision. They have strategically thought through exactly what they want, looked at the specifications they need (which are very different from the last time they bought equipment), secured funding, made sure the "shop folks" were on board, and have begun to source suppliers.

Finally, after senior management has considered all options, prepared the workforce for the change, and are sure they know exactly what they want, they buy the equipment. Management was careful to pick the right supplier, not just the least expensive. They took great care to make sure the specifications met their needs. They tested the equipment and checked all references.

Once they were satisfied, a ten-year payment plan was established with a very aggressive interest rate. The payments are $10,000 a month for 120 months.

After the decision is made and the equipment is purchased, management is excited about how this new technology could change their business. A few weeks later the equipment is delivered and installation begins. It is a time-consuming process, but everyone believes it will be well worth the time and attention.

Senior management, after they "signed on the bottom line," *never, ever, followed up again*. They *never* went to the plant to see how the install was going. They *never* called the foreman for updates. They *never* asked their operators how the new equipment was working. In fact, after everything was installed, they *never* asked the foreman to check in on the new investment or to make any adjustments as the machinery was broken in. Senior management just let it be and figured the "factory settings" were enough and at the end of the first year they would look at how the equipment performed.

In addition to *never* checking, management also did not look for new and better ways to leverage the new technology. The new piece of equipment may be able to enhance their business in unforeseen ways, but management is not interested. When an operator suggests a revolutionary new way to improve the bottom line, management ignores the input. They think, "When we want your opinion, we'll ask for it." Their job is done. They bought the machine and now must move on to "bigger" and "more important" issues.

The idea of planning for the purchase and install makes perfect sense. The lack of follow-up is ridiculous. In the real world, this would never happen. An investment of this type would be monitored, adjusted, maintained, and tweaked. The "factory settings" would be viewed as a starting point, and everyone would know this. In addition, if there were issues with the new equipment in the early stages of install, nearly every resource available would be deployed to make sure it began functioning properly.

The Moral of the Story

Now, let's look at how it works in many organizations in regard to recruiting and retention. First, we need to make some assumptions. Our first assumption is a hiring company would want to retain its talent. If someone were productive, a business would want to keep him or her for years. (If someone is unproductive and is replaced or leaves, our analogy still works, since the person's income is replaced by a new hire.) The next assumption in our story is that a company might hire two folks a year, pay them $45,000 to start, offer some kind of benefits, and pay appropriate employment taxes. This new employee's "fully loaded" compensation would be roughly $60,000. With two new hires, that would be $120,000 per year, or $10,000 per month.

This is the same amount of money invested in these two employees, over ten years, as the $1 million piece of equipment. In fact, with raises along the way, it is an even more significant investment than the equipment. These employees may well be as capable of revolutionizing a business (or department, product line, customer service culture, etc.) as the machine could ever be.

The sad reality is, in many, if not most cases, a $1 million piece of equipment receives more time, energy, care, and maintenance than an employee will ever receive. This will no longer work. If employees are going to be as productive as possible, be engaged, and drive results, they require time and attention as well.

In the 21st century, business leaders who realize that recruiting and retention are not separate strategies, but extensions of each other, will thrive. Business leaders who believe recruiting is one thing and retention begins with a good on-boarding process are in for a rude awakening. Just like our story, where sourcing the equipment was only the first step, employee productivity requires installation and maintenance.

Hiring the best and keeping the best begins by *supporting* the best. Hiring an employee in the 21st century is nearly identical to how a company would implement the $1 million machine purchase and implementation (not necessarily how ACME did it in our story!).

What ACME Did	What ACME Should Also Have Done
• Looked at what was needed NOW, not from previous purchases • Looked at specifications • Tested the specifications against assumptions • Made sure operators were on board • Tested the equipment/had a demo • Checked references • Secured funding • Signed agreement/celebrated decision • Installed equipment	• Followed up with foreman • Received regular updates from the foreman • Had foreman regularly check on progress • Adjusted factory settings • Looked for additional ways to leverage technology • Provided regular maintenance
What Employers Should Do	**Hiring Manager Follow-Up**
• Develop accurate job descriptions (for the job *now*, not the last hire) • Define *exactly* what skills are needed • Develop hiring profile • Make sure workforce is Gen Y ready • Train interviewers in behavioral-based interviewing • Check references • Have rewards and recognition aligned • Send offer letter • Thorough on-boarding process	• Monitor new hire progress • Develop/implement "real time feedback" process • Provide regular feedback • Ask/listen/respond • Provide regular career development coaching

Factory Settings

In our story we talked about "factory settings" and how nearly everyone realizes a new piece of equipment will require adjustments after the initial install. However, in our travels we are amazed at how often employers feel that, after high school, trade school, or university (in other words, "the factory"), no more adjustments may be necessary, or at least not for some time. On-boarding is often thought to be all that is needed to get someone off to a great start, and we do not mean just showing people around and making "drive by" introductions.

It is important to understand how easily Gen Y can feel overwhelmed in the beginning. This is just a partial list of some of the new things they will be struggling to learn:

- Position/job description
- Manager/supervisor's name
- Explanation of your company and philosophy
- List of your key people and their jobs
- Co-workers' names
- Company directory
- Retirement/pension/401k arrangements
- Pay, bonuses, and raises
- Payroll procedures: when paid, deductions, etc.
- Human resource issues
- Union delegate and information, if applicable
- Recycling or environmental programs
- Expense account procedures
- Work and break times
- Awards or incentive programs
- Safety issues
- Ombudsman or whistle-blowing procedures

- Safety incident reporting procedures
- Workers' compensation claims
- Layout of facility
- Rules/procedures for using phone
- Drug and alcohol policies and any testing
- Conditions for termination (for example, at-will employment)
- Quality management or other programs
- Hours and how recorded (for example, flex or comp time)
- Contacts for emergencies after hours
- Sexual harassment policy
- Parking
- Travel procedures and policies
- Lunch facilities
- Locker rooms
- Tools and equipment
- Vacation policies
- Sick leave policies

Not all jobs involve all of the above, but most include the majority of them. While this list seems detailed, many more items have been left out, including where the bathrooms are! Also, many of the items have both physical and social components to learn. For example, a new employee has to learn what time lunch is, where the lunchroom is, how the cafeteria works, and so forth. That's the easy part. The more stressful part is the frequently unspoken social aspects of the lunchroom—for example, whether certain groups have staked out certain tables or the etiquette of joining people already at a table.

Key Point

Being a new employee can be overwhelming to anyone.

A lot will be novel to your new Gen Yers. Help them integrate and process it all. Be sensitive to the time it will naturally take for them to become oriented. Be as helpful and attentive as possible.

Just like with a fine piece of equipment, adjustments and preventative maintenance are critical to its smooth and productive operation. Any foreman worth his or her salt will tell you that preventative maintenance minimizes downtime, too!

Prepare Your Current Employees for Gen Y

Are your current employees ready for the new Gen Y employees? As discussed, Gen Y has been unfairly stereotyped. It is crucial that these stereotypes not exist in your organization or in the hearts and minds of your employees. If your organization has a negative view of Gen Y, your new Gen Y hires will pick up on it, and it will hurt opportunities for team building.

It is incumbent upon you as a leader to check the pulse of your organization on this issue. How do your current employees feel about Gen Y? Have they bought into the stereotypes and misconceptions about Gen Y? What are their expectations for these future employees? Are they dreading working with them or looking forward to it? Do they understand why Gen Y is the way they are and what makes them "tick"? Do they understand the skills Gen Y brings with them to the company? And, most importantly, can they accept Gen Y's differences and work with them?

Key Point

Do whatever you need to do to eliminate prejudice before your new Gen Y employees arrive!

The Basics: Recruit for Your Brand

To know the kinds of people you want to recruit, you have to make explicit what your own organizational personality, culture, or brand is. A company that sees technology as its advantage should hire different types of people than a company that sees customer service as its advantage.

Most companies have very similar candidate profiles, except for their academic majors. Not enough companies have thought about what sets them apart and makes their brand different. When you understand your brand, it will help you hire people who will fit you *and* your customers better.

With the help of your management team, take time to develop your value proposition *as an employer*. Most organizations understand their value proposition *as a business*, yet rarely have we seen leadership teams take the time to develop a list of attributes that set them apart as an employer.

Key Point

Decide on your special brand as an employer and project it.

As you develop this list, make sure you do not just list adjectives and attributes. Have your team describe each point, why it is important, and how it sets you apart from the *hiring* competition. Once this list is finished, make sure your recruiters can link each item back to the recruit's goals and vision.

Consultant's Corner: Your Hiring Value Proposition

One very successful company we work with was having difficulty linking their value proposition to the recruiting process. They had developed a great list of items that set them apart from the hiring competition; yet they were unable to drive these advantages home during the recruiting process.

Their list included things like:

- Family atmosphere
- Ability to contribute immediately
- Opportunities based on performance, not tenure

We offered our client a technique often used in benefits selling. This technique links the benefit to the recruit.

- Because of . . .
- You can . . .
- Which means that . . .
- Which really means that . . .

For example:

- *Because of* the fact that we reward performance,
- *You can* set yourself apart almost immediately.
- *Which means that,* even though you have only been here a short time, you could assume significant responsibilities.
- *Which really means that* you will be in control of your destiny and can fast-forward your career by years and work on some very exciting strategic projects.

Develop Specific Candidate Profiles

The first major recruitment tool you need is a Candidate Profile. Unfortunately, most profiles—when they exist at all—are boringly generic. They contain standard criteria not particularly tailored to your real job needs. You must think carefully about the kind of person you really want and what competencies you are looking for. Be specific, not generic. Relying on gut feelings just doesn't make it. Gut feelings depend on our emotions on any given day, not on legitimate criteria. Create as precise a profile as you can, considering not only job skills but also intangible characteristics.

Developing a precise job profile can be a learning experience, particularly if you involve current job holders in the effort. Some companies require a specific profile of technical skills.

Then their focus is the skills needed for the job and, accordingly, they must have a current and accurate job description. (Developing a job description is discussed below.) Other companies may focus on intangibles like motivation or personality in their candidate profiles.

Develop Accurate Job Descriptions for the Job *Now*

The third key tool you need to successfully recruit Gen Y is a relevant and accurate job description. Just as in our story, a company would not buy new equipment based on five-year-old specs. There obviously has to be a fit between candidates and job descriptions, so you must be sure your job descriptions are precise and current. If only because of changes in technology, most jobs change in the course of five years. Gen Y will be reading your job description carefully and may call you on discrepancies between it and reality if they are hired.

Many organizations don't provide enough real details about the job to applicants. Gen Y wants to know the real nitty gritty of day-to-day work. You and your recruiters must provide a full picture of what the work is actually like. Done right, this can protect you from the danger of too high expectations on the part of Gen Y.

The best way to create an accurate job description is to enlist the aid of employees who hold that job or a similar one. What are the day-to-day components of the job? What are the skills required? Capture job-holders' valuable input and craft a job description that reflects reality. Do not count on older, possibly dated job descriptions. Capture a job description for what is required *now*.

Another tool to use is 360-degree feedback. This type of analysis is typically used to examine job *performance*. It gives managers comprehensive feedback from everyone in the group.

Voices of Experience: Jakob Rolsted, JENSEN Group

JENSEN Group, a company that manufactures and sells large, institutional laundry equipment, initially struggled to attract Gen Y workers. Gen Yers looked at JENSEN Group as being part of the manufacturing industry, believing that a job with the company would mean working with your hands, not your head.

JENSEN Group needs workers who are capable of both—a qualification that's attractive to Gen Y workers—but putting that across to prospective employees was tricky. "We are a place that people can come to and learn a great deal, get experience, and advance in their careers," said Jakob Rolsted, production manager at the group's Bornholm, Denmark, location. "You can learn many valuable things."

JENSEN Group had to figure out how to be proactive to attract talent and get the word out about available jobs in the company, as well as what sort of careers are available in the global industrial laundry industry.

JENSEN Group partnered with local schools to generate ideas about how to attract young workers and saw an opportunity to collaborate with local schools in Denmark. Rolsted launched "tech nerd week," which gave students an opportunity to learn about JENSEN Group and the industry in a day camp–like setting. Students were given a project and paired with staff members, including electricians, engineers, and metal workers, to develop a feel for real people and their jobs. The camp showed students the knowledge they could reap if they took a job with the company, thus making them attractive employees in a worldwide industry. During the camp, JENSEN Group showed students video conferences among employees throughout the world—the United States, Switzerland, Germany, etc.—all using the inter-company language of English. "If you want to have a job at certain levels, you must work for it," Rolsted said. "You must work on your skills and your language skills." He noted that it's important to show the value of blue-collar jobs because JENSEN Group needs both types of workers. "Recruiting talent is often thought of as recruiting white collar workers; however, talent is talent," he said. "It's not just limited to white collar."

(*continued*)

Gen Yers who work with JENSEN Group learn a number of skills—from technology and business to language and communications—that will help them progress along their "career lattice." Baby Boomers looked at their working lives as a career ladder, but Gen Y workers view it as more of a lattice—instead of waiting for the next rung to open up, they will make a lateral move or even a backward move to achieve their view of career success. For Rolsted and other workers in the industry, it's more of a 3-D lattice—throughout their careers, there are many opportunities to learn, take on new roles, and implement those skills anywhere in the world. For his career, it's not a one-dimensional lattice of moving from role to role—he's taken what he's learned to jump from skill to skill, location to location, and culture to culture.

Once JENSEN Group workers gain knowledge of the industry, it's also important to ensure they'll be ready to take over when older generations retire, Rolsted noted. As older generations retire, there has to be a plan to replace them, he said. Mentoring, guiding, coaching, and knowledge transfer are important for both blue- and white-collar workers across generations, he said. As the older generations move toward retirement, they're responsible for ensuring the next generation obtains a level of mastery so they're able to replace older workers in the future.

Train Your Interviewers!

A key to conducting better interviews is to have better *interviewers*. Interviewing is a skill that can be taught. Some people may be naturally good interviewers, especially if they're interviewing for a job they supervise. They may be good at identifying candidates they wouldn't want to work with and those they would get along with. Some people have a knack for judging others. But the best rule of thumb is to pick interviewers who have excellent people skills, and carefully train them to use systematic and validated criteria.

The importance of having trained interviewers cannot be overstated. Gen Y can accept or reject a job based solely on the interviewer! If an interviewer is inattentive, unprofessional, a poor interviewer, or does not know enough about the company or the job, a talented candidate will be put off.

Interviewers must be able to balance talking and listening. They cannot spend too much time "selling" the job to applicants. They must be able to ask questions and listen. Gen Y is particularly sensitive to this. They want to tell you about themselves. Besides, it is vitally important that you find out Gen Y's needs and goals as soon as possible. It will impress Gen Y that you care about their personal visions. Interviewers must also have solid knowledge about the organization.

It is especially important that interviewers be aware of their own unconscious negative tendencies, things that could alienate Gen Y during the initial interview. Chapter 10 discussed personality profiling in detail. This analytical tool will give your interviewers "game film" to review. They may be subconsciously controlling the conversation, cutting off the candidate, bullying, or being too impatient. Any of these tendencies can cost you your Gen Y candidates. Fortunately, once a good interviewer is aware of these behaviors, he or she can control them.

Behavior-Based Questions Provide More Relevant Information

The top goal of a job interview is to find out the applicant's past experience relative to key knowledge, skills, and abilities needed for success in the job. Interview questions must be designed for this. Many Gen Y applicants will not have had relevant job experience. If you don't have a candidate's record of performance in similar jobs, you need to ask performance oriented questions. Answers can be based on school experience, volunteer work, leisure activities, and so on.

You are in a better position to judge your applicants' abilities if they describe several specific instances when they had to deal with the types of issues the job entails. Simply ask applicants to describe the situation, what they did to address it, and what happened as a result.

This assumes that you have analyzed the job and know what key skills it requires. Be sure you know what qualities your applicants must have when you hire them. For example, people in customer service must be comfortable answering questions, know how to use a database (with the information they need), have a friendly attitude, be patient, be able to handle angry customers, and so on. People in sales must learn about your products or services, be comfortable talking with prospects, and be able to take rejection.

Once you have identified key skills for a job, distinguish between those that applicants *must* have and those that they can learn on the job. It's often more important to hire people with the right attitudes than those with the right skills. Skills can be taught, but attitudes are tough to change.

Look for Real Situational Information

You can see the benefit of asking questions that are behaviorally anchored. Traditional interview questions often ask applicants to rate their own abilities: "How good are you at working in a team?" Of course, they'll give themselves a positive rating! Behavior-based questions force applicants to be more specific and give examples. "Describe a time when you worked with a team at school and what you liked and disliked about it." By probing for details, you can learn more about how the applicants think and their underlying assumptions.

Behavior-based questions help you find out whether candidates have experience that can generalize to a job. A related approach is to use questions that describe a hypothetical work situation similar to those they will encounter on the job. These can help you understand how candidates think about the types of situations they will face on the job.

There's No Substitute for Reality

Remember, however, that hypothetical examples are a weak substitute for actual behavioral responses. In one case, an applicant didn't have any work experience and was unable to come up with work examples. The interviewer then asked, "What would you do in that situation?" The applicant gave answers that fit what the organization was looking for.

To get at actual behavior, the interviewer changed the focus to volunteer work or college projects that involved working with others. When they went over the same questions using *actual* behavior, the responses were different.

It's no secret that people will say things that make themselves look good. They will also say what they think you want to hear. When they report on their actual behavior, you have a somewhat better chance of learning what they would actually do and what they are actually like.

Consultant's Corner: Behavior-Based Questions

We often work with our clients to help them develop a set of specific competencies required for each job. Once we have finalized the list, we are able to create specific behavior-based questions for each area.

Sample Competency Questions

RESULTS-DRIVEN: Achievement-oriented: Achieves and exceeds goals; pushes self and others for results.

Example: Give me an example of a goal that you set in the past and tell me about your success in reaching it.

(*continued*)

VERSATILE: Adjusts effectively to new work demands, processes, structures, and cultures.

Example: Tell me about a time you had to handle multiple responsibilities.

INFLUENTIAL: Makes an impact on people, events, and decisions; affects the thinking or actions of others by means of example or personality.

Example: Describe a time when you affected others' decisions or thinking processes.

CUSTOMER-FOCUSED: Aware of customer needs; makes decisions with customer in mind; builds strong customer relationships.

Example: Tell me about a situation when you had to deal with a very upset customer. What did you do? What was the result?

On-Boarding: Have a Plan

You must strategize before new hires arrive. Who are your ambassadors? Your mentors? Your buddies? How should they interact with new Gen Y employees? You must have people in place to help the new hires connect with the team.

Research shows that newcomers to groups tend to band together. When they are uncertain about a situation, they will bond with anyone who seems to be in the same situation. Such newcomer bonding can make your new Gen Y workers feel more in control and safe in a strange environment—your company. However, the norms they develop may not be the norms you want.

Left to their own devices, new Gen Y employees will form a group with each other, and they can develop an "us versus them" mentality. If one Gen Yer is dissatisfied, the rest may be disproportionately influenced. Your goal is to help new Gen Y hires form relationships with many other employees so that the decision of one Gen Y hire will not automatically influence them all.

Be aware of how strong this effect can be, and make sure that your new workers are influenced the way you want them to be. It's very important that you create programs that link newcomers to positive influences and role models. If you do these things before Gen Y arrives, you will have positioned your organization to effectively and successfully on-board Gen Y.

Have a Gen Y Mentor

Institute a reverse-mentoring program. Assign a Gen Yer to one of your Baby Boomer or Xer managers, or even to yourself. Allow the Gen Y employee to mentor you about his or her world, what's important, and how to connect with his or her generation.

Gen Y can give you a view of your organization, your customers, and your marketplace without the filters of experience and preconceptions. Gen Y can give you a fresh perspective and insights that you might never see on your own.

Reverse Mentoring

Jack Welch, author, past CEO of General Electric, and once the top-rated executive in America, pioneered reverse mentoring when he ordered hundreds of his top managers to create reverse-mentoring relationships with their newest employees. (At that time he was mainly interested in the new employees filling in their managers on technology.)

Communicate Your Expectations

After you have listened to Gen Y's initial thoughts and impressions and answered their immediate questions, use the early days to give Gen Y important messages of your own. You must communicate the following messages to Gen Y early and often.

Re-Sell Your Brand

While Gen Y needs job descriptions and technical information, this is also the time to tell them what your organization stands for and to enlist them to represent your standards. Gen Y can be motivated to excel when they believe in what you're doing. Re-sell your brand to new employees and tell them how they can contribute.

Re-Sell Your Vision

Take the time in your early discussions with your new Gen Y employees to tell them again what your company vision is. Ask them what their visions are and what their goals are. Show them how their vision and yours are linked. Reinforce your firm belief that they can achieve their goals by working with you in your organization.

Establish Your Leadership

One of the more intriguing discoveries we uncovered in our research is the fact that Gen Y *wants to be led*. They are looking for strong leaders and, although Gen Y may push, they do not respect pushovers. It is important for leaders to set the standards early. What are your corporate values? Discuss these with your new hires. What are your cultural norms? Make sure these norms, things like being on time, following up, respecting people's space, respecting people's time, and proper appearance are understood and are "nonnegotiable."

Expand Gen Y's Horizon

As we have discussed throughout this book, Gen Y has a different mindset about commitment to an organization because of their increased freedom and lack of familial responsibilities. They are looking for a one- to two-year work experience, not a long-term commitment. Your challenge is to stretch Gen Y's horizon, and the sooner you start doing that, the better. Help them identify and commit to a goal that is bigger than a one- to two-year commitment. As we will discuss below, you will want to engage them as soon as possible in projects that are longer term.

Follow Up: Promise Feedback and Deliver It

Gen Y wants feedback and appreciation. This issue has been addressed in depth. Baby Boomer bosses may operate by the old rule that no news is good news—as long as they don't say anything, everything is fine. This will not work for Gen Y. To get a supportive message across, you have to send out three times the feedback that you think is necessary, and you have to say ten positive statements for every negative one. We're all oversensitive to negative feedback, but Gen Y on a new job is more so.

While daily feedback may sound like too much, Gen Yers would like to be acknowledged every time they do something well. It's a little like saying thank you. If you automatically acknowledge a job well done, Gen Y will appreciate it and develop a bond with you and your organization.

As early as possible, sit down with your new Gen Y employee and agree upon a review schedule. Will you have a one-on-one every two weeks? Once a month? Every two months? If on Day One you set the date for a future performance management review, Gen Yers will know that you are serious about monitoring their progress and listening to their ideas and concerns. Make the appointments and keep them.

Keep Gen Y Informed

All employees want to know what is going on around them, but Gen Y wants to know even more so. Keep your Gen Y employees in the loop. Schedule state-of-the-business meetings to keep your Gen Y talent aware of anything new in the company. Allow plenty of time for questions and answers. Consider other ways you can communicate. Perhaps there is a better way to reach your younger employees than the one you are now using.

Provide Feedback

Gen Y needs and wants feedback. They are used to instant feedback. An annual review is too little, too late. Gen Y needs more.

Conduct a Walk-Through

One thing we regularly do for our clients is a "walk-through" of their facilities. Often small changes can have a big impact on recruiting and retention. What we are looking for are the subtle messages the physical space sends:

- Where is customer parking?
- Where is executive parking?
- Where do new hires park?
- Who has the spaces closest to the door (or in the shade or undercover), and who has to park around back?
- Are new hires all in the same location or are they interacting with all of the employees?

It's not always the biggest adjustments that have the biggest impact.

Strategic Planning for Retention

Even if you develop a culture that accepts Gen Y and promotes their full integration, you are still going to have more turnover today than we did with earlier generations. This is going to be a fact of life moving forward. It is critical that you and your team incorporate this reality into all of your strategic plans. It is a new cost of doing business.

To quote legendary football coach Vince Lombardi, "We're going to chase perfection in the hopes of catching excellence." As you develop your strategic plans, it will be critical for your team to understand and move proactively to the new paradigm Generation Y presents.

Items to consider for your strategic plan include:

- Recruiting and retention goals
- Recruiting and retention owners
- Sustainable business strategies
- Resource allocation for:
  - On-boarding
  - Leadership development
  - Change management

One-on-One Performance Management

An excellent tool for giving Gen Y employees feedback is the one-on-one review. Take the time to meet with your Gen Yers individually to discuss what they are doing and how they are doing it. Give them feedback on what they are doing right and wrong. Let them know how they can do things better. Give them the opportunity to ask questions. Gen Y wants to know where they stand. Remember to reinforce your *mutual* vision and ask them whether they are making progress toward their personal goals.

Here is an overview of how to communicate with Gen Y:

Set Up

- Once per month
- Set date and time two weeks in advance
- Informal setting
- "No major problems"—setting can be informal
- "Some problems"—office or more formal setting
- Be aware of employee's style
- Review employee's vision and goals

Substance

- Establish agenda
- Any special projects?
- Link to performance targets
- Prepare yourself to listen
- Use open-ended questions to begin and dig deeper
- Use close-ended questions to confirm
- Reach consensus/agreement on good performance and performance short of expectations
- Agree on action/timing

Follow-Up

- Short write-up is required, best within seventy-two hours
- Use phrases like: *I believe*, *You should*, *We agreed*, NOT, *Don't ever*, *We said*, *You should have*
- Link write-up to the performance targets
- Reinforce current good performance
- Specifically state where "you've agreed" the performance is short of expectations
- Specifically state the action points "you've agreed" will occur
- Specifically state any actions the manager will take to help the employee reach his or her goals and expectations

Conclusion

Attracting and retaining the best talent requires leaders to align their teams and resources to execute on the plan. In the past, recruiting and retention were looked at as two separate things, whereas in the 21st century these elements are intertwined. Retention of an employee does not start on the first day and with the successful completion of an on-boarding program. It begins with the initial interview and flows through the entire organization. Retaining talent means everyone is accountable, not just the manager or HR. *Everyone!* New employees, like a fine piece of expensive equipment, require regular "maintenance," "tune-ups," and constant vigilance.

Sara's Gen Y Profile

Name: Sara

Location: Northeast

Age: 27

Background:

- Graduated from a large state university in the Northeast with a bachelor's in English writing and political science
- Earned a master's in journalism from a large university in a Northeast city
- Works as a marketing manager for a digital startup owned by a large global media conglomerate

Sara, who worked for the daily student newspaper when she was in college, opted to earn a master's in journalism, as opposed to seeking a job at the beginning of the recession, when jobs for reporters were few and far between.

After graduating from journalism school, Sara worked her way up through a large media conglomerate, ultimately landing a marketing manager position at a digital startup within the company.

She said her job challenges her, gives her opportunities to learn on a daily basis, and is "financially comfortable." She said opportunities for growth in her role and in the company are two reasons for staying in this position.

She works hard, but she said that a better work/life balance is something she thinks about. "Right now I don't have a lot to manage in my personal life, but given the frequent headlines about work/life balance, it's certainly something I think about for the future," she said.

Sara said she doesn't find many differences between colleagues her age and older co-workers.

(*continued*)

"I think it's difficult in general to find hard-working people," she said. "I wouldn't say it has to do with your generation."

For Sara, the characteristics of a good job are

- Feeling challenged and motivated
- Opportunities for continuing education
- A fair salary
- Good leaders and a positive work culture

Sara is motivated by:

- Money and success
- Feeling like she's good at what she does

● ●

CHAPTER FOURTEEN

LEADERSHIP CHALLENGES

As advocates, researchers, and students of Gen Y, we have been exposed to volumes of data, studies, articles, and opinion pieces about this generation. Up to this point of the book we have tried to dispel much of the misinformation and offer our insights and strategies for 21st century leaders. This chapter may seem a bit different. Now we want to lay out the five challenges we see for leaders and where we think Gen Y may fall short and require a strong 21st century leader.

We hope this chapter does not contradict what we have said in previous chapters, especially Chapter 4 on Myths. While we want to point out the myths and challenge leaders to think differently, we also want leaders to understand there can be some real frustrations to leading and motivating this cohort. We do not want eighty million Gen Yers painted negatively in broad strokes, and we want leaders to recognize the reality of 21st century leadership. There will be frustrating moments, even for the most talented 21st century leader.

In this chapter we want to show five leadership opportunities that may arise with Gen Y. To lead folks through, over, and around these issues will require authentic leadership. Leaders will need to have provided real-time feedback, explained the why, and have stood their ground when necessary. Helping your Gen Y employees grow and develop will require patience, as well as a willingness to listen, challenge, guide, and advise. It will also require leaders to stand firm and demand (yes, demand) certain outcomes and behaviors.

At the risk of contradicting our previous points, we want to address five issues and behaviors that are very real coaching opportunities for leaders and possible developmental areas for Gen Y employees.

Coaching Opportunity 1: Gen Y Can Be Easily Distracted

One of the things we often hear from supervisors and managers of Gen Y is how easily they are distracted. We believe this is true and a major challenge for leaders. However, we also believe this is true for *all* of the generations, and Gen Y is taking the brunt of the criticism.

Let's look at some of the research and data. Northwestern Mutual conducted a study of all of the generations to determine their reactions to the pace of society, ability to stick to long-term goals, and how much they are distracted.

The findings are very interesting across all of the generations. Baby Boomers and Traditionalists are *more likely* to say the pace of society makes it harder to stick with long-term goals. In fact, Gen Y is the *least* likely of all of the generations to be distracted by the pace of society.

Our belief is that "distraction" is a societal issue and not just a Gen Y issue. However, Gen Y presents *different* leadership challenges because of their experience *and* inexperience.

Gen Y, as technology natives, have always lived in a world with global news, instant information, hundreds of television stations and the Internet. Their experience has always afforded them dozens, if not hundreds, of options in nearly every aspect of life. They have grown quite used to "switching channels" if they do not like what is happening in real time. This applies to literally every area of their lives. Switching from sport to sport, piano to dance, team to team, or even major to major is the norm for Gen Y.

We believe that because Gen Y has always had multiple options for nearly every decision in their lives, they can lose focus. We also believe this leadership challenge is magnified and defined by mobile/electronic devices. In other words, leaders are missing a real opportunity to develop their folks because they may think this lack of focus/distraction is *purely* driven by "smart phones." It is true that Gen Y is more distracted than any other generation by the immediacy of technology (Northwestern Mutual, 2013). However, organizations often treat the "symptom" rather than curing the disease.

Treating the "symptom" is banning cell phones, texting, reading email, etc., from meetings and one-on-one interactions. We have heard countless managers demand, out of frustration, that all cell phones be silenced at meetings. Their goal is twofold. First, they do not want the speaker to be interrupted, and second, they want to make sure the audience is paying attention. The first goal is usually met and silenced phones do not interrupt the speaker. The second goal, however, may or may not be met.

"Curing the disease" is much harder for leaders. It can and will be frustrating for leaders to help Gen Y gain greater focus and minimize distractions. The first step for leaders is to realize that electronic devices are only a symptom. The real issue is coaching folks to develop the *discipline* of focus.

Coach's Corner: Maintaining Focus

Maintaining one's focus is difficult in all walks of life. The best example in basketball is the free throw. When you're at the free throw line and, right behind the basket, everyone's waving their towels and their Styrofoam pointers, they're jumping up and down to try to create the illusion that the basket is moving, they're screaming. How do you stay focused? One technique that we use

(*continued*)

is a "go to sentence." Before we shoot the free throw a sentence like, "slow, soft, smooth" or "up, over, and in."

The player will say this to himself in a relaxed manner to help focus on his ritual for the free throw. The other thing that is important is to do the same thing each time. Rely on your habits in your moments of pressure where focus could be the most difficult.

It is important what message you send yourself. Positive self-talk. Positive self-affirmation. It is very similar to the "go to sentence." Dr. Denis Waitley, a renowned sports psychologist, has professed how critical it is to talk to yourself the right way when you don't make the shot. Instead of calling yourself every name in the book, immediately say something like, "That's not like me. The next one is over and in." or "That's not like me. This one's going in." If someone's playing golf, using the analogy, if someone shoots a bad shot he might throw his clubs or call himself an idiot. His internal computer just registers that. It all becomes a self-fulfilling prophecy. Having the ability to move on to the next play, having positive affirmations and positive self-talk after you just made a mistake or had an unsuccessful try is what maintaining focus is all about.

In Chapter 9 we discussed the reticular activating system (RAS) and how it works. Leaders need to open their employees' RAS by clearly explaining goals and expectations. Once Gen Y understands the goal, they will be more open to information and less mentally distracted by what was previously "useless noise." When people deem information to be useless (a speaker, boring meetings, boring tasks, etc.), they have a tendency to tune it out. When Gen Y knows the *purpose* (the why has been explained), they will be more likely to focus on task completion.

A 21st century leader will need to *continually* challenge folks to stay focused and to develop the discipline of staying on task. This has always been a frustrating part of leadership, and will continue to be with Gen Y. A good leader will realize that this time-honored issue has taken on new challenges and will understand what is different now and look to "cure the disease" and not "treat the symptom." Smart phones are a symptom. Developing the discipline and focus is the cure.

Coaching Opportunity 2: Gen Y May Quit Too Soon

In Chapter 4, we talked about the myth of Gen Y being disloyal and job-jumpers. Gen Yers really are looking for reasons to stay and not jump from company to company. We talked about the need to develop "career lattices" versus "career ladders" that give Gen Y options to move from position to position in order to develop their skills.

As a leader, your role is to help Gen Y realize it is critical to their long-term success to move from position to position (or even company to company) for the *right* reasons. Since Gen Y is used to having so many options and may become distracted, they may well want to move to a different position for the wrong reasons. On the positive side, a "career lattice" provides options and growth potential. If used inappropriately, it may provide an easy out and have people actually "quitting" a challenge before it is overcome. They may move to another rung on the lattice too soon. Even if they stay within the same company, they may well have "quit" their jobs.

This is where real-time feedback and career coaching are critical. If a 21st century leader is spending time with his or her folks, helping them to navigate the "career lattice," holding them accountable, and providing both positive and constructive feedback, it will be much easier to guide them to do "the right thing for the right reason." Gen Y (or anyone, for that matter) should not be able to move easily because they have failed at a task, found it to be too hard, are bored, intellectually know what to do but have not executed, or simply because "the grass looks greener."

We will address these, but first we want to say there may be times when someone moves for any of these reasons—and it is the right move. For example, if someone fails at a task and is not really capable of accomplishing it but would thrive somewhere else, then a move is in order. Another example may be when someone has mastered a task and is now bored; a new challenge may also be in order. These are "the right reasons."

We are huge proponents of setting people up to succeed by aligning their strengths and talents to the job at hand. If leaders have misaligned talent and task, then a move is in order. However, if that is not the case and leaders do not coach their folks properly, they might unconsciously be enabling Gen Y to "quit too soon."

We have seen many situations in which a talented employee is assigned a role and has been less than successful. It happens all the time. Seasoned leaders know it is not the failure that counts, but how the setback is overcome. If your Gen Y employee has the talent to complete the job successfully and has yet to succeed, allowing him or her to move to another position on the lattice is a mistake. We believe this starts a chain reaction that subliminally tells the organization it is OK to lose. The leadership message should be: "Win and then move on." In our experience, once one overcomes an initial setback and begins winning, the desire to move on goes away.

Coach's Corner: Never Quit on a Miss

Perhaps the greatest glory exists not in succeeding in and of itself but in succeeding after some fall or adversity. That's what movies are made about. Our world isn't nearly as swept away when success comes automatically. If, in fact, it comes after some struggle, therein lies a true seed of greatness in my mind.

We do talk about the fact that almost any great accomplishment is preceded by some kind temptation to give in because of the difficulty. We talk about, and give examples all the time, about what people are overcoming and the challenges they are overcoming. That cuts across all endeavors.

When we shoot free throws at the end of practice, we always give players goals. Goals always include making so many in a row, ending on a swish. Again, if we can end the right way, that's positive momentum.

I think a lot of guys from Koby Bryant to Michael Jordan manage their workouts similarly. They hold themselves accountable to making so many shots before they can move to the next step. The workout's not over until a standard is met.

We have several concerns about allowing our Gen Y employees to move on the lattice for the wrong reasons. First is the message it sends and the unseen culture it begins to develop. Results do matter, and accountability is critical for any business to succeed. By allowing moves to another position too soon, before real results are achieved, a leader is silently condoning failure.

This will have an enormous impact on the culture and very negative ramifications for the Gen Yer down the road. Leaders should be coaching their folks to "win, then move" (if still desired).

The next concern we have about moving too soon or for the wrong reasons is that, until a task is mastered, there is really little "institutional knowledge" or "knowledge capital" developed for the business. Leaders have to realize that one of their most precious assets is the knowledge capital held by their workers.

If Gen Y workers are allowed to shift positions simply because they have failed (when they clearly have the capability) without overcoming their failures, they will be moving without having gained the necessary confidence *and* without having gained the "institutional knowledge" of how to successfully complete the task. This is a critical point.

Moving to another position on the "lattice" means the current position now needs to be filled. If the person moving cannot help with the transition/handoff to the new person, then the lattice concept becomes unsustainable and a "house of cards." It is destined to fail and crumble.

Over the long haul, we believe enabling Gen Y (or any employee) to move to another position for the wrong reasons will definitely backfire. A boss may think he or she is being Gen Y–friendly and accommodating employees, when in fact these are weak leaders who are enabling their employees. The only things weak leaders attract are weak followers. Gen Y is looking for strong leadership. If allowed to "quit too soon," a talented Gen Y employee will soon realize the boss has not been a good leader. Ultimately, they will quit anyway and seek out better leadership.

Our final concern about moving a Gen Y employee after a failure is the long-term effect it has on the employee. While Gen Y has many talents, the one thing that is truly impossible for a thirty-year-old to have is thirty years of experience. With most things in life, work included, the more one does something, the better one becomes at it. Gen Y needs to stay in a position on the lattice long enough to gain the proper confidence, experience, and the *mastery* that come with successfully completing a job. This leads us directly to our next coaching opportunity.

Coaching Opportunity 3: Gen Y Wants to Advance Before They Are Ready

In an effort to become "Gen Y–friendly" we fear that many companies will take the "career lattice" discussion and use it inappropriately. It *is* critical for businesses to discard the old career ladder model and expand/define additional opportunities and create a lattice. However, it is equally critical, if not more critical, for leaders to develop the skills to help Gen Y navigate the career lattice.

Over the long haul, Gen Y, just like every previous generation, will have to turn their potential, talent, intelligence, drive, and knowledge into *results*. Along the way, in order to have a sustainable career, they will also have to gain experience and *master* many skills.

If Gen Y is allowed to "quit too soon" or move to another position because they are "bored" or view the "grass as greener," then it will become increasingly more difficult for them to master the skills required for a long and successful career. This is especially troubling to us because Gen Y does not expect to retire. With that thought in mind, it is important for them to master skills that may need to carry them for a fifty-year career.

Twenty-first century leaders must coach Gen Y to see the broader view. Career coaching and development will become a critical skill for leaders. It will be important for leaders to have frequent career discussions and help Gen Y employees to understand the long-term picture. Gen Y may become distracted, or bored, or view another opportunity as better, without first having mastered the skills of their current position. Real-time feedback and "explaining the why" will be the best tools a leader can use to develop Gen Y's mastery.

Twenty-first century leaders must help Gen Y understand mastery is only accomplished by working, practicing, and spending time on a given task. In fact, we would argue that less talented people who spend time developing their skills will outperform more talented, less practiced people.

Geoffrey Colvin, author of *Talent Is Overrated: What Really Separates World-Class Performers from Everybody Else*, proposes that the concept "natural talent" is a myth. While certainly some folks find it easier to perform certain tasks than others, Colvin contends that in many respects "natural talent" may be irrelevant. What is relevant is *working* to master a task.

Voices of Experience: Tyler Palko

Tyler Palko has always been a leader. Before becoming a leadership consultant, he was the starting quarterback for the University of Pittsburgh Panthers from 2004 to 2006 and spent five years in the NFL.

Palko said he began building his leadership skills at a young age in backyard football games and neighborhood basketball games.

(*continued*)

He thinks people largely have the wrong idea of leadership, which is why they sometimes need an outside coach and game film. "It's not just yelling and screaming," he said. "It's leading by example, handling adversity, and training someone to take over for you when you leave." But that's not an easy thing to do, he notes, especially for his generation—Gen Y.

The "instant gratification" that some members of his generation expect can be problematic when it comes to building future leaders, he said. "Everything's an algorithm now, and that's helped, but not with human capital development," he said. "Developing leaders—it's not something you can learn on a computer. You can't watch somebody do it. It's a trained skill that you have to learn."

Palko said the biggest challenge in overcoming generational divides is that the level of patience among members of Gen Y and older workers is notably low. Members of Gen Y think that, because they went to college, obtained a degree, and can efficiently use computers, they have it all figured out, he said. Meanwhile, older generations think they have all the answers because they have twenty or thirty years of experience. "The merger of knowledge is the answer, but people fight it," Palko said, describing himself as a "Baby Boomer in a Gen Y body."

As a consultant, he uses what he learned as a quarterback to help businesses build leaders. It's just like building athletes, he explained—it's important to understand what you know and what you don't know and slowly build up to a "full playbook" of skills and knowledge.

In your first year—whether you're a freshman quarterback or an entry-level employee—it's important to learn 10 percent of the playbook and become really good at it, Palko said. Regardless of how much you want to keep progressing, you have to buy into perfecting 10 percent first. The following year, dedicate your time to perfecting 40 to 50 percent of the playbook, Palko recommended.

By the second year on the team or on the job, you're faster, stronger, and more confident because you've been slowly gaining bits of information. The following year, shoot for perfecting 75 to 80 percent of the playbook, he said.

By your final year (if you're a college football player, that is), "you should be, in essence, calling your own plays," Palko said. "Moving forward in business, it's the same thing," he said.

Business owners sometimes think they can hire someone who just graduated from Harvard who can do the job. "That can ruin people in sports and that can ruin people in business," Palko said, noting that football *and* business are a growing and maturing process. You're not going to be perfect the minute you walk into the stadium—or the office.

Gen Y cannot be allowed to "quit too soon" before achieving some kind of success. Good leaders, with a solid real-time feedback system, have to be prepared to coach folks through challenging times. Leaders need to help Gen Y see the longer-term vision.

In Chapter 12 we talked about vision, alignment, and execution. Gen Y has a vision for themselves, and leaders must link all of the current decisions to the "big picture." Not everyone finds "the vision thing" easy. In fact, for many leaders it is not at all natural. That is why leaders need some game film to help them improve in this area. As Colvin points out, it may not be relevant what one's natural skills are. If "visioning" and linking Gen Y's vision to career steps is difficult for a leader, it's not an excuse. Leaders in the 21st century must work at it, and having game film will help.

In Chapter 9 we discussed world-class performers and what sets them apart. One of the elements we have recently researched is "self-talk." The human mind does not argue with itself. If a Gen Y employee (or anyone) begins to tell him- or herself that he or she *can't* do something, then it will become fact.

As leaders develop their coaching skills, two things have to be kept top of mind. First, they must not limit themselves as leaders with negative self-talk. If they have not developed certain leadership skills at this point or if some of them feel "unnatural," they must dedicate the time and the discipline to develop these new skills. Game film will help them create strategies to develop in all areas, especially those areas that may be counterintuitive.

Second, leaders must be keenly aware of any "negative self-talk" from their Gen Y or other employees. If Gen Y employees believe they are "not good at" or "can't do" something, that will become a reality in their minds. This may well be a career-long belief that dramatically limits further opportunities.

Today's leaders must accept the challenge of providing real-time feedback and career guidance to all Gen Y employees. They need to listen closely for "negative self-talk" in others (and avoid it in themselves). Leaders must link Gen Y's vision to the big picture, and they must make sure Gen Y is moving on the lattice after having gained the appropriate experience, confidence, and mastery of the task at hand.

Coach's Corner: Putting in the Time

Geoffrey Colvin, in the book *Talent Is Overrated*, theorizes that expertise takes 10,000 hours of targeted practice. While Mozart was a prodigy, the reality is that he started so young that he had his 10,000 hours in early. Tiger Woods started when he was three, so by the time he was fifteen he had his 10,000 hours.

One example we have is James Harden. He graduated from high school a year young. Nonetheless, he had a brilliant freshman year at Arizona State. Even though he probably could have been a first-round draft pick after his first year, he was courageous and honest enough with himself to know that, for the long haul, it benefited him to have one more year in college.

In large part, he dedicated that year to continuing to transform his body. He had long been considered someone who had to get in better shape, who had to get strong. Part was just natural maturation, and he really dedicated himself to the continuance of transforming his body.

After his sophomore year he went to the Chicago pre-draft combine and, in his group, he was actually ranked number 1 on all physical athletic tests. He came out with the best composite scores. He turned what was initially a criticism into a strength through natural maturation and very hard work, together with our sports performance coach, Rich Wenner.

The other thing he did as a left-hander was to really dedicate himself to improving his right hand. As he returned to school he spent a lot of time working on going right. Over time, he became equally gifted with both his right and left hands.

Coaching Opportunity 4: Knowing Something Is Not the Same as Doing Something

Another significant coaching opportunity we see for leaders is helping Gen Y turn knowledge into results. This might be one of the most frustrating challenges leaders will face with Gen Y. In our research and interviews, we have found experienced leaders almost confounded by Gen Y's breadth of knowledge and yet limited results. Many leaders have told us some variation of: "It is extremely frustrating. Sally is a well-educated, smart, talented, and likable person. For all purposes, she should be a superstar. She knows what to do, but doesn't always do it."

Key Point

Knowledge is only an ingredient for success. Action is another.

Leaders need to coach Gen Y on how to turn "knowing" into "doing." This concept is foreign to previous generations. Traditionalists, Boomers, and Xers all inherently knew they would ultimately be judged on what they *did*, not on what they *knew*. Knowledge was simply a means to the end (results) and not the end in itself.

In many ways Gen Y has heard a different message. They have grown up with instant access to information. They have become great researchers and are able to dig out information on nearly any topic. Gen Y has always been able to "google it." Similarly, when faced with a problem or challenge, Gen Y can also reach out to others around the world and ask for help and input. They can see what others have done in similar situations.

This is all a very good thing. The coaching challenge is that Gen Y needs to understand that simply *knowing* what to do is not enough. Turning that knowledge into the proper action is what drives results. Simply having knowledge, intelligence, education, high test scores, and research is not enough.

Leaders have to help Gen Y understand *why* information/knowledge is just the first step. This is counterintuitive for other generations. Previous generations did not need this kind of coaching. Gen Y does. Previous generations did not have the ability to research something instantly. In fact, for everyone other than Gen Y, research actually was *doing* something and produced a *result.* It required a strategy, hours in the library, reading twenty articles to find one nugget, and learning the Dewey Decimal System. We do not mean to discount 21st century research techniques. We simply want to point out that there was more "doing" involved in research in 1980.

In addition to helping Gen Y understand the why, leaders must also help Gen Y with the "how." How does one apply the knowledge? How does one make the right decisions? How does one excel at this job? These are a leader's coaching opportunities.

Previous generations grew up with a "trial and error" philosophy. They were told that "experience is the best teacher" and "if at first you don't succeed, try, try again." Many past training programs were as simple as, "Here is the manual; go figure it out." While trial and error is one way to learn, it may not always be the best—and certainly is not the most productive.

Key Point

Results are about application, not academic understanding.

A 21st century leader has to take a step back and realize Gen Yers can *know* almost anything at any time. That doesn't mean they *understand* it or can *apply* their knowledge. A leader's job is to help them link knowledge to action that leads to results.

Coaching Opportunity 5: Gen Y Is Not "Hungry" Enough

This seems to be a common refrain as businesses try to find ways to motivate Gen Y. Over and over, we hear things like, "They [Gen Y] just don't want to put in the same effort we [previous generations] did. They want what we have without putting in the work. We were hungrier than they are and were willing to work for it." Business leaders are often challenged with how to motivate Gen Y, since previous generations seemed to be "hungrier" and provided more "self-motivation." When a talented Gen Y employee does not seem to be working hard (or up to his or her potential), there is a tendency to assume the person is just not "hungry" enough. Previous generations, the theory goes, provided their own motivation and realized they had to work hard to get ahead.

We *do* think this is a leadership challenge in the 21st century. Motivating Gen Y requires a very different leadership approach. Getting the most out of Gen Y employees is not as "simple" as it may have been for previous generations. Leaders need to learn that motivating employees is not as "automatic" as it once was. This can be frustrating for leaders as they feel their way through the challenge.

In the past, workers were much more likely to look beyond poor-to-mediocre leadership and focus on "the next rung on the ladder." They had several motivations that simply do not exist for Gen Y. First, in many instances they "had a family to feed," having married young and had children. Second, previous generations "bought the job" (or had a long-term lease), and believed they simply had to grind their way through poor leadership. Finally, in many ways previous generations equated career advancement with earning more money, thus expanding their purchasing power. The "American dream" dictated buying a house and a car, as well as providing for the family.

The challenge for today's leaders is to realize many of the "auto pilot" motivators for previous generations no longer exist. Sure, compensation is still a motivator, but for very different reasons. Gen Y does not need more money to "feed the family" as soon as previous generations did. Also, Gen Y will not "grind their way through poor leadership," nor are they looking to own a job and move up the corporate ladder. The "auto pilot" is gone. Twenty-first century leaders must take a more active role in managing the controls and motivating their workers.

A major first step in this process for leaders is to stop believing what motivated *them* is what motivates Gen Y. Gen Y is less motivated by what money can buy as it relates to material goods. There are literally dozens of studies that show Gen Y is simply less materialistic than previous generations. They don't need a luxury watch; they have a smart phone, thank you very much!

In Chapter 5 we talked about the Recession Generation and how the downturn has affected this cohort. Gen Y was not materialistic *prior* to the recession and is even less so now. This is a generation of informed shoppers, skilled at managing tight budgets. Gen Y will seek out the best deals available, shop the Internet, and find a good second-hand store in order to find what they want. If what they want seems extravagant or beyond their current budget, they will do without. Gen Y is not very likely to put "nice-to-have" purchases on their credit cards. This has several implications.

The first is that Gen Y will simply not put up with a poor situation because they need the money for material things. They would rather do without than be unhappy. Second, not being locked into discretionary debt gives Gen Y more freedom of job movement. Finally, Gen Y is less motivated by "stuff" and more motivated by other things.

So how do you make Gen Y "hungry"? The key is to look at what motivates them, not at yourself. At some point we both may have been motivated by "stuff" and what career success might have been able to provide. Gen Y looks beyond that.

Throughout the book we have touched on what motivates Gen Y. We have talked about providing strong leadership, regular and real-time feedback, a career lattice, and a link between their vision and a career plan, to name a few. Here we want to add two more: trust and stretch goals.

In previous chapters, we talked about how Gen Y wants flexibility, and they do. Additionally, there is an underlying message that is communicated to Gen Y when they are given flexibility—trust. Providing flexibility means a leader trusts that the employee is working, even though he or she may not be present. It means a leader trusts the employees to do their jobs. In all of our research we have found *trust* to be a key motivator for Gen Y.

Another motivator for Gen Y, closely linked to trust, is to provide stretch goals and assignments. Twenty-first century leaders must learn to challenge Gen Y to look beyond the immediate and to stretch themselves in new and often uncomfortable ways. Challenges motivate Gen Y. Challenges also have an element of trust. By challenging Gen Y, a leader is saying, "I trust you are capable of growing, developing, and doing even more." The key for leaders is to coach and support them along the way.

We do realize why Gen Y can be viewed as being less "hungry" than previous generations. We also recognize this can prove to be frustrating for leaders who are trying to motivate their teams. The loss of "societal auto pilot motivators" does require a much more hands-on approach. The leaders who adopt this mentality will see the results and have a much more motivated and engaged workforce.

Conclusion

Gen Y does pose some unique leadership challenges. These challenges will force leaders to evolve and add new leadership skills. The pace of society has increased, as has the proliferation of smart phones and other devices. Leaders need to recognize "distraction" is not simply an overreliance on one's phone.

The career lattice is a necessary element for any organization, but it must be implemented properly. Leaders *cannot* allow folks to quit too soon or to move before they are ready. Career coaching is becoming a critical skill for 21st century leaders.

A leader must push Gen Yers to take all of their skills, abilities, and knowledge and turn them into results. Knowledge without application is fairly useless in the marketplace. Motivating Gen Y to produce results will also require 21st century leaders to understand a new set of motivators. The things that motivated folks twenty-plus years ago simply do not exist for Gen Y.

Bill's Gen Y Profile

Name: Bill

Location: Northeast

Age: 33

Background:

- Graduated with a bachelor's degree in English writing from a large state university in a Northeast city
- Earned a master's degree in journalism and mass communications from a smaller private university in the same city
- Works in communications in the donor relations department of a large state university

Bill is happy with his current job, calling his current environment "congenial, if bureaucratic." He said a pleasant atmosphere, opportunities for professional development, fair compensation, and a focus on work/life balance make the job appealing. "I'm fortunate to not have to take home work," he said. "That makes it easy."

He said that his personal life is more important than his professional life, but they feed off each other. "If I'm personally satisfied, I perform my job better," he said. "If I'm professionally satisfied, my personal life benefits."

He said the qualities and attributes of a successful worker don't differ from one generation to the next, but he said the biggest frustration he faces is when older colleagues claim ignorance or indifference when it comes to technology. "Sometimes it's someone calling me to respond to an email I sent," he said. "I then have to explain to them that I sent the email because I need an emailed response that I can print and include with whatever I am submitting."

For Bill, the characteristics of a good job are

- A pleasant work atmosphere
- Support for personal and professional growth
- Opportunities for advancement
- Fair compensation and flexible scheduling

Bill is motivated by:

- Personal ambition
- Desire to provide for his family

CHAPTER FIFTEEN

LEADERSHIP
A Timeless Principle

In the first chapter of the first edition of this book we posed a few simple questions. We asked you, the reader, to imagine that you had known in 1995 how important the Internet was going to be. Or if you had known about the dot-com bubble through 2001, or the real estate bust of 2007. What might you have done differently?

In closing this book we want to take that a bit further. We want to ask you to think about how you felt in 1995 when this thing called the Internet began to take off? How did you feel when you began to see companies launch an initial stock offering and be worth a billion dollars, with little to no revenue? How did you feel when someone bought a house and sold it thirty days later for twice the price?

You may even have bought and sold one of these homes. Or perhaps you were able to get in on an IPO and make a great deal of money. You may even have had a great Internet strategy and transformed your business. Many people did. Also, many people did not.

Principles vs. Rules

What is certainly true about all three of these transformational events is that, until long-held, rock-solid principles were put into place, nothing was self-sustaining. The Internet had to find its place, businesses went bankrupt during the bubble burst, and the housing market, arguably, put the entire world economy at risk. Timeless principles needed to be put into place and combined with these new opportunities. Once that was accomplished, things began to get markedly better.

We believe timeless principles were ignored and people and businesses suffered. Rules (and laws) were broken, and new rules were not put into place to ensure timeless principles were upheld. If you notice, we are making a distinction between "rules" and "principles." Principles are timeless. Honesty, integrity, and *authentic leadership* are a few of the timeless things we are talking about.

Rules, on the other hand, are meant to be adapted to new situations. When there is a transformational event, often the old rules simply do not work or can be ignored. Failure to adopt new rules, or bending the old rules, can create chaos. The financial markets prior to the Great Recession are just one tangible example. New rules have to be developed for new situations. Old rules, applied to a new situation, is a recipe for disaster.

We also believe that some business leaders are confusing *principles* with *rules*. Hard work is a guiding principle for most successful people. When we asked Tamara Tunie, an award-winning actress and producer, her secret to success, she simply said, "Work your butt off!"

One example is hard work. That is a principle most business leaders do not ever want to change. However, flextime is a "rule." The principle of hard work is not compromised by adapting one's rule to allow flex time. Business leaders, in our opinion, should take some time to think about the rules they have in place and whether they are confusing timeless principles with the need to adapt/create new rules.

History, especially recent history, is full of examples where businesses either failed to adapt rules or failed to hold tight to timeless principles. Many businesses are now gone because they did not adapt their "rules" to the Internet and its transformational power. For example, many businesses believed that they *had to have* brick-and-mortar locations to survive. They felt that was a "business principle." They learned it was just a rule. Conversely, many people suffered when timeless principles like honesty were compromised.

We believe principles are timeless and rules are temporary. Please do not get us wrong. We are not saying, "Rules are meant to be broken." We are saying that rules are meant to be adapted to new situations. In many ways, recognizing the need to adapt old rules, having the vision to see what needs to happen, and implementing the changes needed, are a leader's job.

One thing for certain, Gen Y is a transformational event that requires leaders to rethink their rules, but not their principles. As Peter Drucker, the Austrian-born American management consultant, said, "The one thing you can predict with absolute certainty is demographics." The shear numbers of Gen Y make them a transformational event. Gen Y will require new rules. They *will not* require, or even want, new principles. Gen Y wants to work for strong leaders.

Leadership Is a Timeless Principle

Gen Y is dying for leadership—real, authentic, and timeless leadership. They want leaders who will give them feedback, guide them on their career journeys, listen to them, correct them when needed, and compliment them when appropriate. All timeless principles.

For the first time in history, 21st century leaders are faced with the challenge of leading four generations of breadwinners. Each generation has a different way of approaching things, and it is a leader's job to blend these strengths and challenges into a cohesive team.

Each generation will, quite naturally, push back on "the other." Gen Y will push back on the older generations just as much as the older generations will push back on Gen Y. It is simply the way the human mind works. The fundamental attribution error and the actor observer bias nearly guarantees this push-back.

However, the good news is that, once people better understand "the other," it becomes easier to collaborate, communicate, and work together. Conflict can be reduced, productivity can improve, and innovation can occur. Many times just "getting to know" the "other" boosts morale and creates a more engaged workforce.

Leaders Must Look in the Mirror First

Leaders much first confront their own prejudices about Gen Y. If you buy into the myths about this generation, it is difficult, if not impossible, to lead Gen Y. It is also nearly impossible to lead your team of non–Gen Yers to a better understanding of this cohort. It is important to understand the seven myths:

1. Gen Yers are slackers or lazy.
2. Gen Y needs instant gratification and wants a trophy for just showing up.
3. Gen Yers are disloyal and job-jumpers.
4. Gen Y is self-centered and narcissistic.
5. Gen Y is pampered and spoiled.
6. Gen Y lacks respect for authority.
7. Gen Y feels entitled.

Becoming World-Class

World-class performers are not just the "rich and famous." One does not need to be famous to be world-class. There are world-class performers all around us. You may even be one yourself.

What we do know about you, whether you are a world-class performer or not, is that you are committed to being a better leader. You would not be reading a book like this one if you did not want to become a better leader—perhaps even a world-class leader. Our research into world-class performers reveals nine similar characteristics/traits/habits all of them have.

World-class performers and leaders:

1. Use performance feedback or "game film."
2. Turn unconscious, negative tendencies into conscious, positive choices.
3. Practice energy management.
4. Realize that what is required for improvement may be counterintuitive.
5. Develop a clear vision.
6. Seek out Coaches/Mentors.
7. Develop tactical and measurable action plans.
8. Recover from losses quickly.
9. Use positive self-talk.

All world-class performers use "game film" to study their tendencies. We have a strong belief in DiSC profiles, especially The Work of Leaders profile. Having "game film" helps one understand him- or herself and others better. It allows leaders to see some of their "unconscious tendencies" and to act counterintuitively when necessary.

Having "game film" and a coach, if appropriate, also helps leaders to increase their EQ (emotional intelligence) as well as deliver on their brand promise. All world-class performers in our research work on their "people skills" and realize that having the technical skills is a given. People skills are what allows them to reach new heights.

Gen Y's Attitude and Superior Skills

The Great Recession has not diminished Gen Y's enthusiasm or their deep belief in making a difference in their lives and the lives of others. The terrible economy this generation lived through, either early in their lives or early in their careers, has not broken them. In fact, it has emboldened them. They know they can persevere. A majority of Gen Y, in spite of the challenging times they inherited, still believe they will achieve a higher standard of living than their parents did.

Gen Y remains optimistic about the future. The wisdom Gen Y gained was just that, wisdom. The Great Recession did not create a generation of malcontents and skeptics. They have not become cynical and downtrodden. They have become a bit more realistic about how uncontrollable events can derail their plans and about how they need to overcome and adapt to events.

We believe that, much like the Great Depression molded the Greatest Generation, the Great Recession will mold Gen Y in similarly positive ways. In both cases, these generations were forced to overcome the worst economies in history. Both generations persevered.

Gen Y will bring some real skills to the workplace that can be implemented immediately. Previous generations often had a steep learning curve for nearly every aspect of a new job. Gen Y has several skills that may well be better than their more experienced co-workers have, without any ramp-up time. In fact, they most likely will possess certain superior skills on day one:

1. Gen Y is tech-savvy.
2. Gen Y is diverse.
3. Gen Y understands the global marketplace.
4. Gen Yers have good self-esteem.
5. Gen Y has a sense of security and is ambitious.
6. Gen Y has life experience in the marketplace.
7. Gen Y is research-oriented.
8. Gen Yers are problem solvers.

The New Realities

Leaders who realize the changes Gen Y are driving, and the changes in how they are living, will be able to adapt their organizations in order to attract and retain the best talent. These ten new realities simply cannot be ignored:

1. Gen Y is delaying marriage and parenthood.
2. There is no stigma associated with moving back home.
3. When Gen Y leaves, no one is at fault.
4. Gen Y "leases" a job, not "buys."
5. Multiple jobs are a badge of honor.
6. Your leadership is continually being evaluated.
7. Their circle of influence is also watching.
8. The extended family is coming back for Gen Y.
9. Gen Y has a vision for themselves.
10. There is an "ambition gap" between Gen Y men and women.

Turning Knowledge to Action

Strong leaders realize that knowing what to do is not the same as doing it. Leaders in the 21st century need to work equally hard at casting a strong vision (and then aligning that vision with their employees' individual visions), creating alignment throughout the entire organization, and then executing on the plan.

In order to attract and retain the best talent, leaders will need to drive the necessary organizational change and bring all of the generations on board. While they are accomplishing this buy-in and support, focus must also be given to aligning all of the hiring and retention systems. Starting with pre-employment practices and moving all of the way to career development practices, everything must align.

One key area to align is the performance management systems. Gen Y wants real-time feedback. Systems must be put in place to give one-on-one feedback in real time. The traditional "annual review" must be adapted to a new workforce.

Leaders need to learn, and then teach, managers and supervisors how to conduct productive one-on-one meetings that involve giving real-time feedback. Feedback should not just be corrective input, but also timely affirmations.

The Platform Is Burning

We opened this book by discussing why this subject is so important. Gen Y is the future of work and will impact the work world for decades. Every member of Gen Y is now either in the workforce or preparing to enter. The time is now! Gen Y will demand the changes or will simply find an employer who "gets it." Employers who "get it" will have access to the best talent available.

In no way do we believe becoming an employer of choice in the 21st century will be easy. Just the opposite. It will require real work. It will require looking at your principles and adapting your rules. It will require alignment of four different generations. It will require having a clear vision. It will require alignment of all of your practices and people. It will require relentless execution of your strategy. In short, it will require strong and timeless leadership.

We believe *the* key differentiator for Gen Y will be leadership. They will choose to follow strong leaders while working to become one themselves.

Our coach, and dear friend, Dave Maloney, used to tell us "fatigue lessens the desire to win." While he meant that as a motivator to get us into better shape, it has proved to be a life lesson and not just a basketball lesson. If we allow ourselves to become weary, we allow ourselves to think losing is an option.

Do not become weary. Losing is not an option. Be a strong leader. Gen Y, and every generation, will follow a strong leader.

If we can help in any way, please visit www.genynow.com. Let us know your feedback and whether you have any questions.

REFERENCES AND RESEARCH[*]

Alessandra, A.J., O'Connor, T., & Alessandra, M.J. (1996). *The platinum rule: Discover the four basic business personalities—and how they can lead you to success*. New York: Warner Books.

Alexander, R. (n.d.). Where are you on the global pay scale? www.bbc.co.uk/news/magazine-17512040.

Alsop, R. (2014, January 10). The crucial skill new hires lack. www.bbc.com/capital/story/20130828-the-crucial-skill-new-hires-lack.

American Student Assistance (asa.org.). (n.d.). Student loan debt statistics—American Student Assistance. www.asa.org/policy/resources/stats/.

Ballor, G. (2012). Young, smart, and broke? Tips for Generation Y. http://genwhypress.com/2012/01/25/young-smart-and-broke-tips-for-generation-y/.

Bar-On, R., & Parker, J.D.A. (Eds.). (2000). *Handbook of emotional intelligence*. San Francisco: Jossey-Bass.

Bradberry, T., & Greaves, J. (2005). *The emotional intelligence quick book*. New York: Simon & Schuster.

Brett, S. (2010). Do Gen Y really not understand commitment? www.smh.com.au/lifestyle/life/blogs/ask-sam/do-gen-y-really-not-understand-commitment-20100823-13dsw.html.

Buckingham, J., & Buckingham, M. (2012). Note to Gen Y workers: Performance on the job actually matters. http://business.time.com/2012/09/28/note-to-gen-y-workers-performance-on-the-job-actually-matters/.

[*] All websites were accessed either January 10, 2014, or March 5, 2014.

Buisnessnewdaily.com. (n.d.). "Gen Y: Your Work BFF?" 10 January 2014 www.businessnewsdaily.com/2434-gen-work.html.

Caldwell, C. (2012). Second-hand sales on the rise. http://earth911.com/news/2012/04/13/thrift-shopping-on-the-rise/.

Campbell, P. (2011). Positive self talk can help you win the race—or the day. http://m.psychologytoday.com/blog/imperfect-spirituality/201106/positive-self-talk-can-help-you-win-the-race-or-the-day.

Caruso, D.R., & Salovey, P. (2004). *The emotionally intelligent manager*. San Francisco: Jossey-Bass.

Chester, E. (2005). *Getting them to give a damn: How to get your front line to care about your bottom line*. New York: Kaplan Business.

Clark, D. (2013). Three ways millennials can succeed at work. www.forbes.com/sites/dorieclark/2013/09/05/three-ways-millennials-can-succeed-at-work/.

Cohen, L., & DeBenedet, A.T. (2011). Are helicopter parents here to stay? http://ideas.time.com/2011/11/08/roughhousing-the-answer-to-helicopter-parenting/.

Coine, T. (n.d.). It's not just Generation Y experiencing feedback deprivation. http://sustainablebusinessforum.com/tedcoine/186751/it-s-not-just-generation-y-experiencing-feedback-deprivation.

Collins, J.C. (2001). *Good to great: Why some companies make the leap . . . and others don't*. New York: HarperCollins.

Colvin, G. (2008). *Talent is overrated: What really separates world-class performers from everyone else*. New York: Penguin.

Cost of turnover calculator. (n.d.). http://us.drakeintl.com/hr-tools/cost-of-turnover-calculator.aspx.

Debt.org. (n.d.). Debt demographics – Statistical breakdown of consumer debt in the U.S. www.debt.org/faqs/americans-in-debt/demographics/.

El-Shamy, S. (2004). *How to design and deliver training for the new and emerging generations*. San Francisco, CA: Pfeiffer.

Emmerling, R.J., & Goleman, D. (2003). *Emotional intelligence: Issues and common misunderstandings*. *Issues in emotional intelligence* [On-line serial], 1(1). Available at www.eiconsortium.org.

Epmsonline.com. (n.d.). Going green: How does Gen Y perceive your green initiative. www.epmsonline.com/uncategorized/going-green-how-does-gen-y-perceive-your-green-initiative.

Epsmonline.com. (n.d.). Work life flexibility is #1 job requirement for Generation Y. https://www.epmsonline.com/generational-understanding/worklife-flexibility-is-1-job-requirement-for-generation-y.

Fastweb.com. (n.d.). Shocking student debt statistics. http://www.fastweb.com/financial-aid/articles/3930-shocking-student-debt-statistics.us.drakeintl.com.

Fenn, D. (n.d.). What makes Generation Y optimistic about business? http://www.cbsnews.com/8301-505143_162-41840362/what-makes-generation-y-optimistic-about-business/.

Forbusinessake.com. (2013). Getting diversity right for Generation Y. http://forbusinessake.com/2013/06/28/getting-diversity-right-for-generation-y/.

Fox, E.J. (2012). Work from home soars 41% in 10 years. http://money.cnn.com/2012/10/04/news/economy/work-from-home/index.html.

Frankel, V.E. (2006). *Man's search for meaning*. Boston, MA: Beacon Press.

Gardner, H. (1983). *Frames of mind: The theory of multiple intelligences*. New York: Basic Books.

Giang, V. (2012). Gen Y worker tells us why his generation has commitment issues. http://www.businessinsider.com/gen-y-workers-have-commitment-issues-2012-10.

Giang, V. (2013). Why Gen Y workers have no idea what their managers expect from them. http://www.businessinsider.com/study-reveals-expectation-gap-between-managers-and-their-workers-2013-9.

Gibson, R. (n.d.). Essential tools to make your boss love remote working (.n.d.). www.generationy.com/essential-tools-remote-working/.

Goleman, D. (1995). *Emotional intelligence*. New York: Bantam.

Goudreau, J. (2013). 7 surprising ways to motivate Millennial workers. http://www.forbes.com/sites/jennagoudreau/2013/03/07/7-surprising-ways-to-motivate-millennial-workers/.

Hamel, G., & Prahalad, C.K. (1994). *Competing for the future*. Boston, MA: Harvard Business School Press.

Hansen, R. (n.d.). Perception vs. reality: 10 truths about the Generation Y workforce. http://www.quintcareers.com/Gen-Y_workforce.html.

Hartwell, S. (n.d.). Gen Y is more positive than other generations. http://www.examiner.com/article/gen-y-is-more-positive-than-other-generations.

Hawley, C. (n.d.). Understanding the Gen Y debt better. *Huffington Post*. www.huffingtonpost.com/saveup/understanding-the-gen-y-d_b_3613508.html.

Henderson, J. M. (2012). Millennial women speak out about the gender ambition gap. It's real and they're living it. www.forbes.com/sites/jmaureenhenderson/2012/05/16/millennial-women-speak-out-about-the-gender-ambition-gap-its-real-and-theyre-living-it/2/.

Holland, K. (2013). Gen Y managers perceived as entitled. www.usatoday.com/story/money/business/2013/09/07/gen-y-managers/2759873/.

Institute for Global Labour. (n.d.). How U.S. teens spend their time and money.www.globallabourrights.org/reports/how-u-s-teens-spend-their-time-and-money. www.globallabourrights.org/reports/how-u-s-teens-spend-their-time-and-money.

Iwise.com. (n.d.). Kotter's 8 stage process for major change. www.iwise2.com/kotters-8-stage-process-major-change.

Jamrisko, M., & Kolet, I. (2013). College costs surge 500% in U.S. Since 1985. www.bloomberg.com/news/2013-08-26/college-costs-surge-500-in-u-s-since-1985-chart-of-the-day.html.

Janis, I. (1972). *Victims of groupthink: A psychological study of foreign-policy decisions and fiasco*. Boston: Houghton-Mifflin.

Johnson, M., & Johnson, L. (n.d.). The rise of the Gen Y 'sharing economy. http://m.huffpost.com/us/entry/891413.

Kaufman, M. (2013). How company culture needs to adapt to the so-called me, me, me generation. www.forbes.com/sites/michakaufman/2013/09/16/gen-y-entitled-or-empowered-how-company-culture-needs-to-adapt/.

Kerner, N. (2013). Trying to understand Gen Y? Get comfortable with being uncomfortable. http://www.forbes.com/sites/onmarketing/2013/07/03/trying-to-understand-gen-y-get-comfortable-with-being-uncomfortable/.

Knot yet! The benefits and costs of delayed marriage in America. (n.d.). http://twentysomethingmarriage.org/in-brief/.

Kotter, J. (n.d.). Leading change. Kotter's 8 stage process for major change | iWise2. www.iwise2.com/kotters-8-stage-process-major-change

Lencioni, P. (2002). *The five dysfunctions of a team*. San Francisco, CA: Jossey-Bass.

Lewin, K., Lippitt, R., & White, R.K. (1939). *Journal of Social Psychology, 10*, 271–301.

Loder, A. (2012). Gen Y struggles with declining wages. http://stateimpact.npr.org/new-hampshire/2012/03/07/gen-y-struggles-with-declining-wages/.

Lucas, S. (n.d.). How much does it cost companies to lose employees? www.cbsnews.com/8301-505125_162-57552899/how-much-does-it-cost-companies-to-lose-employees/.

Luhby, T. (2008). How to lure Gen Y workers? Do good. http://money.cnn.com/2008/08/14/news/companies/recruiting_the_new_generation/.

Malcom, H. (2013). Unlike Boomers, Millennials appear to be super savers. www.usatoday.com/story/money/personalfinance/2013/05/11/mass-affluent-millennials-retirement/2148469/.

Market-truth.com. (n.d.). The power of online reviews. www.market-truth.com/power-online-reviews/.

Martin, C. (2011). Gen Y speaks out on performance reviews. www.forbes.com/sites/work-in-progress/2011/07/15/gen-y-speaks-out-on-performance-reviews/.

Mathews, G., Zeidner, M., & Roberts, R. D. (2002). Emotional intelligence: Science and myth. Cambridge, MA: MIT Press.

Mayer, J.D., Salovey, P., Caruso, D.R., & Sitarenios, G. (2003). Measuring and modeling emotional intelligence with the MSCEIT V 2.0. *Emotion, 3*, 97–105.

Mayoclinic.com. (n.d.). Positive thinking: Reduce stress by eliminating negative self-talk. www.mayoclinic.com/health/positive-thinking/SR00009/NSECTIONGROUP=2.

McGillis, K. (2013). Gen Y shuns credit cards. www.learnvest.com/2013/06/gen-y-shuns-credit-cards/.

Mielach, D. (n.d.). Gen Y seeks work-life balance above all else. www.businessnewsdaily.com/2278-generational-employee-differences.html.

Milford, J. (n.d.). Is Gen-Y afraid of credit cards? http://elitedaily.com/news/business/is-gen-y-afraid-of-credit-cards/.

millennialbranding.com. (2013). The Gen Y workplace expectations study. http://millennialbranding.com/2013/09/gen-workplace-expectations-study/.

Muir, K. (n.d.). Generation Y fails commitment test. www.sunshinecoast-daily.com.au/news/generation-y-fails-commitment-test/1199834/.

Murphy, M. (n.d.). Top 5 myths about Generation Y in the workplace. www.leadershipiq.com/top-5-myths-about-generation-y-in-the-workplace/.

Murray, K. (n.d.). Gen Y not as different as you think. www.massey.ac.nz/massey/about-massey/news/article.cfm?mnarticle_uuid=12F1EF8F-C9C3-D5A8-5272-4803B5E35985.

Nelson, B. (1994). *1001 ways to reward employees*. New York: Workman.

Northwestern Mutual. (2013). Planning and progress 2013. www.northwesternmutual.com/news-room/Documents/technology_society.pdf.

O'Donnell, J. (2013). Gen Y can guide their offices with tech savvy. www.usatoday.com/story/money/business/2013/06/10/millennials-boomers-workplace-challenges/2398403/.

Palmer, K. (2012). Why Gen Y is so financially frustrated. http://money.usnews.com/money/personal-finance/articles/2012/03/20/why-gen-y-is-so-financially-frustrated.

Parker, J. (2012). Why Gen Y may face least secure retirement. http://usatoday30.usatoday.com/money/perfi/retirement/story/2012-04-22/cnbc-gen-y-financial-hurdles-retirement/54446740/1.

Parker, K. (2012). The boomerang generation: Feeling OK about living with mom and dad. www.pewsocialtrends.org/files/2012/03/PewSocialTrends-2012-BoomerangGeneration.pdf.

Peak, L. (2011). Gen Y: Can they survive a performance review? www.thefiscaltimes.com/Columns/2011/02/09/Employers-Confront-the-Millennials.

Patten, E., & Parker, K. (2012). A gender reversal on career aspirations. www.pewsocialtrends.org/2012/04/19/a-gender-reversal-on-career-aspirations/.

Pear, R. (2013). Median income rises, but is still 6% below level at start of recession in '07. www.nytimes.com/2013/08/22/us/politics/us-median-income-rises-but-is-still-6-below-its-2007-peak.html.

Perman, C. (2013). Are Millennials really the 'Me' generation. www.usatoday.com/story/money/business/2013/08/24/millenials-time-magazine-generation-y/2678441/.

Petrides, K., & Furnham, A. (2000). Gender differences in measured and self-estimated trait emotional intelligence. *Sex Roles*, *42*, 449–461.

Pinkerton, J. (2013). The rise of Gen Y in the workplace. http://certification.comptia.org/news/2013/08/21/the-rise-of-gen-y-in-the-workplace.

Pogue, D. (n.d.). Critical mass: How to maintain the power of online reviews. www.scientificamerican.com/article.cfm?id=critical-mass.

Ponce De Leon, S. (n.d.). The social evolution for Generation Y. www.socialbusinessnews.com/the-social-evolution-for-generation-y/.

Prlog.org. (n.d.). Generation Y and education. www.prlog.org/10575597-generation-and-education.html

Rampell, C. (2011). A generation of slackers? Not so much. www.nytimes.com/2011/05/29/weekinreview/29graduates.html?_r=0.

Reeves, R. (1961). *Reality in advertising*. New York: Knoph.

Ries and Trout, (1981). Positioning,

Ryan, S. (n.d.). Suffering the helicopter generation. www.edmontonjournal.com/life/Suffering+helicopter+generation/3337796/story.html.

Salovey, P., & Mayer, J.D. (1990). Emotional intelligence. *Imagination, Cognition, and Personality*, 9, 185–211.

Schawbel, D. (n.d.). 74 of the most interesting facts about the Millennial Generation. http://danschawbel.com/blog/74-of-the-most-interesting-facts-about-the-millennial-generation/.

Schawbel, D. (2011). Who's at fault for high Gen-Y turnover? www.forbes.com/sites/danschawbel/2011/11/22/whos-at-fault-for-high-gen-y-turnover/2/.

Statisticbrain.com. (n.d.). Student loan debt statistics. www.statisticbrain.com/student-loan-debt-statistics/.

Stern, L. (2010). Generation Y: Educated, underemployed and in debt. www.reuters.com/article/2010/05/19/us-column-personalfinance-idUSTRE64I4M220100519.

Stillman, J. (n.d.). The kids are risk averse: Will the recession scar Gen Y? www.cbsnews.com/8301-505125_162-38945328/the-kids-are-risk-averse-will-the-recession-scar-gen-y/.

Straw, J., Scullard, M., Kukkonen, S., & Davis, B. (2013). *The work of leaders: How vision, alignment, and execution will change the way you lead.* Hoboken, NJ: John Wiley & Sons.

Thefinancialbrand.com. (n.d.). Gen-y stressed most over debt, making savings a distant dream. http://thefinancialbrand.com/30161/millennials-worry-about-financial-problems/.

Tripathi, S. (n.d.). Attracting the best young talent: What makes Gen Y tick? www.londonlovesbusiness.com/business-in-london/london-loves-talent/attracting-the-best-young-talent-what-makes-gen-y-tick/6565.article.

Trunk, P. (n.d.). Why Gen Y doesn't fear the lousy job market. www.cbsnews.com/8301-505125_162-45040260/why-gen-y-doesnt-fear-the-lousy-job-market/.

Trunk, P. (n.d.). Why Gen Y is better at your Job than you are. www.cbsnews.com/8301-505125_162-45040304/why-gen-y-is-better-at-your-job-than-you-are/.

Ulrich, D., & Smallwood, N. (2007). *Leadership brand: Developing customer-focused leaders to drive performance and build lasting value*. Boston, MA: Harvard Business School Press.

Wanous J.P. (1980). *Organizational entry: Recruitment selection and socialization of newcomers*. Reading MA: Addison-Wesley.

Webmd.com. (n.d.). The power of positive talking. www.webmd.com/balance/express-yourself-13/positive-self-talk?page=2.

Wells Fargo. (2013). https://www.wellsfargo.com/press/2013/20130522_MorethanhalfofMillennials.

Zionts, S. (2012). Secondhand is the new black: Consignment shops boom in tough economy. http://smallbusiness.foxbusiness.com/entrepreneurs/2012/01/12/secondhand-new-black-consignment-shops-boom-in-tough-economy/.

ABOUT THE AUTHORS

Buddy Hobart founded Solutions 21 in 1994. Today, the firm is a global enterprise that provides services in four primary practice areas: Client Development, Leadership Development, Strategic Planning, and Process Improvement. He has led Solutions 21 in providing leadership and management solutions to companies around the world, ranging from startups to Fortune 500 enterprises.

Buddy is an author, speaker, entrepreneur, leadership expert, and radio host. He has written four other books and has been quoted in publications such as *USA Today* and *The Wall Street Journal*. He hosted his own radio show, "The Consultant's Corner," and his research on world-class performers is widely used to develop leadership institutes for companies around the globe.

Buddy has spoken to conferences, businesses, associations, and conventions around the world on topics such as World-Class Performers, Leadership, "Game Film," and Gen Y. He is recognized as an energetic and enthusiastic speaker, often receiving "best speaker" recognition and the highest audience ratings possible.

Herb Sendek is the men's head basketball coach at Arizona State University. In many ways, Herb is a "coach's coach." He is a coach's son and learned very early the value of teamwork and hard work. He has instilled these values in his players and his assistant coaches. Herb has the largest "coaching tree" in all of Division I basketball. Herb takes his leadership role seriously with both his players and his assistant coaches. More Division I coaches worked for Herb at one point than for any other coach of all time.

Herb works daily with Gen Y and believes their work ethic and commitment to teamwork rival any previous generation. His values of "one," as in "one team" and "one heartbeat," are readily embraced by Gen Y.

In addition to being one of the most successful mentors of Division I coaches of all time, he has also produced his share of outstanding players. Many of his players go on to play professionally, and all of his players go on to excel in their life's work. Herb has been coaching at the highest level since he was thirty years old. He has been Coach of the Year in every conference he has coached in, including the Mid-American, Atlantic Coast, and PAC-10 conferences.

INDEX

Page references followed by *fig* indicates an illustrated figure; followed by *t* indicates a table.